More praise for NEWSTART® Lifestyle Cookbook

"The *NEWSTART® Lifestyle Cookbook* is filled with delicious recipes made from 'clean' ingredients. . . . we especially enjoyed the breakfasts, desserts, and breads, and the many helpful hints. We will recommend this book."

John McDougal, M.D., and Mary McDougall
The McDougall Program

"The scientific evidence now has become substantial that the closer an individual approximates a plant-based diet, using good quality and varied food while minimized consumption of added fat, salt, and sugar, the greater the health benefits. The *NEWSTART® Lifestyle Cookbook* is a good place to start."

T. Colin Campbell, Ph.D.
Director, China-Oxford-Cornell Project
on Diet, Lifestyle, and Disease

"Many today are convinced that they should be 'eating better.' Few find it easy to make the shift. This book can make the difference and make it attractive."

Dr. Ralph Winter,
Founder, U.S. Center for World Mission and
William Cary International University

"The recipes in the *NEWSTART® Lifestyle Cookbook* provide an excellent guide for [diabetic] patients and their families. The recipes are easy to prepare, nutritious, and delicious."

Mark Sklar, M.D.
Researcher, Georgetown University Medical Center
Washington, D.C.

". . . simple, sound, practical, economical, and delicious. What more can you wish from a cookbook?"

Hans Diehl, Dr. HSc., M.P.H
International Nutrition Research Foundation

"In our never-ending search for delicious food combinations that are also nutritious and scientifically sound, Weimar's *NEWSTART® Lifestyle Cookbook* must have a place at the top of our list."

Dr. Raymond and Dorothy Moore
The Moore Foundation, Authors of *Home Made Health*

"The *NEWSTART® Lifestyle Cookbook* is a splendid gift for anyone wanting to eat more healthfully."

John Robbins
Author of *Diet for New America* and *Reclaiming Our Health*

Weimar Institute's
NEWSTART®
LIFESTYLE COOKBOOK

MORE THAN 260 HEART-HEALTHY RECIPES
FEATURING WHOLE PLANT FOODS

Compiled and edited by

Sally J. Christensen and Frances Piper de Vries

WEIMAR
INSTITUTE

THOMAS NELSON PUBLISHERS
*Nashville * Atlanta * London * Vancouver*
Printed in the United States of America

Nutrient Analysis Information

Nutrient analysis for this book was done with Nutritionist II, III, and IV (N-Squared Incorporated). Optional ingredients are not included in the calculations. When there is a choice of two or more ingredients, the analysis is based on the first one mentioned. In recipes that call for "salt, to taste," the salt has not been included in the analysis. Percentages shown in parentheses are the calorie ratio to total calories.

Published in Nashville, Tennessee, by Thomas Nelson, Inc.

Photography and food styling by Nina Courtney, Sacramento, California.

Pyramid artwork by Dave Eaton.

Clip art from Food and Drink Spot Illustrations, Susan Gaber, Copyright © 1982, Dover Publications and ClickArt Incredible Image Pack 65,000, Copyright © 1996, T/Maker Company.

The Bible version used in this publication is THE NEW KING JAMES VERSION. Copyright © 1979, 1980, 1982, 1990, Thomas Nelson, Inc., Publishers.

ISBN 0-7852-71406

Printed in the United States of America.

2 3 4 5 6 QPH 02 01 00 99 98 97

Cover Photo: Korean Jhapchae, Korean Cucumber Salad, Millet Peanut Balls, Zesty Tomato Relish, and Orange Cream Pie.

DEDICATION

The growing awareness of the benefits of a plant-based diet has made the cookbooks of Weimar Institute a trusted resource in kitchens around the world. Many of these recipes were standbys when Weimar Institute first opened as a wellness center in 1978. Through the years, our cookbooks have undergone several revisions. We hope you will enjoy this latest edition, complete with nutrient analysis, which will replace *Recipes from the Weimar Kitchen* and the *NEWSTART® Homestyle Manual*. Many family and professional cooks have tested, refined, adapted, and shared their recipes and comments with us. To all of you who have contributed in so many ways, the **NEWSTART® Lifestyle Cookbook** is dedicated. Bon appetit!

WEIMAR INSTITUTE

Weimar Institute is a nonprofit, Christian wellness center, located in the Sierra foothills between Lake Tahoe and Sacramento. It attracts guests from around the world seeking to regain health using natural methods. Under strict medical supervision, thousands of people with heart disease, diabetes, arthritis, and other illnesses, have completed the NEWSTART® Lifestyle Program and experienced renewed health and vigor. The eight components of the program create a unique blend of strategies that heal. Here is a brief description:

N - NUTRITION: The NEWSTART® diet is plant-based, free of all animal products (vegan), and emphasizes whole, natural foods. It is naturally high in fiber, low in fat, and cholesterol-free.

E - EXERCISE: We are designed to be physically active. Regular exercise is very effective in combating many health problems, both physical and mental. It strengthens the immune system, improves circulation, and reduces stress.

W -WATER: Our bodies are composed mostly of water and virtually every body function is dependent upon water. Six to eight glasses per day are recommended for the average person. Water on the outside of the body may be used to treat pain and infection, and is vital for cleansing the skin.

S - SUNSHINE: Sunlight is one of the healing agents of nature, and is necessary for strong bones. Just 15 minutes of sunlight can provide the daily requirement of Vitamin D. Moderation is the key, avoiding sunburn.

T - TEMPERANCE: Temperance is having a healthful balance in every area of life. It involves avoiding that which is harmful and moderation in that which is good.

A - AIR: Air is the body's most frequently needed resource. Living in an environment where the air quality is good greatly enhances our ability to fight disease. Breathing deeply of fresh, outdoor air promotes a good oxygen supply for the body cells.

R - REST: With proper rest, productivity and disease resistance is increased. Rest is the great rejuvenator. We need quiet physical relaxation after active work, vigorous exercise after mental work, and deep restorative sleep.

T - TRUST IN DIVINE POWER: Trust in God is the most important healing component in the NEWSTART® Lifestyle Program. Stress, fear, and anxiety affect the chemistry and function of every body system. Becoming acquainted with and learning to trust the Creator God, enhances physical, emotional, and spiritual healing.

TABLE OF CONTENTS

THE NEWSTART® DIET

A healthful diet and lifestyle are unique and priceless gifts you give to yourself. Providing tasty, nutritious food for your family and friends is a gift of highest value. The abundance of information and products now available make choosing healthful foods easier than ever. The NEWSTART® diet is based upon the original diet given to us by our Creator. Current research confirms that a whole plant food diet promotes the abundant life God intended for us.

Guidelines for Implementing the NEWSTART® Diet

- Select a diet of whole plant foods–fruits, vegetables, legumes, grains, nuts, and seeds.
- For a balanced diet, choose a wide variety of foods during the course of a week, but only a limited variety within any one meal.
  Enjoy several *fresh* fruits and vegetables each day.
- Complex carbohydrates should make up 65-75% of our caloric intake, fat, 15-20%, and protein, 10-12%.
- Prepare food simply, using it in its most natural state, for optimum nutrition. Avoid highly processed and refined foods.
- Arrange meals at regular times, 4-6 hours apart, with nothing in between except water, thus allowing the stomach time to rest.
- Eat a hearty, generous breakfast, a medium-sized lunch, and a small, light supper, if needed.
- Chew food thoroughly.
- Plan a relaxed, unhurried mealtime, spent in a pleasant atmosphere.

The Preventive Diet Versus the Therapeutic Diet

There are two variations of the NEWSTART® diet—*preventive* and *therapeutic*. The *preventive* diet is designed for those who have no significant health problems and want to remain healthy. A *therapeutic* diet is advocated for those who are at high risk for, or already have, heart disease, hypertension, diabetes, obesity, arthritis, etc.

In addition to the "Guidelines" stated above, a *therapeutic* diet recommends very sparing use of plant foods that are naturally high in fat, such as nuts, olives, avocados, seeds, and soybean products. Suggested total fat intake is 10-15% of total calories. Medical research confirms that reversal of heart disease occurs when the fat level is reduced to 10%. A low salt intake is also recommended.

Recipes in this book are designed for the *preventive* diet, but most can be modified for therapeutic use by reducing or eliminating the high fat foods mentioned above, and limiting salt and high-salt seasonings.

THE NEWSTART® FOOD PYRAMID

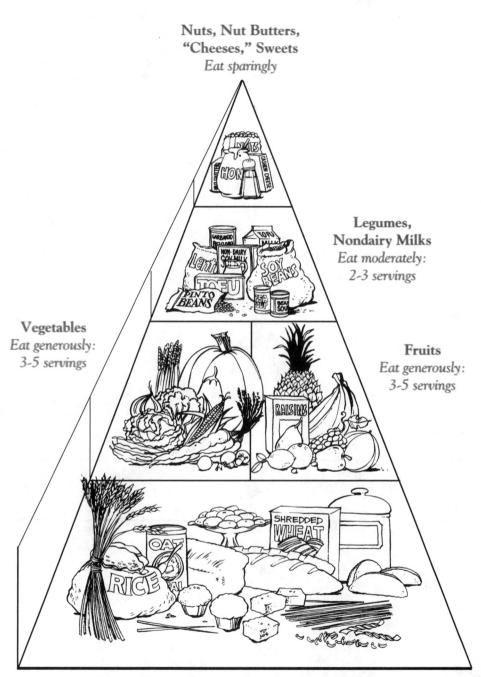

**Nuts, Nut Butters,
"Cheeses," Sweets**
Eat sparingly

**Legumes,
Nondairy Milks**
*Eat moderately:
2-3 servings*

Vegetables
*Eat generously:
3-5 servings*

Fruits
*Eat generously:
3-5 servings*

Whole Grains, Breads, Cereals, Rice, and Pasta
Eat liberally: 6-11 servings

BREADS

*Pictured at left: Breakfast Biscuits, Old World Black Bread,
Corn Muffins, and Basic Whole Grain Bread.*

BREADS

BREAD-MAKING BASICS

Making your own bread has many benefits. Not only is it economical, but home-baked bread can be more healthful and certainly more flavorful than the bread you buy at the supermarket. It is not as difficult as you may think and can be fun, especially if you make it with your family. Though recipes may vary, here are the basic steps to bread-making:

1) Mix dry ingredients, including yeast, using no more than one-third the flour.
2) Add hot water and other liquids, sweeteners, and moisturizers. Beat for 200 strokes or use an electric mixer at medium speed for 2 minutes. The consistency should be stringy and soupy, like pancake batter. If it is too wet, add flour.
3) Stir in flour as needed to make a thick dough. Mix together until you have an even consistency and all flour is moistened.
4) Let the dough rest for 5-10 minutes. The whole-grain fibers are absorbing the liquids. This step is a safeguard against adding too much flour while you knead.
5) Remove from bowl by covering the entire surface of dough with flour. Shake off excess flour and knead a 2-3 loaf ball of dough for 10 minutes. (If you use an electric mixer to knead, add flour slowly until the dough forms a ball that pulls away from the side of the bowl.) Knuckle test—with the surface of the dough lightly coated and your knuckle coated with flour, press gently into the dough. If the dough is soft and pliable and springs back, refilling the hole, you are ready to continue.
6) Cover and let rise in a warm place for at least 30 minutes.
7) Punch out all the air bubbles. Shape into loaves and place in sprayed pans. Fill each pan 2/3 full, then let rise till dough is 11/2-2" above the pan.
8) Bake at 350° F for 35-45 minutes. Test to see if loaves are ready by thumping the bottom and sides of each loaf. A hollow sound signals a thoroughly baked loaf. A dull thud, or moist, soggy sides, indicate the need for longer baking.

One slice of whole wheat bread has
as much fiber as 5-6 slices of white bread.

3

HELPFUL TIPS

If your bread didn't turn out like you had hoped, here are a few helpful tips:

SYMPTOM	POSSIBLE CAUSES
Crumbly, dry	Wrong type of flour; too much flour added; not enough kneading; oven too cool.
Heavy	Old, partially inactive yeast; wrong type of flour; too much flour added; not enough kneading; poor distribution of ingredients; too cool while rising; rising period too short; poor quality of flour (low gluten content).
Coarse	Rising period too long; oven too cool; not enough flour; not enough kneading.
Yeasty taste	Rising period too long; temperature too high during rising.
Sour taste	Rising period too long; insufficiently baked; poor ingredients.

SPECIALTY BREADS

The recipe for Whole Wheat Bread (p. 5) may be used for all types of bread rolls, bread sticks, pizza crusts, etc. The points to remember are the *specific temperatures* and *rising times*.

ROLLS: Bake at 400° F for 15-20 minutes.

BREAD STICKS: Roll pencil-thin. Raise 2-5 minutes. Bake in a preheated 375° F oven until browned, about 10 minutes.

PIZZA OR DESSERT CRUST: Spread dough onto cookie sheet until very thin. Prick with a fork as you would a pie crust. Let rise to desired height. Place in oven (325° F) and bake 15-20 minutes. Next day bake at 400° F for 10 minutes, with topping.

WHOLE WHEAT BREAD

1/4	cup gluten flour
1	cup whole wheat flour
1/3	cup rolled oats
1	tablespoon active dry yeast
1	teaspoon salt
23/4	cups very warm water (130° F)
1/3	cup honey or date butter
2	tablespoons applesauce
41/4	cups whole wheat flour (as required for kneading)

Stir first 5 ingredients together. Add next 3 ingredients and stir 200 strokes. Consistency should be soupy and stringy, like pancake batter. Add 3 cups flour and mix thoroughly. Let stand about 5 minutes. Place dough on a floured board. Knead 10 minutes, adding as little of the remaining flour as necessary to prevent dough from sticking to hands or table. Shape into 2 loaves. Let rise for 40 minutes, then bake at 325-350° F for 30-45 minutes. **Yields two 22 ounce loaves.**

Per 1 ounce slice: 63 calories; 2.5 g protein (15%); 13.4 g carbohydrate (81%); 0.3 g fat (4%); 50 mg sodium; 6 mg calcium; 0 mg cholesterol.

OLD WORLD BLACK BREAD

2	cups lukewarm water
1	tablespoon honey
1	tablespoon active dry yeast
2	cups rye flour
1/2	cup gluten flour or Do-Pep
1/2	cup rolled oats
1/4	cup carob powder
1	tablespoon salt
1/3	cup molasses
2	cups whole wheat flour
2/3	cup unbleached flour (as required for kneading)

Combine first 3 ingredients in a bowl. Stir next 5 ingredients together and add to yeast mixture. Stir in molasses. Let stand for 10 minutes. Add whole wheat flour and unbleached flour as needed until you have a stiff dough. Knead vigorously for 10 minutes, or until dough is moist, but not sticky. Allow to rise until doubled (at least 1 hour). Punch down. Spray your hands with a food release spray and shape dough into a round loaf. Place on a cookie sheet and let rise for 45 minutes in a warm place. Bake in a preheated 350° F oven for 1 hour, or until thoroughly baked. If it gets too brown on top, cover with foil until baking is completed. **Yields one 22 ounce loaf.**

Per 1.5 ounce slice: 177 calories; 6.9 g protein (15%); 37.6 g carbohydrate (81%); 0.8 g fat (4%); 395 mg sodium; 37 mg calcium; 0 mg cholesterol.

BASIC WHOLE GRAIN BREAD
(For Magic Mill or other bread machine)

1	package active dry yeast
23/4	cups whole wheat bread flour
1/4	cup gluten flour
1/2	cup barley flour
1/4	cup quick oats
1	rounded tablespoon date butter or honey
1	teaspoon salt
2	tablespoons applesauce
11/2	cups warm water

Place ingredients into the bread machine in the order listed. Select "White Bread" on the control panel and push "Start." **Yields one 29 ounce loaf.**

Per 1 ounce slice: 54 calories; 2.4 g protein (17%); 11 g carbohydrate (78%); 0.3 g fat (5%); 68 mg sodium; 6 mg calcium; 0 mg cholesterol

ONION ROLLS

2	teaspoons active dry yeast
1/4	cup warm water
5	cups whole wheat flour
1/2	cup chopped onion
1	tablespoon onion powder
1/2	tablespoon barley malt
1/2	tablespoon salt
3/4	cup pitted dates
1/4	cup hot water
3/4	cup water

Dissolve yeast in 1/4 cup warm water. Mix next 5 ingredients together in a large mixing bowl. Process dates and hot water in a blender until smooth. Add yeast mixture and date mixture to dry ingredients. Mix well. Add 3/4 cup water and knead until a soft dough. Add more water or flour as necessary. Let rise for about 20 minutes. Form into small rolls and bake on floured cookie sheets at 350° F for 30 minutes. **Yields about 2 1/2 dozen rolls.**

Per two rolls: 171 calories; 5.8 g protein (13%); 38.4 g carbohydrate (84%); 0.7 g fat (4%); 198 mg sodium; 26 mg calcium; 0 mg cholesterol.

OAT BISCUITS

2	cups very warm water
1	scant tablespoon active dry yeast
1	tablespoon honey
1	tablespoon molasses
3	cups rolled oats
2	cups whole wheat pastry flour
3/4	teaspoon salt

Dissolve yeast in water. Stir in honey and molasses and let stand 5 minutes. Process oats in a blender until a fine flour (1 1/2 cups at a time). Combine oat flour and yeast mixture in a large bowl. Add 1 cup of the whole wheat flour and the salt. Beat vigorously for 150 strokes. Stir in remaining flour. Drop by 1/4 cup portions onto sprayed cookie sheets. Let rise 20-30 minutes, then bake at 400° F for 15 minutes. Very good when split and toasted. If desired, substitute 8-10 dates, blended, for honey and molasses. **Yields 1 dozen biscuits.**

Per biscuit: 157 calories; 6.2 g protein (15%); 30.8 g carbohydrate (76%); 1.6 g fat (9%); 137 mg sodium; 22 mg calcium; 0 mg cholesterol.

BREAKFAST BISCUITS

1/4 cup water
1 tablespoon apple juice
1/2 tablespoon active dry yeast
2/3 cup clean, raw cashews
2/3 cup water
1 cup barley or oat flour
1 cup whole wheat pastry flour
1/2 teaspoon salt

Heat 1/4 cup water and apple juice to 115° F. Pour into a bowl, then sprinkle yeast over mixture. Process cashews and 2/3 cup water in a blender until very smooth. Add to yeast mixture. Stir in remaining ingredients and knead lightly. If dough is a little soft, add more flour. Roll out to 1/4" thick and cut into rounds. Let rise for 20 minutes. Bake in a preheated 350° F oven for 15 minutes, or until golden brown. **Yields 20 23/4" biscuits.**

VARIATION: For **Shortbread**, substitute apple juice concentrate for juice. Roll out on a cookie sheet. Score to desired size and follow above directions.

Per biscuit: 67 calories; 2.2 g protein (12%); 10.3 g carbohydrate (58%); 2.3 g fat (29%); 55 mg sodium; 7 mg calcium; 0 mg cholesterol.

JOHNNY CORNCAKES

2 cups cornmeal
2 cups rolled oats
1/2 cup unsweetened coconut
1 teaspoon salt
21/4 cups hot water
1/2 cup raisins

Mix first 4 ingredients. Lightly process hot water and raisins in a blender. Mix all ingredients together and let stand a few minutes. Spoon onto sprayed cookie sheets. Bake at 325-350° F for 45 minutes, or until bottoms of cakes are golden brown. Serve with jam, if desired. **Yields 21 corncakes.**

Per corncake: 88 calories; 2.5 g protein (11%); 16.8 g carbohydrate (73%); 1.6 g fat (16%); 95 mg sodium; 9 mg calcium; 0 mg cholesterol.

CORN MUFFINS

11/2 cups cornmeal
1 cup barley or whole wheat pastry flour
3 tablespoons Ener-G Baking Powder
11/2 tablespoons Ener-G Egg Replacer
3/4 teaspoon salt
11/2 cups water
6 tablespoons clean, raw cashews
2 tablespoons honey
2 tablespoons applesauce

Preheat oven to 400° F. Mix first four ingredients in a large bowl. Process water and cashews in a blender until smooth. Add honey and applesauce and continue blending until smooth. Pour over dry ingredients and stir just until mixed. Pour into muffin cups—about 3/4 full. Bake about 30 minutes, or until lightly browned. **Yields 1 dozen muffins.**

Per muffin: 133 calories; 2.9 g protein (8%); 25 g carbohydrate (74%); 2.7 g fat (18%); 141 mg sodium; 8 mg calcium; 0 mg cholesterol.

QUICK PIZZA CRUST

1 cup water
1 tablespoon active dry yeast
11/2 cups whole wheat flour
1 cup barley flour or unbleached flour
1 tablespoon honey
1/2 teaspoon salt
2 tablespoons barley flour
2 teaspoons fine cornmeal

Heat water to 115° F. Stir yeast into heated water. Stir in remaining ingredients, except last two. Sprinkle 2 tablespoons barley flour on counter and turn dough out to knead for about 2 minutes. Sprinkle cornmeal onto two 12" ungreased pizza pans or cookie sheets. Divide dough and roll into large circles. Place on pizza pans and bake at 350° F for 20 minutes. **Serves 6.**

Per 1/6 recipe: 199 calories; 6.8 g protein (13%); 42.2 g carbohydrate (82%); 1 g fat (4%); 166 mg sodium; 16 mg calcium; 0 mg cholesterol.

PAN PIZZA CRUST

1/4	cup apple juice
1/4	cup water
1/2	tablespoon active dry yeast
2/3	cup peanuts or clean, raw cashews
2/3	cup water
1	cup oat flour
1	cup whole wheat pastry flour
1/2	teaspoon salt
1	cup finely chopped onion
1/2	teaspoon garlic powder
1/2	teaspoon paprika
1/2	teaspoon salt

Heat apple juice and 1/4 cup water to 115° F. Sprinkle yeast over this mixture. Process peanuts and 2/3 cup water in a blender until very smooth. Pour into a bowl and add yeast mixture. Stir in the flours and 1/2 teaspoon salt. Place on floured board and knead lightly. If dough is a bit soft, add more flour to make a stiff dough. Divide in two and roll into large circles and place on pizza pans. Sprinkle crusts with remaining ingredients and press into dough with finger-tips. Let stand in a warm place for about 15 minutes. Bake in a preheated, 400° F oven for 7-10 minutes, or until golden brown. **Serves 6.**

Per 1/6 recipe: 302 calories; 10.6 g protein (14%); 48 g carbohydrate (61%); 8.8 g fat (25%); 331 mg sodium; 21 mg calcium; 0 mg cholesterol.

MARIA'S TORTILLAS

2	cups water
1	cup rolled oats
1/2	cup walnuts, *or* 1/4 cup sesame seeds
1/2	teaspoon salt
2	cups unbleached wheat flour
2	cups whole wheat flour

Process first 4 ingredients in a blender until smooth. Pour into a bowl and add flours. Knead, then roll small pieces into very thin circles. Bake on a hot, dry griddle for one minute each side. Oil is not necessary. **Yields 2 dozen tortillas.**

Per tortilla: 101 calories; 3.3 g protein (13%); 17.9 g carbohydrate (69%);2 g fat (18%); 46 mg sodium; 10 mg calcium; 0 mg cholesterol.

CHAPATI

2 cups whole wheat bread flour
2 cups whole wheat pastry flour
1/2 teaspoon salt
11/4 cups water

Place flours and salt in a large bowl and stir in enough of the water to make a kneadable dough. Knead for about 5 minutes. Cover dough in bowl and let it rest for 15-20 minutes. Break dough into golf ball size pieces, shaping each one into a ball. Place ball on floured surface and with a rolling pin, roll into a very thin round, about 1/16" thick. Repeat with remaining balls. Heat a dry skillet or griddle to medium. Cook about 15 seconds each side. Flip again and repeat cooking time. Stack on a clean towel and cover to keep warm until ready to serve. **Yields 16 chapati.**

Per chapati: 102 calories; 4.1 g protein (15%); 21.8 g carbohydrate (80%); 0.6 g fat (5%); 11 mg calcium; 69 mg sodium; 0 mg cholesterol.

PITA BREAD CHIPS

6 small whole wheat pita bread pockets
1/2 cup salted water (opt.)

Separate top and bottom layers of pita bread and cut into pie-shaped wedges or cracker-sized pieces. Spray with salted water and place on a cookie sheet. Bake at 250° F for about 10 minutes, or until dry and crisp. **Serves 6.**

Per 2 ounce pocket: 146 calories; 6.2 g protein (16%); 31 g carbohydrate (79%); 0.9 g fat (5%); 214 mg sodium; 19 mg calcium; 0 mg cholesterol.

CRISPY CORN CHIPS

21/2 dozen corn tortillas
1 cup water
1 tablespoon salt or garlic salt

Cut each tortilla into 6 wedges. Mix water and salt and place in a sprayer or shallow bowl. Lightly spray tortillas with salted water, or dip them into salted water. Spread on a baking sheet and toast at 300° F until crispy. **Serves 15.**

Per 2 tortillas or 12 chips: 134 calories; 4.3 g protein (12%); 25.6 g carbohydrate (73%); 2.3 g fat (15%); 534 mg sodium; 87 mg calcium; 0 mg cholesterol.

CORN CRISPS

1	cup coarse cornmeal (polenta)
1/3	cup quick oats
1	teaspoon dill weed (opt.)
1	teaspoon onion powder
1	teaspoon salt
3/4	teaspoon garlic powder
21/2	cups boiling water

Combine all ingredients, except water. Add water and mix together well. Let stand about 8 minutes until thickened. Drop batter by tablespoon onto a sprayed cookie sheet. Bake at 400° F for 30 minutes, or until golden brown and edges begin to loosen from pan. **Yields 3 dozen crisps.**

Per 3 crisps: 46 calories; 1.3 g protein (11%); 9.3 g carbohydrate (78%); 0.6 g fat (11%); 165 mg sodium; 6 mg calcium; 0 mg cholesterol.

COCONUT CRACKERS

13/4	cups water
1/4	cup clean, raw cashews
11/2	tablespoons sesame seeds
1	tablespoon shredded coconut
3/4	cup cornmeal
3/4	cup rolled oats

Process cashews with about 3/4 cup of the water in a blender until very smooth. Add sesame seeds and coconut and continue blending. Add remaining water and other ingredients and blend again until smooth. Pour onto a sprayed cookie sheet and bake at 350° F for 20 minutes. Remove from oven and score to desired cracker size. Return to oven and bake an additional 40 minutes, or until very lightly browned. Check frequently to prevent burning. **Yields 4 dozen 13/4" crackers.**

Per 4 crackers: 71 calories; 2.1 g protein (12%); 10.3 g carbohydrate (56%); 2.6 g fat (32%); 2 mg sodium; 17 mg calcium; 0 mg cholesterol.

DOUGHNUTS

2	cups warm water
2	tablespoons active dry yeast
2/3	cup honey
1/2	cup wheat germ
1/3	cup almond or cashew butter
2	tablespoons lecithin granules
1	teaspoon salt
3/4	teaspoon cardamom
3	cups unbleached flour
23/4	cups whole wheat flour

Sprinkle yeast over water, then add remaining ingredients, except flours. Mix well. Add flours to make a medium-stiff dough. Knead 5 minutes. Let rise until double (about 1 hour). Roll out to 1/2" thick and cut into doughnut shapes. Place on a cookie sheet and let rise another 30 minutes. Bake at 375° F for about 20 minutes. **Yields 3 dozen doughnuts.**

Per doughnut: 113 calories; 3.3 g protein (11%); 21.3 g carbohydrate (72%); 2.2 g fat (17%); 62 mg sodium; 13 mg calcium; 0 mg cholesterol.

SEASONED BREAD CRUMBS

2	cups soft whole wheat bread crumbs
2	teaspoons food yeast flakes
1	teaspoon Bernard Jensen's Protein Seasoning (opt.)
1	teaspoon onion powder
1	teaspoon paprika
1	teaspoon salt
1/2	teaspoon garlic powder

Toss all ingredients together. Bake on a cookie sheet at 200° F until entirely dry and lightly browned. Store in an airtight container. **Yields 1 1/2 cups.**

VARIATION: For **Seasoned Croutons**, cut bread into cubes before tossing with seasonings.

Per 1/4 cup serving: 42 calories; 1.8 g protein (16%); 8.4 g carbohydrate (75%); 0.4 g fat (9%); 436 mg sodium; 19 mg calcium; 0 mg cholesterol.

BREAKFAST

Pictured at left: Waffles Perfect, Blueberry Topping, and Scrambled Tofu.

BREAKFAST

The most important meal of the day!

When you wake up in the morning, your body has been fasting for as many as 12-15 hours. It needs fuel in order to work at peak efficiency.

THE EFFECTS OF A SKIPPED BREAKFAST ARE:
- Short attention span
- Lack of alertness
- Longer reaction time
- Increased tremor
- Low blood sugar
- Decreased work productivity
- In school children: more social and emotional problems, and poorer grades[1]

A GOOD BALANCED BREAKFAST WILL HELP:
- Supply energy when you need it most
- Prevent irritability and fatigue
- Provide 1/3 to 1/2 of the day's total nutritional requirements
- Control weight by promoting regular meals and preventing mid-morning hunger
- Stop the urge to snack
- Stabilize blood sugar levels
- Improve efficiency and safety
- Promote better attitudes and scholastic achievement

"Blessed are you, O land. . . when your princes feast at the proper time for strength and not for drunkenness!" Ecclesiastes 10:17.

WHOLE GRAINS
Every day — Every meal

USE A VARIETY OF WHOLE GRAINS:

Amaranth	Buckwheat	Oats	Sorghum
Barley	Corn	Quinoa	Triticale
Brown Rice	Millet	Rye	Wheat

SUGGESTED USES:

- *Breakfast*: Granola, waffles, pancakes, cereals, muffins, breads.
- *Lunch:* Pastas, patties, pizza, savory loaves, casseroles, breads, rolls, rice, and desserts.
- *Supper:* Zwieback, popcorn, cereal, crackers, muesli, fruit crisps, cookies.

BENEFITS:

- B Vitamins (important for proper functioning of the nerves)
- Minerals
- Complex carbohydrates
- Protein
- Fiber

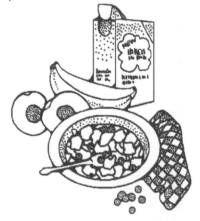

CHOOSE BREAKFAST CEREALS WISELY:

Many prepared cereals have added refined sugar, often "hidden." Read labels carefully. Recommended cereals are: Shredded Wheat, Nutri-Grain, and similar whole grain cereals prepared without excessive sugar, salt, fat, and additives. Nature's Path, Barbara's Bakery, Health Valley, and other brands can be found in natural foods stores or the natural foods section of many grocery stores. Avoid products that contain baking soda or powder (see page 193).

COOKING WHOLE GRAINS: It is wise to rinse grains before cooking, especially amaranth, brown rice, and oat or wheat berries. Quinoa has a bitter resin and should be well rinsed. Dextrinizing (toasting) whole grains improves flavor and shortens cooking time. Toast in a dry skillet over moderately high heat for 3-5 minutes. Stir constantly until golden brown. An alternate method is baking at 200° F for 10-15 minutes, watching carefully and stirring occasionally to prevent burning.

To cook—bring water to boil in a heavy pot with a tight-fitting lid. Salt water if desired, a scant 1/4 teaspoon per cup of water. Stir in the grain, cover, and reduce heat to low. Maintain a gentle simmering throughout cooking time. To prevent stickiness, cook thoroughly and avoid stirring while cooking. Whole grains are cooked when they are tender. (If water is visible in the bottom of the pot, simmer a few minutes without the cover to evaporate this fluid.) When done, cover pot and remove from heat. Let stand for a few minutes, then fluff with a fork and serve, or use as desired.

Whole grains are especially good cooked overnight at 200° F (low setting) in a crockpot, electric bean pot, double boiler, or electric skillet. They can also be steamed, baked, or boiled.

Grain - 1 Cup Dry	Water	Cooking Times	Yield
Amaranth	3 cups	25-30 min.	3 cups
Barley	3 cups	75 min.	31/2 cups
Brown rice	2 cups	60 min.	3 cups
Buckwheat (kasha)	2 cups	15-20 min.	21/2 cups
Bulgur wheat	2 cups	15-20 min.	21/2 cups
Cornmeal (polenta)	1 quart	25 min.	3 cups
Cracked wheat	2 cups	25 min.	21/3 cups
Millet (patties, pudding)	1 quart	45-60 min.	4 cups
Millet (cereal, to replace rice)	2 cups	45-60 min.	3 cups
Oat berries	2-3 cups	45-60 min.	3 cups
Oats (rolled)	2 cups	15 min.	2 cups
Oats (quick)	2 cups	5 min.	2 cups
Quinoa	2 cups	15-20 min.	4 cups
Triticale berries (soak 8 hrs)	21/4 cups	40 min.	31/3 cups
Wild rice	3 cups	60+ min.	4 cups
Whole wheat or rye berries	3 cups	2 hours	3 cups

DELICIOUS MILLET

2	cups water
1	teaspoon salt
1	cup millet grain
3/4	cup chopped dates
1/2	cup toasted, chopped almonds*
1/2	cup unsweetened, shredded coconut

Bring water and salt to a boil. Add millet and bring to boil again. Cover, reduce heat, and simmer about 45 minutes. Just before serving, stir in remaining ingredients. **Yields 41/2 servings.**

*Toast raw almonds in a 350° F oven for about 8 minutes.

Per 1 cup serving: 366 calories; 8.6 g protein (9%); 58.6 g carbohydrate (61%); 12.5 g fat (29%); 447 mg sodium; 61 mg calcium; 0 mg cholesterol.

COMPANY OATMEAL

3	cups water
2	cups rolled oats
3/4	cup raisins
1	large apple, peeled, sliced
1	teaspoon vanilla
1/2	teaspoon salt
1/8	teaspoon coconut extract (opt.)
1/8	teaspoon coriander (opt.)
pinch	cardamom (opt.)

Mix all ingredients together and bake at 350° F for 45 minutes, or simmer in a saucepan for 20 minutes. **Serves 4.**

Per 1 cup serving: 258 calories; 7.4 g protein (11%); 53.8 g carbohydrate (80%); 2.8 g fat (9%); 254 mg sodium; 41 mg calcium; 0 mg cholesterol.

CROCKPOT BREAKFAST

2	quarts water
1	cup pearl barley or wheat berries
1	cup chopped, mixed dried fruit
1	cup raisins
1	teaspoon salt
1/2	teaspoon coriander (opt.)
1	cup toasted, chopped almonds* (opt.)

While crockpot is heating up on high setting, boil water. Add barley and bring to boil again. Pour into crockpot and cover. Turn heat to low setting, and leave on overnight. About 15 minutes before serving, stir in remaining ingredients, except almonds, and place in a serving dish. Sprinkle almonds over top. **Serves 7.**

*Toast raw almonds in a 350° F oven for about 8 minutes.

Per 1 cup serving: 217 calories; 3.4 g protein (6%); 53.7 g carbohydrate (92%); 0.5 g fat (2%); 292 mg sodium; 30 mg calcium; 0 mg cholesterol.

CRACKED WHEAT CEREAL

1	cup cracked wheat
1/4	cup unsweetened, shredded coconut (opt.)
1	quart water
8	pitted dates, chopped
1/4	cup sesame seeds
1	teaspoon salt

Dextrinize (toast) cracked wheat and coconut by stirring constantly in a dry pan over medium heat for several minutes, until lightly browned. Place in a saucepan and add remaining ingredients. Bring to a boil. Reduce heat and simmer for 45 minutes. Sprinkle with chopped nuts, if desired. For variation, add 1 tablespoon carob powder. **Serves 4.**

Per 1 cup serving: 254 calories; 5.7 g protein (9%); 49.1 g carbohydrate (74%); 5.2 g fat (17%); 497 mg sodium; 115 mg calcium; 0 mg cholesterol.

INDIAN CORNMEAL

> 1 quart cold water
> 1 cup coarse cornmeal
> 1/4 cup raisins
> 1 teaspoon salt
> 1 teaspoon vanilla
> 1/4 teaspoon coriander or anise (opt.)

Stir cornmeal into cold water. Cook over low heat, stirring frequently, until thickened and smooth. Stir in remaining ingredients. Pour into a baking dish and bake at 350° F for 45-60 minutes. **Serves 4.**

VARIATIONS: (1) Add 1/4 cup chopped nuts and 1 small apple, shredded; (2) Add 1/4 cup unsweetened, flaked coconut.

Per 1 cup serving: 141 calories; 3 g protein (9%); 30.3 g carbohydrate (85%); 1 g fat (7%); 497 mg sodium; 18 mg calcium; 0 mg cholesterol.

MEAL-IN-ONE BREAKFAST

> 2 cups cooked brown rice
> 1 cup unsweetened, crushed pineapple
> 1/2 cup chopped dates or whole raisins
> 1/4 cup chopped walnuts

Combine all ingredients and serve warm or cold. For variation, substitute 1-2 ripe bananas and 1/2 cup strawberries, blended together, for pineapple. **Yields 31/2 servings.**

Per 1 cup serving: 256 calories; 4 g protein (6%); 50.5 g carbohydrate (75%); 5.6 g fat (19%); 3 mg sodium; 33 mg calcium; 0 mg cholesterol.

FRUITFUL RICE PUDDING

2	cups cooked brown rice
1	cup unsweetened, crushed pineapple
1/4	cup raisins
3/4	cup hot water
1/2	cup clean, raw cashews (scant)
1	ripe medium banana
3	tablespoons orange juice concentrate
1	teaspoon vanilla
1/2	teaspoon almond extract (opt.)

Mix first 3 ingredients in a 8 x 8" casserole dish. Process remaining ingredients in a blender until smooth and pour over rice and fruit. Bake at 350° F for 45 minutes and serve hot. May be made ahead by baking for 30 minutes and reheating just before serving. Garnish with peach or banana slices, if desired. **Serves 4.**

Per 1 cup serving: 323 calories; 6 g protein (7%); 57.6 g carbohydrate (69%); 8.9 g fat (24%); 8 mg sodium; 38 mg calcium; 0 mg cholesterol.

BREAKFAST BANANA SPLIT

1/2	cup cooked millet,* brown rice, or oatmeal (thick)
1	banana, split lengthwise
1/4	cup Pineapple Berry Topping (p. 42)
2	tablespoons Cashew Cream (p. 38)
1	tablespoon chopped nuts or toasted coconut

Use a small ice cream scoop to scoop up cooked cereal. Place in a bowl and position banana halves on each side of cereal scoop. Top with remaining ingredients. **Serves 1.**

*Simmer 2-3 tablespoons millet grain in 1/2 cup salted water for 45-60 minutes.

Per serving: 460 calories; 9.7 g protein (8%); 84.8 g carbohydrate (70%); 12.1 g fat (22%); 52 mg sodium; 53 mg calcium; 0 mg cholesterol.

CREAMY MUESLI

2 1/2	cups rolled oats
3	cups apple, orange, or pineapple juice
2	bananas
1	teaspoon vanilla
1/2	teaspoon salt
1/4	teaspoon maple extract (opt.)
1/2	cup raisins
1	cup shredded apple

Dextrinize (toast) oats on a baking sheet at 300° F for 20 minutes, or until very lightly browned. Watch carefully to prevent burning. Place in a bowl. Process next 5 ingredients in a blender until smooth. Stir into oats and add raisins. Cover and refrigerate overnight. Just before serving, shred apple and stir in. **Serves 6.**

VARIATIONS: (1) Add sliced grapes or other fruits just before serving; (2) Top with chopped nuts.

Per 1 cup serving: 271 calories; 6.3 g protein (9%); 58.5 g carbohydrate (83%); 2.6 g fat (8%); 169 mg sodium; 36 mg calcium; 0 mg cholesterol.

BREAKFAST BAR MUESLI

1 1/2	cups toasted oats*
6	tablespoons chopped dried peaches
6	tablespoons chopped nuts
6	tablespoons raisins
3	cups Fruit Milk, warm or cold (p. 37)

Place dry ingredients in separate serving bowls. Serve Fruit Milk in a pitcher. Place all on table, buffet-style, for each to build his/her own muesli. **Serves 6.**

*Toast on a baking sheet at 300° F for 20 minutes, or until very lightly browned.

VARIATION: Substitute **Pineapple Fruit Sauce** for Fruit Milk: process pineapple juice and a banana and a small amount of cornstarch. Simmer, stirring constantly, until thickened.

Per 1/6 recipe: 241 calories; 7 g protein (11%); 40.9 g carbohydrate (64%); 7.3 g fat (25%); 38 mg sodium; 32 mg calcium; 0 mg cholesterol.

GRANOLA

    1 cup pitted dates
    2 ripe bananas
  1/2 cup water
1 1/2 teaspoons salt
    9 cups rolled oats
    1 cup chopped nuts
    1 cup unsweetened, shredded coconut (opt.)
  1/2 cup sunflower seeds

Process first 4 ingredients in a blender until smooth. Pour over remaining ingredients and stir together. Spread on cookie sheets to about 1/2" thick. Bake at 200° F for about 90 minutes, stirring every 30 minutes, until golden and almost dry. Turn oven off and leave pans in oven to complete drying. Or bake at lowest oven setting and leave on overnight. In the morning the granola will be done without any stirring. Store in an airtight container. **Yields 15 cups or 2 1/2 dozen servings.**

VARIATIONS: (1) Substitute rolled barley or rye for oats; (2) Use 1 1/2 cups apple juice concentrate instead of first 3 ingredients; (3) Add 1 cup chopped dried fruit after baking.

Per 1/2 cup serving: 156 calories; 5.2 g protein (13%); 23.6 g carbohydrate (58%); 5.3 g fat (29%); 99 mg sodium; 22 mg calcium; 0 mg cholesterol.

MAPLE WALNUT GRANOLA

    2 cups chopped dates
1 1/2 cups hot water
  1/2 cup apple juice concentrate
  1/2 cup walnuts
    1 tablespoon vanilla
    1 teaspoon maple flavoring
   12 cups rolled oats
    1 cup slivered almonds
  1/2 cup unsweetened, shredded coconut

Soak dates in hot water while preparing other ingredients. Combine with next 4 ingredients and process in a blender until smooth. Place remaining ingredients in a large bowl and add blended ingredients. Mix well. Spread on cookie sheets and bake at 200° F for 2-4 hours, stirring occasionally, until crisp and dry. **Yields 15 cups or 30 servings.**

Per 1/2 cup serving: 212 calories; 6.7 g protein (12%); 34.5 g carbohydrate (63%); 6.2 g fat (25%); 43 mg sodium; 36 mg calcium; 0 mg cholesterol.

PEACH BREAKFAST CAKE

51/2	**cups soft whole wheat bread crumbs**
1/3	**cup unsweetened coconut**
16	**ounce can unsweetened peaches**
2	**ripe bananas**
1/2	**cup orange or pineapple juice**
11/2	**teaspoons vanilla**
1/8	**teaspoon almond extract**
2	**bananas, sliced**
2	**cups raisins**

Combine bread crumbs and coconut and set aside. Process remaining ingredients in a blender, except last two, until smooth. In a large bowl, mix sauce with bread crumbs and coconut. Place sliced bananas and raisins in a 10 x 13" baking dish and pour sauce/crumb mixture over top. Bake at 350° F for 30 minutes, or until golden brown. Serve warm. **Serves 12.**

Per 3x3.5" piece: 180 calories; 3.1 g protein (6%); 40.5 g carbohydrate (83%); 2.2 g fat (10%); 71 mg sodium; 31 mg calcium; 0 mg cholesterol.

FRENCH TOAST

> 1 cup water
> 5 pitted dates
> 2 tablespoons clean, raw cashews or sunflower seeds
> 1/2 cup orange juice
> 1 tablespoon whole wheat flour
> 1 dozen slices whole wheat bread

Using a blender, process dates and cashews in about half of the water until very smooth. Add juice, flour, and remaining water and continue blending until smooth. Pour into a shallow bowl. Dip bread slices into batter and place on a sprayed cookie sheet. Bake at 400° F until golden brown. Turn and brown other side. May also be browned in a skillet. Top with applesauce, fresh fruit, or fruit topping, if desired. For variation, blend in a banana. **Serves 6.**

Per 2 slices: 171 calories; 5.7 g protein (13%); 31.5 g carbohydrate (70%); 3.6 g fat (18%); 320 mg sodium; 43 mg calcium; 0 mg cholesterol.

BANANA FRENCH TOAST

> 1 1/2 cups sliced bananas
> 3/4 cup soy milk
> 1/4 teaspoon vanilla
> 1/4 teaspoon ground cardamom
> 8 slices whole wheat bread

Spray a nonstick griddle with pan spray and preheat. Place all ingredients, except bread, into a blender and process until smooth. Pour into a pie plate. Dip bread slices into batter, turning to coat both sides. Scrape off excess batter. Place on hot griddle and brown each side 2-3 minutes. Serve with a fruit topping, if desired. **Serves 4.**

Per 2 slices: 230 calories; 6.7 g protein (11%); 44.9 g carbohydrate (73%); 4.5 g fat (16%); 184 mg sodium; 47 mg calcium; 0 mg cholesterol.

GOLDEN FRUIT SOUP

46 ounce can unsweetened pineapple juice
1/2 cup diced, dried apricots
1/2 cup Minute Tapioca
2 bananas, sliced
1 cup diced apples or strawberries
1 cup fresh or frozen sliced peaches
1 cup unsweetened pineapple chunks
1/2 cup seedless green grapes

Combine first 3 ingredients and cook over low heat until thickened, stirring frequently. Remove from heat. Add remaining ingredients. Serve hot or cold. For variation, add any fresh or frozen fruit of your choice. **Serves 8.**

Per 1 cup serving: 209 calories; 1.5 g protein (3%); 52.4 g carbohydrate (95%); 0.5 g fat (2%); 3 mg sodium; 40 mg calcium; 0 mg cholesterol.

APPLE BURRITOS

8 apples, cut in chunks
1/3 cup water
1/4 cup raisins
1 teaspoon vanilla
1/8 teaspoon maple flavoring
8 Maria's Tortillas (p. 10)
12 ounce can apple-grape juice concentrate
3 cans water
5 tablespoons cornstarch or arrowroot

Place first 5 ingredients in a large saucepan and cook until apples are softened. Fill tortillas with apple mixture and roll up. Place, seam-side down, in a baking dish. In a saucepan, mix juice, water and cornstarch. Bring to a boil, stirring constantly until thickened, then pour over burritos. Let set an hour or more for tortillas to absorb juice. Bake at 350° F for 30 minutes. Sprinkle chopped walnuts over top just before serving, if desired. **Serves 8.**

VARIATIONS: (1) Add 1/2 cup chopped walnuts to filling; (2) Substitute juice of choice for apple-grape.

Per burrito: 290 calories; 4 g protein (5%); 65.5 g carbohydrate (87%); 2.7 g fat (8%); 59 mg sodium; 32 mg calcium; 0 mg cholesterol.

BAKED APPLES

4	Golden or Red Delicious apples
1/4	cup chopped dates
1/4	cup chopped nuts
1/4	cup raisins
1/2	cup water
1	teaspoon fresh lemon juice
1	teaspoon vanilla

Pare about 1 inch of peeling off the top of the apples. If apples do not sit straight, cut a thin slice off the bottom. Core and stuff cavity with dates, nuts, and raisins. Place in a casserole dish. Mix remaining ingredients and pour over the apples. Cover and bake at 350° F for 45 minutes or until tender to fork. Top with Whipped Cream (p. 72), if desired. For variation, use Rome Beauty apples and substitute apple juice concentrate for water. **Serves 4.**

Per stuffed apple: 182 calories; 1.8 g protein (4%); 36.2 g carbohydrate (73%); 5.1 g fat (23%); 3 mg sodium; 21 mg calcium; 0 mg cholesterol.

RICE WAFFLES

13/4	cups water
1	cup soaked brown rice*
1/2	cup nuts or sunflower seeds
1	cup cooked brown rice
1/2	cup water
1/3	cup unsweetened coconut (opt.)
1	teaspoon vanilla, *or* 1/2 teaspoon maple flavoring
1/2	teaspoon salt

Process first 3 ingredients in a blender for about 1 minute. Add remaining ingredients and continue blending until smooth. Pour onto preheated waffle iron, sprayed with a pan spray, covering all the grids and edges. Bake until steaming stops, about 10 minutes. **Serves 3.**

*Soak rice in water for several hours or overnight.

Per 8" waffle: 413 calories; 8.7 g protein (8%); 64.1 g carbohydrate (62%); 13.8 g fat (30%); 339 mg sodium; 50 mg calcium; 0 mg cholesterol.

OAT WAFFLES

2 1/4   cups cold water
1/2   cup clean, raw cashews,
     or 2 tablespoons soy milk powder
2-4   dates, or 1 tablespoon honey
2   cups rolled oats
1   teaspoon vanilla
1/2   teaspoon salt

Lightly spray waffle iron with pan spray and preheat between medium and high heat. Place 1 cup of the water into a blender and process with cashews and dates until smooth. Add remaining ingredients and 1 more cup of the water, and blend well. Pour batter onto waffle iron and fill completely, covering all the grids and edges. Bake until steaming stops, about 10-12 minutes. Blend batter again and add remaining 1/4 cup water before baking second waffle. **Serves 5.**

Per two 4" waffles: 215 calories; 7.4 g protein (13%); 28.9 g carbohydrate (52%); 8.4 g fat (34%); 220 mg sodium; 28 mg calcium; 0 mg cholesterol.

WAFFLES PERFECT

1   cup water
1/3   cup nuts (opt.)
5   pitted dates
2   teaspoons vanilla
1   teaspoon salt
3   cups water
2   cups rolled oats
3/4   cup corn flour or millet flour
3/4   cup whole wheat flour

Process first 5 ingredients in a blender until smooth. Add remaining ingredients and continue blending until smooth. For small blenders, blend with less of the water, then pour into a pitcher and add remaining water. Pour onto preheated, nonstick waffle iron, using enough batter to cover grids and edges. Bake until steaming stops, about 12-14 minutes. If batter gets too thick, add more water and blend before pouring. Waffles may be frozen and reheated in toaster or oven. For variation, blend in a banana. **Serves 5.**

Per 8" waffle: 274 calories; 9 g protein (13%); 53.8 g carbohydrate (78%); 2.8 g fat (9%); 398 mg sodium; 35 mg calcium; 0 mg cholesterol.

CORN HOTCAKES

2	cups water
1 1/4	cups corn flour
1/4	cup clean, raw cashews
2	pitted dates
1	teaspoon salt
2	cups cooked corn

Process all ingredients in a blender, except corn, until very smooth. Add corn and turn blender on, then off immediately. Pour onto prepared griddle, like pancakes, cooking first side well before turning. **Serves 10.**

VARIATION: For **Savory Hotcakes**, omit dates and add savory seasonings of choice, such as garlic, onion, etc.

Per two hotcakes: 106 calories; 2.6 g protein (9%); 20.5 g carbohydrate (73%); 2.2 g fat (18%); 199 mg sodium; 7 mg calcium; 0 mg cholesterol.

POTATO PANCAKES

2	raw potatoes
1 1/4	cups soy or nut milk
3/4	cup water
2/3	cup barley flour
2/3	cup whole wheat flour
1	teaspoon honey,
	or 1 tablespoon chopped dates (opt.)
1	teaspoon salt

Process all ingredients in a blender and pour onto medium-hot, nonstick griddle, using 2 tablespoons batter for each pancake. Brown on both sides. Good topped with applesauce. **Serves 8.**

VARIATION: For **Savory Potato Pancakes**, omit honey and add 2-3 minced cloves of garlic. After blending, add 1 tablespoon dried onion flakes.

Per 4 pancakes: 108 calories; 3.9 g protein (14%); 21.6 g carbohydrate (77%); 1.1 g fat (9%); 252 mg sodium; 10 mg calcium; 0 mg cholesterol.

RICE CREPES

11/2 cups water
1/4 cup clean, raw cashews
2 pitted dates
1 cup brown rice flour
1/4 cup firm tofu
1 teaspoon salt

Process cashews and dates in a blender with about half of the water until very smooth. Add remaining water and other ingredients and process well. Allow mixture to stand while nonstick griddle heats. Blend again immediately before pouring crepes, and each time before you pour. Brown over medium heat (325-350° F), cooking first side well before turning. For a 5" crepe, use 1/4 cup batter. May be made ahead and reheated, covered, in oven or microwave. **Serves 6.**

SERVING SUGGESTIONS: Crepe fillings—Mince Pie filling (p. 56), Spinach-stuffed Manicotti filling (p. 128), French Onion Quiche filling (p. 126). Pancake toppings—Fresh fruit and Cashew Cream (p. 38); Fruit-Nut Topping (p. 40); Strawberry Jam (p. 43), etc.

Per two 5" crepes: 151 calories; 4.5 g protein (12%); 24.5 g carbohydrate (63%); 4.3 g fat (25%); 362 mg sodium; 32 mg calcium; 0 mg cholesterol.

WHOLE WHEAT CREPES

11/2 cups soy or nut milk
1/2 cup rolled oats
1/2 cup whole wheat pastry flour
1 teaspoon date sugar

Process all ingredients in a blender, using enough soy milk to make a thin cream. Pour 1/4 cup of batter into a small, heated, nonstick skillet and immediately swirl to coat surface. Turn when underside is lightly browned and brown the other side. Remove from heat and spoon on filling of choice. Roll and place in a casserole dish to reheat, or serve immediately. **Serves 4.**

SERVING SUGGESTIONS: See Rice Crepes recipe above.

Per two crepes: 117 calories; 5.1 g protein (17%); 19 g carbohydrate (64%); 2.5 g fat (19%); 12 mg sodium; 9 mg calcium; 0 mg cholesterol.

SCRAMBLED TOFU

1	pound firm tofu
1/2	cup chopped green onions
1/2	cup sliced mushrooms (opt.)
1/4	cup slivered almonds (opt.)
2	teaspoons Liquid Aminos
11/2	teaspoons All-Purpose Seasoning (p. 167)
1	teaspoon parsley flakes
1/4	teaspoon garlic powder
1/4	teaspoon onion powder
1/4	teaspoon turmeric (opt.)

Drain tofu thoroughly in a colander. Mash in a bowl and mix in remaining ingredients. Bake at 350° F for 30 minutes, or simmer in a nonstick skillet for about 20 minutes, until all liquid has evaporated, stirring frequently. Best if mixed several hours before cooking, to let flavors blend. **Serves 4.**

VARIATION: For **Creamed Tofu Breakfast**, combine with White Sauce (p. 91) and serve over toast.

Per 1/2 cup serving: 169 calories; 18.4 g protein (40%); 5.7 g carbohydrate (12%); 9.9 g fat (48%); 427 mg sodium; 242 mg calcium; 0 mg cholesterol.

OVEN TOASTIES

1	recipe "Cheese" Whiz (p. 154)
14	slices whole wheat bread

Spread bread with "Cheese" Whiz. Cut each slice of bread into 3 lengthwise strips. Place on a cookie sheet and bake at 200-250° F until thoroughly dried, but not browned. **Serves 14.**

Per slice: 124 calories; 3.8 g protein (12%); 15.2 g carbohydrate (46%); 6.2 g fat (42%); 169 mg sodium; 26 mg calcium; 0 mg cholesterol.

GREAT NORTHERN BREAKFAST

3	cups dried white beans
2	quarts water
1	onion, chopped
2	teaspoons salt
1	cup soy or nut milk
1	tablespoon whole wheat flour

Rinse beans under tap water. Place all ingredients, except soy milk and flour, in a crockpot set on high. Cook overnight. In the morning, mix soy milk and flour and stir in. Continue stirring until thickened. Pour over toast. **Serves 13.**

VARIATIONS: (1) For **Great Northern Soup**, use 2 quarts water, 1 1/2 cups soy milk, and 2 tablespoons whole wheat flour; (2) Reduce salt to 1 teaspoon and add 1 teaspoon beef-style seasoning.

Per 1/2 cup serving: 179 calories; 11.2 g protein (24%); 32.6 g carbohydrate (71%); 1 g fat (5%); 314 mg sodium; 72 mg calcium; 0 mg cholesterol.

OVEN HASH BROWNS

6	whole potatoes
1	onion, chopped fine
1/4	cup chopped green onions
1	tablespoon All-Purpose Seasoning (p. 167)
1	tablespoon chopped fresh parsley
1	cup "Cheese" Sauce variation of White Sauce (p. 91)

Parboil potatoes 5-7 minutes, then chill. Grate potatoes and toss with remaining ingredients, except "Cheese" Sauce. Press mixture onto a sprayed cookie sheet and bake at 400° F for 20-25 minutes until brown. Cut into 6 squares and serve with Sauce. **Serves 6.**

VARIATION: For **Potato Roll**, roll up potato "sheet," then top with Sauce.

Per 1/6 recipe: 173 calories; 4 g protein (9%); 34.4 g carbohydrate (76%); 2.9 g fat (15%); 482 mg sodium; 26 mg calcium; 0 mg cholesterol.

NUT MILK

1   quart water
1/2 cup raw, clean almonds, cashews, or
      macadamia nuts

Process nuts in a blender with about 1/2 cup of the water until a very smooth paste. Add remaining water gradually while continuing to blend. Process until very smooth. Chill and stir well before serving. **Yields 1 quart.**

VARIATIONS: (1) Blend in a small amount of honey or softened dates; (2) Blend in fruit, such as a banana or peach.

Per 1 cup serving: 96 calories; 3.2 g protein (13%); 3.3 g carbohydrate (13%); 8.5 g fat (74%); 9 mg sodium; 48 mg calcium; 0 mg cholesterol.

SWEET NUT MILK

1   quart water
2/3 cup clean, raw cashews or almonds
4   pitted dates
1/4 teaspoon salt
1/4 teaspoon vanilla

Process all ingredients in a blender with about 1 cup of the water until very smooth. Pour into a pitcher and stir in remaining water. Strain, if desired. Cover and refrigerate. Shake well before using. This milk is excellent on cereal and for cooking. **Yields 1 quart.**

VARIATIONS: (1) For **Grain Milk**, add 1 cup cooked millet or brown rice and process until smooth; (2) Substitute 1 tablespoon honey or 1/3 cup coconut for dates.

Per 1 cup serving: 153 calories; 3.6 g protein (9%); 13.6 g carbohydrate (33%); 10.5 g fat (58%); 133 mg sodium; 19 mg calcium; 0 mg cholesterol.

OAT MILK

1/3	cup rolled oats
1	cup water
2	tablespoons ground almonds
1/2	teaspoon vanilla
1/4	teaspoon salt
21/2	cups cold water
1	small ripe banana

Process dry oats in a blender until a fine flour, then cook with 1 cup water for 5 minutes. Return to blender and add almonds, vanilla, and salt. Blend until smooth, adding cold water gradually. Add enough cold water to equal 1 quart of milk. Blend in banana just before serving. **Yields 1 quart.**

Per 1 cup serving: 78 calories; 2.2 g protein (11%); 12.2 g carbohydrate (60%); 2.7 g fat (30%); 129 mg sodium; 21 mg calcium; 0 mg cholesterol.

SOY MILK

3	cups water
1	cup prepared soybeans*
1	teaspoon vanilla
1/8	teaspoon salt

Process water and soybeans in a blender until smooth. Strain liquid out through cheesecloth, if desired (save pulp to use in loaves or patties). Stir in vanilla and salt. Keep refrigerated. **Yields 22/3 cups (strained), or 33/4 cups (unstrained).**

*Soak 2 cups raw soybeans in 2 quarts water overnight. After soaking, bring beans and water to a full rolling boil in a large kettle. Lower heat and simmer 5 minutes longer. Pour off foamy liquid and add cold water to stop boiling/cooking process. When cool, drain off water. Yields 4 cups prepared soybeans. Freeze beans in 1 cup quantities, ready for making up fresh milk. Before using, rinse with hot water to thaw them quickly.

VARIATIONS: (1) Blend in 1 banana or other fruit immediately before serving; (2) Omit vanilla for use in savory recipes.

Per 1 cup serving (unstrained): 66 calories; 5.3 g protein (31%); 5.5 g carbohydrate (33%); 2.7 g fat (36%); 72 mg sodium; 39 mg calcium; 0 mg cholesterol.

FRUIT MILK

2   **cups soy or nut milk**
1   **cup orange or pineapple juice**
3   **ripe bananas**

Process all ingredients in a blender until smooth. Serve immediately. **Yields 41/2 cups.**

VARIATIONS: (1) Blend in any favorite fruit; (2) Substitute apricot or peach nectar for orange or pineapple juice.

Per 1 cup serving: 128 calories; 4 g protein (12%); 25.2 g carbohydrate (72%); 2.5 g fat (16%); 15 mg sodium; 14 mg calcium; 0 mg cholesterol.

HOT CAROB MILK

1   **quart soy milk**
11/2   **tablespoons toasted carob powder**
11/2   **tablespoons honey**
1   **teaspoon vanilla**
1/8   **teaspoon almond extract**
pinch   **salt**

Process all ingredients in a blender until smooth. Warm over medium heat, stirring frequently. May also be served cold. **Yields 1 quart.**

Per 1 cup serving: 112 calories; 6.7 g protein (22%); 13.2 g carbohydrate (44%); 4.6 g fat (34%); 63 mg sodium; 19 mg calcium; 0 mg cholesterol.

CASHEW CREAM

    1   cup water
    3/4 cup clean, raw cashews
    8   pitted dates
    1/2 teaspoon vanilla
pinch   salt

Process first 3 ingredients in a blender until very smooth. Bring to a boil, then add remaining ingredients. Reduce heat and simmer until thickened, stirring constantly. May be served warm or cold. May also be used without heating. **Yields 1 cup or 8 servings.**

VARIATIONS: (1) For a creamier, less rich cream, add 1/2-3/4 cup cooked millet or brown rice and process well. Adjust water, if necessary; (2) For a white cream, substitute 1 tablespoon honey for dates.

Per 2 tablespoon serving: 97 calories; 2.1 g protein (8%); 10.4 g carbohydrate (40%); 6 g fat (52%); 36 mg sodium; 9 mg calcium; 0 mg cholesterol.

APPLE RAISIN TOPPING

    4   Golden Delicious apples
    3/4 cup unsweetened, crushed pineapple
    1/3 cup apple juice concentrate
    1/3 cup raisins
    1/8 teaspoon cardamom or coriander
    1/8 teaspoon salt
    1 1/2 tablespoons cornstarch or arrowroot
    2   tablespoons cold water
    1/2 teaspoon fresh lemon juice

Coarsely grate apples. Combine apples with next 5 ingredients and simmer 5-10 minutes until apple shreds are soft. Mix cornstarch with cold water and add to mixture. Simmer until thickened, stirring constantly. When thickened, remove from heat and stir in lemon juice. **Yields 3 1/2 cups or 14 servings.**

SERVING SUGGESTION: Serve over waffles or whole wheat toast, spread with a little nut butter. Top with Cashew Cream (p. 38).

Per 1/4 cup serving: 56 calories; 0.3 g protein (2%); 14 g carbohydrate (95%); 0.2 g fat (3%); 22 mg sodium; 8 mg calcium; 0 mg cholesterol.

APPLE BUTTER

2   cups chopped, fresh apples
1   cup date butter
1   teaspoon fresh lemon juice

Process all ingredients in a blender until very smooth. Keep refrigerated in an airtight container. **Yields 2 cups or 16 servings.**

Per 2 tablespoon serving: 35 calories; 0.2 g protein (2%); 9.2 g carbohydrate (96%); .09 g fat (2%); 0 mg sodium; 4 mg calcium; 0 mg cholesterol.

APPLE SPREAD

2   cups cooked apple chunks or applesauce
1/4   cup raisins
3-4   drops anise flavoring, or to taste

Process all ingredients in a blender until desired smoothness. Keep refrigerated in an airtight container. Serve on waffles or toast. **Yields 2 1/4 cups or 18 servings.**

Per 2 tablespoon serving: 16 calories; 0.1 g protein (3%); 4.2 g carbohydrate (94%); .08 g fat (4%); 0 mg sodium; 2 mg calcium; 0 mg cholesterol.

BLUEBERRY TOPPING

2   cups apple or pineapple juice
6   pitted dates, chopped
1/4   cup Minute Tapioca
2   cups blueberries

Process juice and dates in a blender until very smooth. Simmer with tapioca until thick and clear, stirring constantly. Stir in berries and continue simmering for about 5 minutes. **Yields 2 cups or 8 servings.**

Per 1/4 cup serving: 83 calories; 0.4 g protein (2%); 21 g carbohydrate (96%); 0.2 g fat (3%); 4 mg sodium; 9 mg calcium; 0 mg cholesterol.

FRUIT NUT TOPPING

   1   cup unsweetened, crushed pineapple
   3   fresh peaches
   1   banana
1/4   cup unsweetened, finely shredded coconut
   4   pitted dates
1/2   cup walnuts

Process all ingredients in a blender, except walnuts, until smooth. Add walnuts and blend slightly—leave a little chunky. Serve immediately, over waffles, toast, or cereal, etc. For variation, substitute apples, apricots, or persimmons, for peaches. **Yields 2 1/2 cups or 10 servings.**

Per 1/4 cup serving: 83 calories; 1.4 g protein (6%); 11.1 g carbohydrate (49%); 4.5 g fat (45%); 1 mg sodium; 13 mg calcium; 0 mg cholesterol.

GOLDEN DELIGHT

20   ounce can unsweetened, crushed pineapple
16   ounce can unsweetened peaches or apricots
  3   tablespoons Minute Tapioca

Drain fruit and save juice. Simmer juice with tapioca, stirring constantly. When thickened, stir in fruit and mash. **Yields 3 1/2 cups or 14 servings.**

Per 1/4 cup serving: 45 calories; 0.4 g protein (3%); 11.9 g carbohydrate (96%); .04 g fat (1%); 2 mg sodium; 8 mg calcium; 0 mg cholesterol.

LEMON SAUCE

  2   cups unsweetened pineapple juice
1/4   cup honey or apple juice concentrate
1/4   cup fresh lemon juice
1/3   cup cornstarch or arrowroot
1/2   teaspoon fresh grated lemon peel
1/4   teaspoon salt

Process all ingredients in a blender until very smooth. Heat in a saucepan, stirring constantly, until thickened. **Serves 9.**

Per 3 tablespoon serving: 78 calories; 0.2 g protein (1%); 19.9 g carbohydrate (98%); .04 g fat (1%); 55 mg sodium; 11 mg calcium; 0 mg cholesterol.

GRAPE JAM/TOPPING

2 cups unsweetened grape juice
1 cup raisins
3 tablespoons cornstarch or arrowroot
3 tablespoons cold water

Heat 1 cup of the grape juice and raisins until raisins are plump. Process in a blender until raisins are in small pieces. Add remaining grape juice and bring to a boil in a small saucepan. Mix cornstarch with cold water and add to juice. Simmer until thickened, stirring constantly. Keep refrigerated in an airtight container. **Yields 21/2 cups or 10 servings.**

VARIATION: For **Grape Syrup**, increase grape juice to 3 cups and raisins to 2 cups.

Per 1/4 cup serving: 83 calories; 0.8 g protein (3%); 21.2 g carbohydrate (96%); 0.1 g fat (1%); 3 mg sodium; 12 mg calcium; 0 mg cholesterol.

PEACH PEAR SAUCE

2 cups canned, unsweetened peaches, drained
2 cups canned, unsweetened pears, drained
5 pitted dates, chopped
11/2 tablespoons cornstarch or arrowroot
2 tablespoons cold water

Dice peaches and pears. In a blender, process 1/2 cup of peaches, 1/2 cup of pears, and dates, until smooth. Pour into a saucepan and simmer. Mix cornstarch and cold water, then add to saucepan. Continue simmering, stirring constantly, until thickened. Stir in remaining peaches and pears. **Yields 31/2 cups or 14 servings.**

Per 1/4 cup serving: 45 calories; 0.4 g protein (3%); 11.7 g carbohydrate (96%); 05 g fat (1%); 3 mg sodium; 6 mg calcium; 0 mg cholesterol.

PINEAPPLE BERRY TOPPING

20 ounce can unsweetened, crushed pineapple
1 cup chopped dates
1 cup blueberries
1 cup raspberries

Simmer pineapple and dates, stirring frequently, until dates are soft and mixture begins to thicken. Stir in berries and serve. **Yields 33/4 cups or 15 servings.**

VARIATION: For **Icy Pineapple Berry Jam**, freeze pineapple/date mixture, then process 2 tablespoons of mixture with 2 cups frozen berries and a small amount of juice.

Per 1/4 cup serving: 65 calories; 0.5 g protein (3%); 17 g carbohydrate (95%); 0.2 g fat (2%); 2 mg sodium; 11 mg calcium; 0 mg cholesterol.

RASPBERRY JAM

1 1/2 cups raspberry juice concentrate
1 1/2 cups water
1/4 cup Minute Tapioca
2 cups mashed raspberries

Mix first 3 ingredients together and let stand for 15 minutes. Bring to a boil, then reduce heat and simmer, stirring constantly, until tapioca is clear. Stir in raspberries and remove from heat. Keep refrigerated in an airtight container. For variation, use any juice concentrate or fruit. **Yields 4 cups or 32 servings.**

Per 2 tablespoon serving: 29 calories; 0.4 g protein (5%); 7 g carbohydrate (93%); 0.1 g fat (2%); 1 mg sodium; 6 mg calcium; 0 mg cholesterol.

STRAWBERRY JAM

5   rings dried pineapple
1/2 cup apple, orange, or pineapple juice
2   cups unsweetened frozen strawberries, thawed

Cut dried pineapple into small pieces. Cover with juice and let stand until pineapple is soft. Drain and process with strawberries until smooth, adding juice if necessary. **Yields 31/2 cups or 28 servings.**

Per 2 tablespoon serving: 15 calories; 0.1 g protein (3%); 3.9 g carbohydrate (96%); .03 g fat (2%); 1 mg sodium; 4 mg calcium; 0 mg cholesterol.

STRAWBERRY TOPPING

1   cup apple or pineapple juice
8   pitted dates, chopped
1   tablespoon cornstarch or arrowroot
2   cups unsweetened strawberries

Process first 3 ingredients in a blender until very smooth. Bring to a boil, stirring constantly. When thickened, stir in strawberries. **Yields 2 cups or 8 servings.**

Per 1/4 cup serving: 52 calories; 0.4 g protein (3%); 13.3 g carbohydrate (94%); 0.2 g fat (3%); 2 mg sodium; 10 mg calcium; 0 mg cholesterol.

DESSERTS

Pictured at left: Sesame Candy, Haystack Cookies, Cluster Cookies, Tofu "Cheesecake" with Berry "Cheesecake" Topping, and Ambrosia.

DESSERTS

COMPLEX CARBOHYDRATES

Carbohydrates are the main source of energy for all body functions and muscular activity. They are also necessary for the proper regulation of protein and fat metabolism. Complex carbohydrates should make up 65-75% of our total calorie intake.

The principal carbohydrates found in foods are: sugars, starches, and fiber. Simple sugars, found in honey and fruits, are very easily digested, while double sugars, such as sucrose, require some digestive action. However, starches are much more complex and require prolonged enzymatic action in order to be broken down into simple sugars for digestion. Whole grains and potatoes are examples of starches.

Dietary fibers are complex carbohydrates that are not digested, but which modify the intestinal content in important ways. Generally, "insoluble" fibers add bulk to the intestinal tract, speed transit time, and help prevent constipation. "Water soluble" fibers slow the passage of food through the intestine by forming a type of gel, but do not increase fecal bulk.

All animal products, including meat, poultry, dairy products, eggs, and fish, contain no fiber. All unprocessed plant foods are high in dietary fiber. In America, where the majority of caloric intake comes from animal sources, refined grains, and processed foods, the dietary fiber intake is very low, at an average of 10 grams per day. It is recommended that Americans increase their fiber intake to around 30 grams per day. Many cultures, in which the diet is starch-centered, such as in China, are consuming 60-70 grams per day.[2]

A diet high in refined carbohydrates can result in vitamin or mineral deficiencies. This type of diet also contributes to diabetes, heart disease, high blood pressure, anemia, kidney disorders, and cancer.

There are more than 700 different over-the-counter laxative preparations on the market. Most of these drugs act as stimulants to the colon, and their repeated use can lead to a chronic inability of the colon to act on its own. A diet high in plant fiber is the best method of preventing constipation and maintaining a healthy digestive tract.

Insoluble fibers in the cell walls of plants (cellulose, hemicellulose, and lignin) may protect against diverticulosis,[3] ulcers,[4] irritable bowel syndrome,[5] hemorrhoids, varicose veins,[6] and hiatal hernia.[7] Insoluble fibers are found in wheat bran and other non-digestible, fibrous parts of grains and vegetables, and are often called "roughage."

Another major health benefit fiber provides is its cancer-preventive action. Dietary fiber helps dilute, bind, and remove many carcinogens and toxic substances found in our food supply. The increased stool volume and rapid transit time through the intestine helps prevent these harmful substances from prolonged contact with the bowel wall, thus decreasing their absorption rate. This helps prevent colon cancer, as well as other cancers.[8]

Studies have shown that dietary fiber also binds cholesterol and bile acids, thus reducing the risk of heart disease and gallstones.[9]

Water soluble fibers (pectins and gums) have been shown to greatly improve the control and prevention of diabetes and hypoglycemia. The gel formation from water soluble fibers slows glucose absorption and may reduce erratic swings in blood sugar.[10] Some of the most beneficial soluble fibers are found in beans, oats, barley, and fruits.

CONDITIONS THAT RESPOND TO A HIGH FIBER DIET

A diet high in natural fiber may prevent and help treat the following health problems:

- High serum cholesterol
- Constipation
- Colon and other cancers
- Diverticulitis
- Gallstones
- Irritable bowel syndrome
- Hemorrhoids
- Hiatal hernia
- Diabetes
- Hypoglycemia
- Ulcers
- Varicose veins

GUIDELINES FOR HEALTHFUL DESSERTS

Delicious, wholesome treats will please your family and can be so nutritious that they'll become an occasional breakfast highlight or midday main dish. Whole grains, dried or fresh fruits, nuts and seeds, can be simply prepared in delicious combinations or served elegantly "as is." Pies, pudding, cookies, fruit bars, "smoothies," and fruit crisps, made from wholesome ingredients, will please the most discriminating taste buds.

When nuts and seeds are used in a special treat, limit your meal to simple foods and let the dessert provide the calories which would usually be present in your main dish. Natural desserts that are high in fat are best used at breakfast or lunch.

COMMON SWEETS	ALTERNATIVES
Syrup	Fruit sauce
Ice cream	Smoothies
Jams	Fruit spreads
Soft drinks	Water (between meals)
Candy	Dried fruit
Pastries	Fruit breads, fruit bars, etc.
Cookies	Wholesome cookies

SUGAR FACTS

• Too much sugar depletes the body of B vitamins. B vitamins are essential for healthy nerves. A depletion of B vitamins lowers our resistance to infection and makes us irritable and depressed.

• Too much sugar increases the blood fat levels and tends to clog the arteries. This lowers the body's resistance to disease. Sugar plays a significant role in the buildup of cholesterol.

• Too much sugar contributes to tooth decay, because it slows the fluid flow through the tiny canals of the teeth. The teeth lose their resistance to viral and bacterial invasion and decay results.

• Rich, heavy desserts cause irritation of the stomach, mental dullness, and obesity. Natural sweets can satisfy the "sweet tooth" while furnishing vitamins and minerals.

• Too much sugar weakens the white blood cells, which furnish our main line of defense against invading germs. One white cell can normally attack and destroy 14 invading germs. After eating an excess of sugar, this capability is reduced dramatically. See the table on next page.

Sugar's Effect on One White Blood Cell[11]

Teaspoons of Sugar	Germs Destroyed
0	14.0
6	10.0
12	5.5
18	2.0
24	1.0

Natural Sweets and White Sugar Compared

Food Item	Calories	Calcium (mg)	Iron (mg)	Potassium (mg)	Vitamin C (mg)
Apple	81	10.0	0.3	159	7.8
Honey, 1 T	65	1.0	0.1	11	0
Dates, 2	46	5.4	0.2	108	0
Maple Syrup, 1 T	50	33	.24	26	0
Orange	62	52.4	0.1	237	69.7
Raisins, 2 T	54	8.9	0.4	136	0.6
Strawberries, 1 C	45	20.9	0.6	247	84.5
White sugar, 1 T	48	0	0	0.4	0

Refined Sugar in Common Foods

Food Item	Tsps. Sugar (appr.)
Angel food cake, 4 oz	7.0
Banana split	25.0
Berry pie, 1 slice	10.0
Candy, hard, 4 oz	20.0
Chewing gum, 1 stick	0.5
Chocolate cake, iced, 4 oz	10.0
Chocolate mint, 1 piece	2.0
Cola drink, 12 oz	9.0
Custard pie, 1 slice	10.0
Donut, glazed	6.0
Ice cream sundae	7.0
Jelly, 1 T	4-6.0
Seven-Up, 12 oz	9.0

CHOCOLATE AND CAROB COMPARED

Here is a table designed to help you evaluate chocolate and its suitability as a food compared to carob. Make a decision based on facts and not on taste and habits alone.

CHOCOLATE

- **Methylxanthines:** are contributing factors in breast cancer, and possibly prostate cancer. Caffeine is a methylxanthine. It is wise to discontinue the use of coffee, tea, colas, chocolate, and all forms of methylxanthines.
- **Tannin:** is present in all brands of cocoa from which chocolate is made, and can have harmful effects on the mucous membranes of the digestive tract.
- **Theobromine:** causes headaches, central nervous system irritation, itching, depression, anxiety, and fibrocystic disease of the breast.
- **Sugar:** in large amounts is required to mask the bitter flavor and make it palatable.
- **Fat:** makes up a minimum of 50% of chocolate's calories. Oil, cream, or milk is often added which makes it extremely rich, heavy, oily, and difficult to digest.
- **Contamination:** often occurs during the processing of cocoa beans. The bean pods are left in piles outdoors to ferment for several days. Fermentation is essential to develop the chocolate flavor. Aflatoxins, which are cancer promoting toxins produced by molds, are produced in the beans. In addition, insects, rodents, and small animals may make nests in the piles. Though the beans are later cleaned, roasted, and shelled, contaminants can be present. The U.S. Department of Health and Human Services does allow for some contamination in chocolate from "insects, rodents, and other natural contaminants."[12] Some individuals thought to be allergic to chocolate may actually be allergic to the contaminants in the chocolate.

CAROB POWDER

No methylxanthines.

No tannin.

No theobromine.

Naturally sweet.

Low in fat (about 2% of its calories).

No fermentation necessary; no known allergic reactions.

TOFU "CHEESECAKE"

1 1/2	cups R. W. Knudsen Coconut Nectar
3	tablespoons Emes Kosher Jel
3/4	cup apple juice concentrate
3/4	cup firm tofu
1 1/2	tablespoons fresh lemon juice
2	teaspoons grated lemon peel
3/4	teaspoon grated orange peel
1/2	teaspoon coconut extract (opt.)
pinch	salt
1	Crumble Crust (p. 59)
1	recipe Berry "Cheesecake" Topping (p. 52) or Pineapple "Cheesecake" Topping (p. 53)

Sprinkle Emes Jel over coconut nectar in a saucepan. Heat, stirring constantly, until gelatin is dissolved. Process in a blender with remaining ingredients, except last 2, until smooth. Pour into a bowl and refrigerate. When firm, blend again until smooth and creamy. Pour into Crumble Crust and refrigerate until firm. Serve with "Cheesecake" Topping. **Serves 8.**

VARIATIONS: (1) Substitute ambrosia or pineapple-coconut juice for coconut nectar; (2) Omit Emes Jel and use filling as a sauce or topping.

Per 1/8 recipe: 294 calories; 7.5 g protein (10%); 61.5 g carbohydrate (81%); 2.9 g fat (9%); 137 mg sodium; 77 mg calcium; 0 mg cholesterol.

BERRY "CHEESECAKE" TOPPING

3/4	cup fruit juice concentrate, such as raspberry-apple
1/2	cup water
4	teaspoons cornstarch or arrowroot
1/2	cup fresh or frozen berries (opt.)

Place juice concentrate in a saucepan. Dissolve cornstarch in water and stir into juice. Bring to a boil, stirring constantly, until thickened and clear. Remove from heat and add berries, if desired. When cool, pour over "Cheesecake." Garnish and serve. **Serves 8.**

Per appr. 2 tablespoon serving: 54 calories; 0.2 g protein (1%); 13.2 g carbohydrate (97%); 0.1 g fat (1%); 2 mg sodium; 4 mg calcium; 0 mg cholesterol.

PINEAPPLE "CHEESECAKE" TOPPING

20   ounce can crushed, unsweetened pineapple
1   tablespoon cornstarch or arrowroot
1   tablespoon grated orange peel

Drain pineapple and pour juice into a saucepan. Dissolve cornstarch in juice, then add pineapple. Heat on medium setting, stirring constantly, until bubbly and thickened. When cool, add orange peel and spread over "Cheesecake." **Serves 8.**

Per 1/4 cup serving: 47 calories; 0.3 g protein (2%); 12.2 g carbohydrate (96%); 0.1 g fat (1%); 1 mg sodium; 11 mg calcium; 0 mg cholesterol.

BANANA CREAM PIE

2   cups water
1   cup chopped dates
1/2   cup clean, raw cashews or blanched almonds
3   tablespoons cornstarch or arrowroot
1   teaspoon vanilla
1/8   teaspoon salt
2   bananas
1   baked Nutri-Grain Pie Crust (p. 59)

Process all ingredients in a blender, except last two, until very smooth. Place in a heavy saucepan and cook until thickened, stirring constantly. Cool in refrigerator. When cool, slice bananas and layer with cream filling in pie crust. Garnish with fresh strawberries or toasted coconut, if desired. **Serves 8.**

VARIATIONS: (1) For **Banana Cream Parfait**, spoon filling into parfait glasses with alternate layers of sliced bananas and granola; (2) Layer cream with other fresh fruits, in a pie or parfait glasses.

Per 1/8 pie: 260 calories; 3.4 g protein (5%); 48.8 g carbohydrate (71%); 7.5 g fat (24%); 148 mg sodium; 22 mg calcium; 0 mg cholesterol.

LEMON PIE

12	ounce can pineapple juice concentrate
2	tablespoons Emes Kosher Jel (heaping)
11/2	cups water
1/4	cup fresh lemon juice
2	tablespoons orange juice concentrate
1/4	teaspoon grated lemon peel
1	baked Nutri-Grain Pie Crust (p. 59)

Bring pineapple juice concentrate to a boil. Add Emes Jel and stir until dissolved. Stir in remaining filling ingredients. Place in refrigerator to set up. When firm, process in a blender until smooth. Pour into baked pie crust and chill until firm. Garnish with lemon twist and mint, if desired. Top with Whipped Cream (p. 72), if desired. For variation, blend in 1/2 cup tofu. **Serves 8.**

Per 1/8 pie: 183 calories; 2.3 g protein (5%); 39.4 g carbohydrate (82%); 2.7 g fat (13%); 92 mg sodium; 27 mg calcium; 0 mg cholesterol.

PINEAPPLE LEMON CREAM PIE

2	cups pineapple juice
1/2	cup water
1/3	cup cornstarch or arrowroot
21/2	tablespoons fresh lemon juice
1	tablespoon orange juice concentrate
1	tablespoon pineapple juice concentrate
1/8	teaspoon grated lemon peel
1/4	teaspoon lemon extract, or to taste
1	baked Nutri-Grain Pie Crust (p. 59)

Place pineapple juice in a medium saucepan. Dissolve cornstarch in water and add to saucepan. Bring to a boil, stirring until thickened and clear. Remove from heat. Add remaining filling ingredients and mix well. Cool slightly before pouring into pie crust. Refrigerate until firm. Top with Whipped Cream (p. 72) or Coconut Whip (p. 71), if desired. **Serves 8.**

Per 1/8 pie: 174 calories; 1.7 g protein (4%); 35.7 g carbohydrate (79%); 3.3 g fat (17%); 112 mg sodium; 20 mg calcium; 0 mg cholesterol.

APPLE RAISIN PIE

4	cups sliced Delicious apples
3/4	cup fresh orange juice
1/2	cup raisins
1/3	cup chopped dates
2	tablespoons cornstarch or arrowroot
11/2	tablespoons cold water
1	baked Basic Pie Crust (p. 58)

Cook first 4 ingredients in a saucepan until apples are tender. Mix cornstarch and cold water and add to saucepan. Cook over low heat, stirring gently, until thickened and liquid is clear. Pour into pie crust and allow to set. May be served hot or cold. **Serves 8.**

Per 1/8 pie: 201 calories; 3.4 g protein (6%); 35.5 g carbohydrate (66%); 6.7 g fat (28%); 84 mg sodium; 42 mg calcium; 0 mg cholesterol.

ORANGE CREAM PIE

1/2	cup water
21/2	tablespoons Emes Kosher Jel
10.5	ounce package silken soft tofu, drained
1/2	cup frozen orange juice concentrate
2	tablespoons honey
11/2	cups cubed orange segments*
1	baked Nutri-Grain Pie Crust (p. 59)

Heat water to boiling in microwave oven or in a saucepan. Remove from heat and stir in Emes Jel. Stir until dissolved. Pour into a blender and add tofu, juice concentrate, and honey and process until very smooth. Add orange segments and turn blender on and then off immediately. Repeat as necessary to break up the segments into tiny pieces. Pour into pie crust and chill. **Serves 8.**

*Flavor is enhanced if membrane is removed from segments.

Per 1/8 pie: 197 calories; 3.9 g protein (8%); 37.5 g carbohydrate (73%); 4.4 g fat (19%); 114 mg sodium; 38 mg calcium; 0 mg cholesterol.

"MINCE" PIE

20   ounce can unsweetened, crushed pineapple
3/4   cup ground dried pears (remove hard centers)
3/4   cup ground raisins
1   orange, peeled, seeds removed, ground
1   tablespoon grated orange peel
1   baked Basic Pie Crust (p. 58)
1   recipe Whipped Cream (p. 72) (opt.)

Mix all ingredients thoroughly, except last two. Pour into pie crust and bake at 375° F until heated through, about 20 minutes. Serve hot or cold, topped with Whipped Cream, if desired. Filling can also be used as jam or crepe filling. **Serves 8.**

Per 1/8 pie: 243 calories; 3.9 g protein (6%); 46.8 g carbohydrate (71%); 6.7 g fat (23%); 86 mg sodium; 61 mg calcium; 0 mg cholesterol.

CAROB CREAM PIE

3   cups soy or nut milk
3   tablespoons Emes Kosher Jel
1   cup pitted dates, *or* 5 tablespoons honey
3   tablespoons carob powder
1   tablespoon molasses
1   tablespoon vanilla
1   teaspoon Roma, Postum, or other cereal "coffee"
2   drops mint flavoring (opt.)
1   baked Basic Pie Crust (p. 58)

Heat 1 cup of the soy milk with the Emes Jel and stir until Jel is dissolved. Combine with remaining filling ingredients and process in a blender until very smooth. Pour into a bowl and chill until firm. When firm, blend again (add more milk, if necessary) and pour quickly into pie crust. Chill again until firm. Garnish with lightly toasted coconut, if desired. **Serves 8.**

VARIATION: For **Carob Cream Pudding**, omit Emes Jel and add 3 tablespoons cornstarch or arrowroot. Heat until thickened, stirring constantly. Pour into dessert dishes and chill.

Per 1/8 pie: 220 calories; 6 g protein (10%); 34.8 g carbohydrate (59%); 8.3 g fat (31%); 96 mg sodium; 54 mg calcium; 0 mg cholesterol.

PUMPKIN PIE

1 1/2	cups chopped dates
1 1/4	cups water
1	cup clean, raw cashews
1	tablespoon coriander
1/2	tablespoon cardamom
1	teaspoon vanilla
1/2	teaspoon salt
16	ounce can pumpkin
2/3	cup water
2	teaspoons Emes Kosher Jel
1	unbaked Basic Pie Crust (p. 58)

Process first 7 ingredients in a blender until very smooth. Add pumpkin and stir until well mixed. Bring 2/3 cup water to boil and add Emes Jel. Stir until dissolved. Add to pumpkin mixture and stir well. Pour into pie crust and bake at 350° F for 50 minutes. Shield pie crust edges with foil. Let cool. Top with Cashew Cream (p. 38) or 1/2 cup chopped pecans, if desired. **Serves 8.**

Per 1/8 pie: 319 calories; 6.7 g protein (8%); 46 g carbohydrate (54%); 14.7 g fat (39%); 213 mg sodium; 69 mg calcium; 0 mg cholesterol.

DESSERT PIZZA

1	recipe Basic Pie Crust dough (p. 58)
1/3	cup peanut butter
1 1/2	cup applesauce
1/4	cup raisins
2	tablespoons date or malt-sweetened carob chips
1	tablespoon shredded coconut

Roll pie crust dough into a pizza pan size circle and place on a sprayed pizza pan. Bake 10-15 minutes, or until browned. Let cool slightly, then spread with thin layer of peanut butter, then top evenly with applesauce. Sprinkle with remaining ingredients and return to oven to warm. Leave in just long enough to melt the carob chips. Cut and serve while warm. **Serves 8.**

Per 1/8 pizza: 214 calories; 5.7 g protein (10%); 22.7 g carbohydrate (40%); 12.7 g fat (50%); 134 mg sodium; 38 mg calcium; 0 mg cholesterol.

BASIC PIE CRUST

3/4 cup barley or brown rice flour
1/3 cup almond or cashew butter
1/3 teaspoon salt
3 tablespoons water

Mix first 3 ingredients thoroughly. Add water and mix well. Form into a ball and roll between two layers of plastic wrap. Place in an ungreased 9" pie plate. Prick with fork and bake at 350° F until lightly browned. Suitable for both sweet and savory fillings. **Serves 8.**

Per 1/8 crust: 104 calories; 2.7 g protein (10%); 10.3 g carbohydrate (38%); 6.4 g fat (53%); 90 mg sodium; 29 mg calcium; 0 mg cholesterol.

ALMOND SESAME PIE CRUST

1/3 cup almonds
1/3 cup sesame seeds
1/2 cup water
1/2 cup barley flour
1/2 cup whole wheat pastry flour
1/3 cup soy flour
1/2 teaspoon salt

Process almonds and sesame seeds in a blender until fine. Add water and blend until smooth. Combine with remaining ingredients and knead lightly until dough is not sticky. Roll between sheets of plastic wrap until very thin (1/16"). Place dough in pie pan and prick with fork. Bake at 375° F until golden brown. **Serves 8.**

Per 1/8 crust: 129 calories; 5.9 g protein (17%); 13.6 g carbohydrate (40%); 6.5 g fat (43%); 126 mg sodium; 36 mg calcium; 0 mg cholesterol.

CRUMBLE CRUST

1/2	cup chopped dates
1/2	cup hot water
1	cup Grape-Nuts cereal
3/4	cup rolled oats, lightly blended
1/4	teaspoon salt

Soften dates in hot water, then process in a blender until smooth. Combine with remaining ingredients and press into a sprayed pie pan with dampened fingers. Use a little more Grape-Nuts, if necessary. Bake at 375° F for 10 minutes. Cool and fill. **Serves 8.**

Per 1/8 crust: 111 calories; 3.1 g protein (11%); 25 g carbohydrate (85%); 0.6 g fat (4%); 161 mg sodium; 14 mg calcium; 0 mg cholesterol.

NUTRI-GRAIN PIE CRUST

2 1/4	cups Nutri-Grain Wheat Flakes cereal
3/4	cup unsweetened, finely shredded coconut
6	tablespoons apple, orange, or pineapple juice concentrate

Place Nutri-Grain flakes in a plastic bag and crush well with a rolling pin, or process in a blender until semi-fine. Place crumbs in a bowl and stir in remaining ingredients, making sure that juice concentrate is mixed evenly. Place in a sprayed 11" pie pan and press into place with a rubber spatula or your hands. Bake at 400° F for about 7 minutes, or until golden brown. **Serves 8.**

Per 1/8 crust: 93 calories; 1.4 g protein (6%); 17 g carbohydrate (69%); 2.7 g fat (25%); 89 mg sodium; 7 mg calcium; 0 mg cholesterol.

WAFFLE CAKE

3   Rice Waffles (p. 29) or Waffles Perfect (p. 30)
2   cups pudding variation of Carob Cream Pie (p. 56)
2   bananas, sliced
1   cup Carob Fudge Frosting (p. 60)
1   cup Banana Cream (p. 70)

Use a circular waffle iron for making waffles, or cut waffles into circles. Layer waffles with pudding and bananas. Frost the cake with Carob Fudge Frosting and serve with Banana Cream. **Serves 8.**

Per 1/8 cake: 364 calories; 8.8 g protein (9%); 58.2 g carbohydrate (61%); 12.8 g fat (30%); 219 mg sodium; 43 mg calcium; 0 mg cholesterol.

CAROB FUDGE FROSTING

3/4   cup boiling water
1/2   cup chopped dates
1/4   cup carob powder
1/2   cup peanut butter
1   teaspoon vanilla
1/8   teaspoon salt

Process first 3 ingredients in a blender until very smooth. Pour into a bowl and add remaining ingredients. Stir well and chill. **Yields 1 1/2 cups or 12 servings.**

Per 2 tablespoon serving: 89 calories; 3 g protein (12%); 9.3 g carbohydrate (38%); 5.4 g fat (50%); 72 mg sodium; 14 mg calcium; 0 mg cholesterol.

CAROB MOUSSE

1	pound silken soft tofu, cut in chunks
1/4	cup honey
3	tablespoons toasted carob powder
2	teaspoons vanilla
1/2	teaspoon grated orange peel

Place all ingredients in a blender and process until very smooth and creamy. Pour into serving dishes and chill. **Serves 5.**

Per 1/3 cup serving: 132 calories; 7.5 g protein (21%); 18.9 g carbohydrate (52%); 4.4 g fat (27%); 9 mg sodium; 109 mg calcium; 0 mg cholesterol.

COCONUT RICE PUDDING

2	cups "lite" coconut milk
15	dates, pitted, *or* 1/2 cup chopped dates
1	tablespoon honey
1/2	teaspoon grated orange peel
2	cups cooked short grain brown rice
1/4	cup currants or raisins
2	tablespoons unsweetened, shredded coconut

Process coconut milk and dates in a blender until very smooth. Pour into a large saucepan and mix well with remaining ingredients. Cover and simmer over low heat for about 20 minutes, stirring occasionally. Serve warm or chilled. **Serves 6.**

Per 1/2 cup serving: 215 calories; 2.2 g protein (4%); 41.4 g carbohydrate (74%); 5.3 g fat (22%); 36 mg sodium; 19 mg calcium; 0 mg cholesterol.

RICE PUDDING

1	quart soy or nut milk
2	cups water
1	cup long grain brown rice
1	cup short grain brown rice
1	teaspoon salt
2	cups water
1/2	cup whole, blanched almonds*
1/4	cup honey
2	tablespoons Minute Tapioca
1/2	teaspoon vanilla
1/16	teaspoon almond extract
1/2	cup slivered, blanched almonds*
1	whole, blanched almond*

Place first 5 ingredients in a large, heavy saucepan, and bring to a boil. Reduce heat and let simmer, uncovered, stirring occasionally, until rice is creamy and the liquid is entirely absorbed. Refrigerate. Process whole, blanched almonds in a blender with about 1 cup of the remaining water, until very smooth. Add second cup of water and continue blending until smooth.

Strain mixture through a cheesecloth and pour liquid into a saucepan (save pulp for use in patties, loaves, etc.). Add honey and tapioca. Bring to a boil, then reduce heat and cook until tapioca is clear, stirring constantly. When thickened, remove from heat, stir in flavorings, and refrigerate until chilled. When cool, process in a blender until smooth. Stir into rice, being sure to break up any clumps. Stir in slivered almonds, and add one whole, blanched almond. Garnish and serve. **Serves 10.**

*Boil raw almonds in water for 1 minute. Drain and cool, then pinch off skins.

This is a traditional Danish dessert served at Christmas dinner. It is best when served cold, topped with a warm cherry sauce. Berry "Cheesecake" Topping (p. 52) may be used. Before serving, one whole, blanched almond is stirred into the bowl. The pudding is then served and eaten very carefully, for whoever finds the whole almond, and presents it, unbroken, receives a special gift.

Per 1/2 cup serving: 275 calories; 8.1 g protein (11%); 41.3 g carbohydrate (59%); 9.4 g fat (30%); 215 mg sodium; 52 mg calcium; 0 mg cholesterol.

TAPIOCA PUDDING

1	quart hot water
1	cup blanched almonds*
1/3	cup honey
1/3	cup small pearl tapioca
1	teaspoon coconut extract
1	teaspoon vanilla
1/4	teaspoon salt

Process almonds with 1 cup of the hot water in a blender until very smooth. Add remaining water and continue blending a little longer. Strain mixture through cheesecloth and pour liquid into a saucepan (save pulp for use in patties, loaves, etc.). Add remaining ingredients and bring to a boil. Turn heat to low and stir with a whisk until tapioca is clear. Pour into dessert dishes and chill. **Serves 8.**

*Boil raw almonds in water for 1 minute. Drain and cool, then pinch off skins.

Per 1/2 cup serving: 152 calories; 4 g protein (10%); 20.4 g carbohydrate (50%); 7.4 g fat (41%); 71 mg sodium; 51 mg calcium; 0 mg cholesterol.

CREAM PUDDING DELIGHT

2	cups hot, cooked millet*
2	cups unsweetened, crushed pineapple, with juice
3	rings dried pineapple (soaked in juice)
1/2	banana
1	tablespoon vanilla
1/4	teaspoon salt
1	cup Grape-Nuts Cereal
2	cups sliced fruit, such as bananas, strawberries, kiwi, blueberries, etc.

Process first 6 ingredients in a blender until very smooth. Layer ingredients in a 9 x 9" pan, or parfait glasses, starting with Grape-Nuts on the bottom, then pudding, then fruit, etc. **Serves 9.**

*Simmer 1/2 cup millet grain in 2 cups salted water for 45-60 minutes.

Per 3" square: 161 calories; 2.9 g protein (7%); 38.2 g carbohydrate (90%); 0.5 g fat (3%); 144 mg sodium; 20 mg calcium; 0 mg cholesterol.

APPLE CRISP

5 Golden Delicious apples, cored, diced
1 cup unsweetened, crushed pineapple
1 cup raisins
2 cups Granola (p. 25)
1 cup Cashew Cream (p. 38)

Simmer apples, pineapple, and raisins, in a saucepan, or bake in the oven, until apples are tender. Place in a casserole dish or individual dessert dishes and top with granola and Cashew Cream. **Serves 8.**

Per 1/8 crisp: 294 calories; 5.6 g protein (7%); 53.3 g carbohydrate (67%); 9 g fat (26%); 93 mg sodium; 37 mg calcium; 0 mg cholesterol.

APRICOT CRISP

3   cups unsweetened pineapple juice
1/2 cup chopped dates
1   teaspoon vanilla
3   tablespoons arrowroot or cornstarch
3   tablespoons cold water
6   cups apricot halves
3   cups Granola (p. 25) or Grape-Nuts cereal

Process dates with about 1 cup of pineapple juice in a blender until very smooth. Pour into saucepan and add remaining juice and vanilla. Bring to a boil. Mix arrowroot and cold water and add to saucepan. Cook several minutes, stirring constantly, until thick and clear. Arrange apricots in a 9 x 12" baking dish. Pour sauce over apricots and top with Granola or Grape-Nuts. Bake at 350° F for 30 minutes. **Serves 12.**

VARIATIONS: (1) Substitute peach slices for apricot halves; (2) Substitute peach or pear juice, or apricot nectar, for pineapple juice.

Per 3" square: 201 calories; 3.7 g protein (7%); 43 g carbohydrate (81%); 2.7 g fat (12%); 55 mg sodium; 40 mg calcium; 0 mg cholesterol.

PEACH CRISP

6	cups canned, unsweetened peaches
2	cups peach juice from canned peaches
1	small, ripe banana
1/2	cup dates
3/4	teaspoon coriander
3	tablespoons Minute Tapioca
1	recipe Nutri-Grain Pie Crust mixture (p. 59),
	or 3 cups Granola (p. 25)

Drain peaches and set aside 2 cups of juice. Process juice with banana, dates, and coriander in a blender until smooth. Add tapioca. Place peaches in a 10 x 14" casserole dish. Pour sauce over peaches. Top with Nutri-Grain Pie Crust mixture or Granola and bake at 350° F for 40-50 minutes. **Serves 8**.

Per 1/8 crisp: 283 calories; 3.2 g protein (4%); 64.9 g carbohydrate (85%); 3.5 g fat (10%); 120 mg sodium; 36 mg calcium; 0 mg cholesterol.

APRICOT DESSERT

2	cups unsweetened apricot nectar
1/4	cup soy or nut milk
2	tablespoons cornstarch or arrowroot
1/4	cup diced, dried apricots or currants
1/4	cup coarsely chopped pistachios
1/2	teaspoon vanilla
1	recipe Cashew Cream (p. 38)
	or Whipped Cream (p. 72) (opt.)

Bring apricot nectar to a boil. Meanwhile, dissolve cornstarch in milk. Add to boiling nectar and boil for one minute, stirring constantly. Let cool slightly and stir in remaining ingredients, except Cashew Cream. Pour into a serving dish or individual dessert dishes and chill. Top with chilled Cashew Cream just before serving. Garnish with pine nuts or pistachios, if desired. **Serves 4.**

Per 1/2 cup serving: 157 calories; 2.8 g protein (7%); 29 g carbohydrate (70%); 4.3 g fat (23%); 8 mg sodium; 24 mg calcium; 0 mg cholesterol.

APPLE BREAD PUDDING

4	cups sliced apples
1/2	cup raisins
2	tablespoons flour
1	teaspoon coriander
1/8	teaspoon salt
2 1/2	slices whole wheat bread, cut in 1/2" cubes
2	cups raspberry-apple juice
2	tablespoons cornstarch or arrowroot
1	tablespoon fresh lemon juice
1	tablespoon vanilla
pinch	salt

Lay apples in a large, sprayed, baking dish. Mix next 4 ingredients and sprinkle over apples. Place bread cubes in a bowl and pour 1 cup of raspberry-apple juice over top, being sure that all bread is moistened. Arrange cubes over apple slices. Mix remaining juice and ingredients in a small saucepan and cook until thick and clear, stirring constantly. Pour over fruit and cubes and bake in a preheated 350° F oven for 50-60 minutes. Cover the last 15 minutes to avoid burning. Serve hot or cold. **Serves 6.**

Per 1/6 recipe: 173 calories; 1.8 g protein (4%); 40 g carbohydrate (90%); 1.1 g fat (6%); 108 mg sodium; 27 mg calcium; 0 mg cholesterol.

AMBROSIA

1	cup pineapple juice
2	teaspoons small pearl tapioca
1	cup sliced bananas or grapes
1	cup cubed oranges
1	cup cubed pineapple
1/2	cup shredded coconut

Cook juice and tapioca together until tapioca is clear, stirring constantly. Remove from heat. Stir in remaining ingredients and chill. **Serves 6.**

Per 1/2 cup serving: 104 calories; 1 g protein (4%); 21.1 g carbohydrate (76%); 2.5 g fat (21%); 2 mg sodium; 24 mg calcium; 0 mg cholesterol.

HOMEMADE "ICE CREAM"

3 1/2 cups water
2/3   cup clean, raw cashews
1 1/2 cups hot, cooked millet*
1/2   cup honey, *or* 3/4 cup pitted dates
2   teaspoons vanilla
1/4   teaspoon salt

Process cashews with about 1 cup of the water in a blender until very smooth. Add millet and remaining water and continue blending. Add remaining ingredients and blend until very smooth. Pour into an ice cream freezer and follow directions for dairy ice cream. **Serves 11.** (From *Something Better*.)

*Simmer about 6 tablespoons millet grain in 1 1/2 cups salted water for 45-60 minutes.

VARIATIONS: (1) For **Carob "Ice Cream,"** add 2 tablespoons carob powder; (2) For **Maple Walnut "Ice Cream,"** add 1 teaspoon maple flavoring and 1/2 cup finely chopped walnuts; (3) For **Fruity "Ice Cream,"** add 1-2 cups strawberries, peaches, or other fruit.

Per 1/2 cup serving: 112 calories; 1.6 g protein (6%); 18.3 g carbohydrate (63%); 3.9 g fat (31%); 49 mg sodium; 7 mg calcium; 0 mg cholesterol.

TUTTI-FRUTTI "ICE CREAM"

1   quart pineapple-coconut juice or ambrosia juice
3/4   cup orange juice concentrate
3/4   cup clean, raw cashews or soy milk powder
3   cups unsweetened, crushed pineapple
4   large bananas
1   teaspoon vanilla
1/4   teaspoon salt
1/8   teaspoon coconut extract (opt.)

Divide and prepare recipe in two batches if using a 1 1/2 quart blender. Process first 3 ingredients in a blender. With blender running, add remaining ingredients and continue blending until very smooth. Mix batches well and pour into an ice cream freezer and follow directions for dairy ice cream. **Serves 19.**

Per 1/2 cup serving: 166 calories; 2 g protein (5%); 24.3 g carbohydrate (56%); 7.8 g fat (40%); 71 mg sodium; 177 mg calcium; 0 mg cholesterol.

PINEAPPLE SHERBET

20   ounce can unsweetened, crushed pineapple
1   very ripe banana
1/2   cup orange juice concentrate

Process all ingredients in a blender until very smooth. Pour into a shallow bowl and freeze until mushy. Whip with a beater and refreeze until firm. **Serves 3.**

Per 1/2 cup serving: 112 calories; 1.2 g protein (4%); 28.3 g carbohydrate (94%); 0.2 g fat (2%); 3 mg sodium; 22 mg calcium; 0 mg cholesterol.

STRAWBERRY SLUSH

2   cups crushed ice
3/4   cup pineapple juice or apricot nectar
1/2   banana
2   tablespoons fresh or frozen strawberries

Process all ingredients in a blender until smooth. Pour into dessert dishes or parfait glasses. **Serves 3.**

Per 1 cup serving: 54 calories; 0.4 g protein (3%); 13.5 g carbohydrate (94%); 0.2 g fat (3%); 1 mg sodium; 13 mg calcium; 0 mg cholesterol.

GRAPE ICE

12   ounce can grape juice concentrate
3   juice cans water
8   ounce can unsweetened, crushed pineapple
1   ripe banana

Process all ingredients in a blender until very smooth. Freeze until mushy, then whip with a beater. Freeze again and serve when firm. **Serves 8.**

Per 1 cup serving: 106 calories; 0.5 g protein (2%); 26.6 g carbohydrate (96%); 0.2 g fat (2%); 7 mg sodium; 13 mg calcium; 0 mg cholesterol.

FRUIT SMOOTHIES

1 1/2	cups soy or nut milk, or fruit juice
4	ripe bananas, frozen, sliced
2	cups frozen berries or other fruit

Place soy milk in a blender and while blending, gradually add frozen fruit. Continue blending until smooth. Serve immediately. **Serves 6.**

Per 1 cup serving: 112 calories; 2.9 g protein (9%); 24.3 g carbohydrate (79%); 1.6 g fat (12%); 9 mg sodium; 19 mg calcium; 0 mg cholesterol.

CAROB SMOOTHIES

3	cups soy or nut milk
10	pitted dates, *or* 2 tablespoons honey (opt.)
1/4	cup carob powder
8	ripe bananas, frozen, sliced

Process first three ingredients in a blender until very smooth. With blender running, gradually add bananas and continue blending until smooth. Serve immediately. **Serves 8.**

SERVING SUGGESTIONS: (1) Top with granola, chopped nuts, coconut, fruit sauces, or chopped dried apples (Oven-dry apple slices at 250° F until brown, but not hard—they harden as they cool.); (2) Use in a banana split.

Per 1 cup serving: 169 calories; 4 g protein (8%); 38.8 g carbohydrate (81%); 2.3 g fat (11%); 13 mg sodium; 25 mg calcium; 0 mg cholesterol.

BANANA POPSICLES

6	ripe bananas
1	recipe Carob Fudge Frosting (p. 60)
3/4	cup chopped nuts or toasted coconut

Cut bananas in half, width-wise. Insert popsicle sticks in cut ends. Coat with frosting, then roll in nuts or coconut. Dilute frosting with a little water, if necessary, so it is easy to spread. Cover a shallow pan with a sheet of waxed paper or plastic wrap, and place popsicles on the pan. Cover with plastic wrap and freeze. **Serves 12.**

Per popsicle: 188 calories; 5.2 g protein (10%); 24.2 g carbohydrate (47%); 9.9 g fat (43%); 74 mg sodium; 39 mg calcium; 0 mg cholesterol.

"FUDGESICLES"

2	cups water
3/4	cup chopped dates
3/4	cup walnuts
1/2	cup soy milk powder
2	tablespoons toasted carob powder
1/2	teaspoon vanilla

Soak dates in water for about 30 minutes. Process all ingredients in a blender until very smooth and creamy. Pour into plastic cups and insert popsicle sticks. Freeze until firm. **Serves 6.**

VARIATION: For **Carob Coated "Fudgesicles,"** melt carob chips in a double boiler, diluting with enough soy or nut milk to make a creamy sauce, thin enough for dipping. Stir constantly to avoid burning. Dip frozen "Fudgesicles" into sauce, then immediately put back into cups and refreeze briefly.

Per 1/2 cup serving: 222 calories; 4 g protein (7%); 27.8 g carbohydrate (46%); 12.7 g fat (47%); 83 mg sodium; 362 mg calcium; 0 mg cholesterol.

BANANA CREAM

1/2	cup pineapple juice
1/4	cup clean, raw cashews
2	tablespoons chopped dates
3	frozen bananas, sliced
1/2	cup water
1/4	teaspoon maple flavoring
1/8	teaspoon vanilla

Process pineapple juice and cashews in a blender until very smooth and creamy. Add dates and continue blending. Add remaining ingredients and continue blending until very smooth. Freeze slightly and serve. **Yields 21/4 cups or 9 servings.**

Per 1/4 cup serving: 59 calories; 0.9 g protein (5%); 11.4 g carbohydrate (72%); 1.6 g fat (23%); 1 mg sodium; 6 mg calcium; 0 mg cholesterol.

STRAWBERRY CREAM

11/2   cups cold water
1/4   cup clean, raw cashews
1/2   cup cooked brown rice
1   cup strawberries
1/4   cup honey or pitted dates
1   teaspoon fresh lemon juice
1/4   teaspoon salt

Process cashews with about 1 cup of the water in a blender until very smooth. Add rice and remaining water and blend well. Add remaining ingredients and blend until very smooth. Serve immediately. For variation, substitute cherries, raspberries, or other berries, for strawberries. **Yields 21/2 cups or 5 servings.**

Per 1/2 cup serving: 118 calories; 1.6 g protein (5%); 21.7 g carbohydrate (70%); 3.4 g fat (25%); 102 mg sodium; 12 mg calcium; 0 mg cholesterol.

COCONUT WHIP

1   tablespoon Emes Kosher Jel
14   ounce can "lite" coconut milk
2-3   tablespoons clover or other light-colored honey
1   tablespoon lecithin granules
1   teaspoon vanilla
1/2   teaspoon lemon juice
1/8   teaspoon salt

Sprinkle Emes Jel over coconut milk in a saucepan. Heat, stirring constantly until gelatin is dissolved. Process in a blender with remaining ingredients and pour into a shallow dish and refrigerate. When firm, blend again just before serving. **Yields 2 cups or 16 servings.**

Per 2 tablespoon serving: 29 calories; 0.0 g protein (0%); 3.5 g carbohydrate (47%); 1.7 g fat (53%); 27 mg sodium; 0.5 mg calcium; 0 mg cholesterol.

WHIPPED CREAM

1	cup extra-rich, cold soy or nut milk
2	tablespoons honey or date butter
1	teaspoon vanilla
1/8	teaspoon coconut extract (opt.)
pinch	salt
2	tablespoons Instant Clear Jel

Process all ingredients, except Clear Jel, in a blender until very smooth. While blending, add the Clear Jel. Continue blending until desired consistency is obtained. Add more Clear Jel, if necessary. Serve immediately. **Yields 1 1/4 cups or 10 servings.**

Per 2 tablespoon serving: 32 calories; 1 g protein (12%); 5.6 g carbohydrate (69%); 0.7 g fat (19%); 18 mg sodium; 2 mg calcium; 0 mg cholesterol.

BANANA DATE COOKIES

3	bananas, mashed
1	teaspoon vanilla
1/2	teaspoon salt
1	cup unsweetened, shredded coconut
1	cup chopped, packed dates
1	cup chopped dried fruit, such as papaya or pineapple
1	cup raisins or dried currants
1/2	cup chopped walnuts
1	cup rolled oats

Stir vanilla and salt into mashed bananas. Add remaining ingredients, except oats, and mix together. Stir in oats. Drop by spoonful onto sprayed cookie sheets and bake at 350° F for 25 minutes. For variation, omit coconut and increase rolled oats to 2 cups. **Yields 3 dozen 1 1/2" cookies.**

Per two cookies: 128 calories; 2.1 g protein (6%); 23.6 g carbohydrate (68%); 4 g fat (26%); 57 mg sodium; 18 mg calcium; 0 mg cholesterol.

CAROB CHIP COOKIES

    11/4   cups water
       1   cup clean, raw cashews or walnuts
     3/4   cup pitted dates
       2   teaspoons vanilla
     1/2   teaspoon salt
    11/4   cups barley, brown rice, or whole wheat pastry flour
       1   cup date or malt-sweetened, nondairy carob chips*
       1   cup raisins

Process cashews and water in a blender until very smooth, then add next 3 ingredients and continue blending until smooth. Pour into a mixing bowl and add remaining ingredients. Mix well. Drop by spoonful onto sprayed cookie sheets and bake at 350° F for 20-25 minutes. **Yields 40 cookies.**

*See Glossary.

Per two cookies: 145 calories; 2.2 g protein (6%); 24.2 g carbohydrate (62%); 5.6 g fat (32%); 55 mg sodium; 15 mg calcium; 0 mg cholesterol.

CLUSTER COOKIES

       1   cup puffed brown rice
       1   cup Nutri-Grain Flakes cereal
     3/4   cup toasted, chopped walnuts
     1/2   cup raisins
     1/4   cup Grape-Nuts cereal
     1/8   teaspoon salt
       2   cups date or malt-sweetened, nondairy carob chips*

Mix all ingredients, except carob chips, in a medium-size bowl. Place carob chips in a double boiler and melt over medium-low heat. Stir constantly to prevent burning. When melted, immediately add to dry ingredients and stir well. Spoon onto wax paper and let cool. **Yields 21/2 dozen 11/2" cookies.**

*See Glossary.

Per cookie: 86 calories; 0.9 g protein (4%); 12.2 g carbohydrate (51%); 4.8 g fat (45%); 29 mg sodium; 13 mg calcium; 0 mg cholesterol.

GOLDEN MACAROONS

3/4	cup water
2/3	cup chopped dates
1	cup grated raw carrots
1	teaspoon almond extract
1/2	teaspoon salt
2	cups unsweetened coconut
1/4	cup soy flour
1/4	cup whole wheat flour

Process water and dates in a blender until smooth. Mix with carrots, almond extract, and salt. Add remaining ingredients and mix well. Drop onto sprayed cookie sheet with small ice cream scoop and bake at 350° F for 20 minutes, or until lightly browned. For variation, 1/2 cup honey with 1/4 cup water may be substituted for dates and 3/4 cup water. **Yields 2 dozen macaroons.**

Per two cookies: 93 calories; 1.9 g protein (7%); 12.6 g carbohydrate (50%); 4.7 g fat (42%); 88 mg sodium; 14 mg calcium; 0 mg cholesterol.

GRANOLA CRUNCHIES

2	cups granola
1/2	cup peanut butter
2	tablespoons honey
1 1/2	teaspoons vanilla
pinch	salt
	finely shredded coconut or finely chopped nuts (opt.)

Mix all ingredients together with hands, except coconut, until well mixed. Form into balls, dipping hands in water, if necessary. Roll in coconut and freeze. **Yields 2 dozen crunchies.**

Per two crunchies: 128 calories; 4.5 g protein (14%); 12.7 g carbohydrate (38%); 7.1 g fat (48%); 85 mg sodium; 11 mg calcium; 0 mg cholesterol.

HAYSTACK COOKIES

2	cups pitted dates
1	cup raisins
3/4	cup pineapple or orange juice
3	cups unsweetened, shredded coconut
1	cup chopped walnuts or almonds
3/4	cup barley or whole wheat pastry flour
1/3	cup rolled oats
1/2	teaspoon salt

Process dates, raisins, and juice in a blender until smooth. Add to remaining ingredients and mix lightly. Drop onto ungreased cookie sheets with small ice cream scoop and bake at 325° F for 20-25 minutes, or until browned. **Yields 44 1**1/2**" cookies.**

Per two cookies: 161 calories; 2.3 g protein (5%); 24.8 g carbohydrate (57%); 7.3 g fat (38%); 49 mg sodium; 18 mg calcium; 0 mg cholesterol.

OATMEAL COOKIES

1/2	cup almond butter
1/2	cup honey
1/2	cup unsweetened, crushed pineapple
1/2	teaspoon vanilla
1	cup barley or whole wheat pastry flour
1/2	teaspoon salt
3/4	cup rolled oats
1/2	cup wheat germ
1/2	cup unsweetened, finely shredded coconut
1/2	cup chopped nuts (opt.)
1/2	cup raisins or date-sweetened carob chips

Whip almond butter and honey together in a bowl until creamy. Stir in pineapple and vanilla, then pour into a blender and blend well. Pour back into the bowl and add flour and salt. Beat together, then add oats and wheat germ, and continue beating. Stir in remaining ingredients. Drop by spoonful onto sprayed cookie sheets and bake at 325-350° F until lightly browned (about 20 minutes). **Yields 2 dozen 2" cookies.**

Per cookie: 113 calories; 2.5 g protein (9%); 17.4 g carbohydrate (59%); 4.3 g fat (33%); 51 mg sodium; 22 mg calcium; 0 mg cholesterol.

SCANDINAVIAN CAROB COOKIES

1 1/4	cups hot water
3/4	cup chopped dates
2	teaspoons vanilla
1/4	teaspoon salt
1/2	cup almond butter
1/3	cup toasted carob powder
1	teaspoon Postum, Roma, or other cereal "coffee"
6	tablespoons barley flour
1 1/2	tablespoons Ener-G Baking Powder
1	tablespoon Ener-G Egg Replacer
3/4	cup chopped walnuts

Process first 4 ingredients in a blender until smooth. Add almond butter, carob powder, and Postum, while continuing to blend. Sift flour, egg replacer, and baking powder together. Pour batter into bowl and fold in dry ingredients and nuts. Spray and flour bottom of 10 x 14" pan and spread mixture in pan. Bake at 350° F for 35 minutes. When cool, cut into squares. **Yields 2 dozen cookies.**

Per cookie: 89 calories; 1.8 g protein (8%); 9.9 g carbohydrate (41%); 5.6 g fat (52%); 24 mg sodium; 26 mg calcium; 0 mg cholesterol.

CAROB FUDGE

4	cups date or malt-sweetened, nondairy carob chips*
1	cup almond or peanut butter
1	cup chopped nuts
1	cup raisins

Place carob chips and almond butter in a double boiler over low heat. Heat just until chips begin to melt, stirring constantly. Remove from heat. Combine with nuts and raisins and mix together well. Press mixture into a flat casserole dish and chill. **Yields 32 pieces.**

*See Glossary.

Per 1x2" piece: 185 calories; 2.5 g protein (5%); 20.5 g carbohydrate (40%); 12.6 g fat (55%); 9 mg sodium; 50 mg calcium; 0 mg cholesterol

POLYNESIAN FRUIT BARS

3	cups rolled or quick oats
1 1/2	cups orange juice
1	cup unsweetened coconut
1	cup oat flour*
1	banana, mashed
1/2	cup chopped nuts
1	teaspoon salt
20	ounce can unsweetened, crushed pineapple
2	cups chopped dates

Mix all ingredients together, except pineapple and dates. Use more orange juice to hold mixture together, if necessary. Press half of mixture firmly into a 9 x 12" glass baking dish. Cook pineapple and dates until thickened, then spread over oat mixture. Top with remaining oat mixture and bake at 350° F for 30 minutes. When cool, cut into bars. Keep refrigerated. **Yields 16 bars.**

*Can be made by processing rolled oats in blender.

Per bar: 237 calories; 5 g protein (8%); 44.2 g carbohydrate (71%); 5.9 g fat (21%); 151 mg sodium; 31 mg calcium; 0 mg cholesterol.

DRIED FRUIT BALLS

1 1/2	cups walnuts
1	cup dried apricots
1	cup pitted dates
1	cup raisins
2/3	cup rich soy or nut cream
1	teaspoon grated orange peel
1/8	teaspoon salt

Place first 4 ingredients in a food grinder and grind until fine. Add remaining ingredients and mix well. Chill, then shape into small balls. For variation, roll balls in shredded coconut or finely chopped nuts. **Yields 4 dozen 1" balls.**

Per two balls: 103 calories; 1.9 g protein (7%); 15.2 g carbohydrate (54%); 4.9 g fat (39%); 14 mg sodium; 15 mg calcium; 0 mg cholesterol.

SESAME CANDY

1   cup honey
1   teaspoon salt
1   pound hulled sesame seeds

In a skillet, bring honey and salt to a boil. Add sesame seeds and stir vigorously. Cook until seeds are golden brown, stirring constantly. Pour onto a sprayed cookie sheet and spread as thin as possible as it begins to cool. Immediately cut into squares and place on wax paper. Cool completely and serve. Store in refrigerator. For variation, add chopped nuts before spreading on cookie sheet. **Yields 2 dozen pieces.**

Per 2.5" piece: 155 calories; 5 g protein (12%); 13.1 g carbohydrate (32%); 10.4 g fat (56%); 97 mg sodium; 29 mg calcium; 0 mg cholesterol.

TROPICAL FRUIT FONDUE

1   cup water
1   tablespoon cornstarch or arrowroot
3/4   cup chopped, dried papaya
1/3   cup unsweetened coconut
1/4   cup soy milk powder
3   rings canned, unsweetened pineapple
1   teaspoon coconut extract (opt.)
2   apples, cut in chunks
2   cups fresh strawberries
1   large Rice Waffle (p. 29), cut in bite-size pieces

Dissolve cornstarch in water and cook until clear, stirring constantly. Combine remaining ingredients, except fruit chunks and waffle pieces, and process in a blender until smooth. Add heated water and cornstarch and continue blending until smooth. Pour into a fondue pot and place in the center of your table. Arrange bowls of fruit chunks and waffle pieces on table. Provide fondue skewers or forks for dipping fruit and waffle pieces into fondue. **Serves 4.**

VARIATIONS: (1) For **Tropical Pudding**, increase cornstarch; (2) For **Tropical Pops**, freeze fondue sauce in popsicle trays; (3) Pour fondue sauce into a baked pie crust and freeze for **Tropical Cream Pie.**

Per 1/4 recipe: 294 calories; 4.5 g protein (6%); 51.1 g carbohydrate (66%); 9.5 g fat (28%); 176 mg sodium; 291 mg calcium; 0 mg cholesterol.

CALIFORNIA FRUIT FIZZ

1/2 large cantaloupe melon
1 ripe mango
12 ounce can tangerine juice concentrate
1 quart or more sparkling water with orange essence
8 mint sprigs (opt.)

Scoop out cantaloupe seeds, then cut off and discard rind. Cut melon into chunks. Peel, pit, and cut mango into chunks. Combine with melon and place in a blender. Add juice concentrate and process until smooth. Pour into a 2 quart pitcher and stir in sparkling water—enough to make 2 quarts juice. Pour into tall, slender glasses or wine flutes and garnish with mint sprigs. **Yields 2 quarts or 8 servings.**

Per 1 cup serving: 97 calories; 1.5 g protein (6%); 23.5 g carbohydrate (92%); 0.3 g fat (2%); 6 mg sodium; 36 mg calcium; 0 mg cholesterol.

GOLDEN WASSAIL

1 quart apple juice
1 quart unsweetened pineapple juice
1 cup unsweetened apricot nectar
1 cup orange juice
1/8 teaspoon cardamom
1/8 teaspoon coriander

Simmer all ingredients in a large kettle. Serve hot. Garnish with orange slices or mint, if desired. **Yields 2 1/2 quarts or 10 servings.**

Per 1 cup serving: 128 calories; 0.6 g protein (2%); 31.7 g carbohydrate (96%); 0.2 g fat (2%); 5 mg sodium; 28 mg calcium; 0 mg cholesterol.

GRAVIES & SAUCES

GRAVIES & SAUCES

THE FACTS ABOUT FAT

Fats are necessary in our diet. They provide a key source of fuel, carry fat-soluble vitamins (A, D, E, K), provide the body with essential fatty acids, and help to flavor our food. Fat is also needed for the building of cell membranes, to cover nerve fibers, to insulate and pad our frame, to provide warmth, and to form vital chemicals and hormones.

Triglycerides are made up of three fatty acids attached to a carrier of glycerol. This is the "fat" we are all familiar with, which makes up the deposits of fat in the body and is the main source of stored energy. Triglycerides are found in all dietary fats and oils, alcohol, and sugars.

Saturated fatty acids are the portions of fat that have the maximum number of hydrogen atoms attached to the carbon skeleton—they are saturated with hydrogen. Foods that are highly saturated are generally solid at room temperature, such as lard, butter, and bacon fat.

Unsaturated fatty acids have one or more sites where the carbons are not carrying the maximum number of hydrogen atoms. Unsaturated fats are liquid at room temperature, and usually come from plant sources. Most vegetable oils are unsaturated. Some are more unsaturated than others. Food manufacturers often artificially saturate plant oils (identified as "partially hydrogenated"). These altered fats are harmful to the body, since the body cannot make proper-functioning chemicals and hormones from these fatty acids.

Cholesterol is a fatty, waxy substance made by the body, and is a component of cell membranes, serves as nerve insulation, and is the base for various hormones, Vitamins D and K, and bile salts, which emulsify fat. Only animal products contain cholesterol. The body makes all the cholesterol that it needs. Dietary cholesterol is harmful, due to oxidative changes that occur during cooking, which trigger atherosclerosis and degenerative disease. (The use of raw animal products introduces other health risks, primarily the risk of infectious disease.) Excess fat intake also increases the amount of cholesterol the body makes.

FAT AND DISEASE

Several cancers, such as breast, prostate, colon, and pancreatic cancers have been linked to the total fat in the diet, as well as to meat intake. In the United States, the average person has a dietary intake of 35-45% fat (by calories), when it should be about 15-20%. The United States also has the highest incidence of degenerative diseases in the world, including heart disease, general arteriosclerosis, osteoarthritis, hypertension, and diabetes.

The more fat consumed, the greater the incidence of degenerative disease.

Unutilized fat and cholesterol are stored in the blood and tissues, and form plaque inside the blood vessels, causing atherosclerosis. In time, the plaque narrows the blood vessels and reduces the amount of blood flow. This causes the heart to compensate by elevating the blood pressure and limiting the flow of blood to vital tissues. Severe clogging of blood vessels to the heart causes angina (heart pain), and failure. Restricted blood flow to the brain results in impaired thinking, headaches, senility, loss of hearing, and strokes. Narrowing of the arteries to the back, hips, and knees, can cause arthritis.

Excess fat causes the red blood cells to stick together and reduces their oxygen-carrying capacity. About one hour after a fatty meal, this clumping begins. Six hours after the meal, the clumping can become so severe that blood flow actually stops in some vessels. Several hours later, the clumps break up and blood flow returns to the tissues.[13] Excess fat also causes cellular insensitivity and resistance to the effects of insulin. An elevated blood sugar is the result.[14] In the United States, a new diabetic is diagnosed every minute.

If we eat a wide variety of fruits, grains, nuts, and vegetables, in adequate quantities to maintain our ideal weight, there is no need to add any additional refined fats. Fats, such as butter, oil, and margarine, have virtually no vitamin or mineral content and no fiber. They are pure fat. Especially for those with a weight problem, the elimination of these fats from the diet can be of great help.

By reducing fat and cholesterol intake sharply, plaque formation can be halted and even reversed. Medical research confirms that reversal of heart disease occurs when the fat level is reduced to 10%. A low fat intake is also vital in reversing adult onset diabetes.

HELPFUL TIPS ON MAKING GRAVY

• **Tip #1:** Instead of melting fat, stirring flour into it, browning the flour/fat combination, then adding liquid, try this approach: Brown whole grain flour in a dry skillet or in the oven. You can do several cups at a time and have browned flour on hand whenever you want to make gravy. Stir several spoonfuls of browned flour into a small amount of cool liquid (water, vegetable juice, etc.). Stir until flour is completely dissolved and no lumps remain. Pour the dissolved mixture into a saucepan or skillet, add remaining liquid and blend with a wire whisk. Bring mixture to a boil, stirring frequently to prevent burning. Season as desired.

• **Tip #2:** For still greater ease, use arrowroot or cornstarch. Dissolve powder in a small amount of cool liquid, then mix well with remaining liquid in saucepan and bring to a boil. Season as desired.

• **Tip #3:** Tasty gravies are made by blending cooked beans. To achieve a creamy texture and the desired consistency, blend in some nut or grain milk.

• **Tip #4:** Bring water or vegetable broth to a boil. Meanwhile fill a glass half full of cool water and add just enough flour to make a thick, smooth paste—not too thick, but not runny either. When the liquid in the saucepan is boiling hard, slowly stir in the thickened flour paste, adding only enough to reach the desired consistency.

• **Seasoning:** Chopped mushrooms, onion, celery, garlic, pimiento, bell pepper, or other vegetable tidbits add both flavor and texture to gravy. Most cooks prefer to steam the vegetables before thickening their juices for gravy. Some favorite seasonings include beef or chicken-style seasoning, bay, parsley, oregano, Italian seasoning, sweet basil, cumin, or Vegex, Liquid Aminos, etc. Make your own seasoning mix by blending dried vegetables together.

BROWN GRAVY

3	tablespoons whole wheat flour
2	cups water
1/2	tablespoon All-Purpose Seasoning (p. 167)
1/2	tablespoon Vegex or Liquid Aminos
1/2	teaspoon onion powder
1/4	teaspoon garlic powder

Brown flour in a nonstick skillet, stirring constantly. Stir in water slowly. Add remaining ingredients and simmer for 15 minutes, stirring constantly. **Yields 2 cups or 8 servings.**

VARIATIONS: (1) Add chopped onion; (2) Substitute soy or nut milk for water.

Per 1/4 cup serving: 13 calories; 1 g protein (28%); 2.4 g carbohydrate (68%); 0.1 g fat (4%); 143 mg sodium; 5 mg calcium; 0 mg cholesterol.

COUNTRY-STYLE GRAVY

2	cups hot water
1/2	cup clean, raw cashews
2	tablespoons cornstarch or arrowroot
2	tablespoons Liquid Aminos
2	teaspoons onion powder
1	teaspoon food yeast flakes (opt.)
1/2	teaspoon salt
1/2	teaspoon smoked yeast

Process cashews in about 1 cup of the hot water in a blender until very smooth. Add remaining ingredients and continue blending until smooth. Pour into a saucepan and bring to a boil, stirring constantly. Cook until thickened. For variation, omit salt and add 2 teaspoons All-Purpose Seasoning (p. 167). **Yields 21/2 cups or 10 servings.**

Per 1/4 cup serving: 49 calories; 1.5 g protein (12%); 4.2 g carbohydrate (32%); 3.2 g fat (56%); 260 mg sodium; 7 mg calcium; 0 mg cholesterol.

GRANDMA'S FAVORITE GRAVY

1/2	onion, chopped
2	cups water
3/4	cup cooked garbanzos
1/4	cup Liquid Aminos
1/4	cup whole wheat flour
1/4	teaspoon salt
1/8	teaspoon ground celery seed

Simmer onion in a small amount of water. Process garbanzos with about 1 cup of the water in a blender, then add remaining water and other ingredients and continue blending until smooth. Add to onion and bring to a boil, stirring with a wire whisk. Reduce heat and simmer for 15-20 minutes, stirring constantly, until thickened. **Yields 1 quart or 16 servings.**

Per 1/4 cup serving: 18 calories; 1.1 g protein (24%); 3.1 g carbohydrate (67%); 0.2 g fat (9%); 251 mg sodium; 6 mg calcium; 0 mg cholesterol.

MUSHROOM GRAVY

2	cups soy or nut milk
2/3	cup water
1/3	cup whole wheat flour
1	tablespoon All-Purpose Seasoning (p. 167)
2/3	cup canned mushroom pieces
1 1/2	teaspoon parsley flakes

Bring soy milk to a boil. Process remaining ingredients in a blender, except mushrooms and parsley, then add to boiling soy milk. Stir rapidly with a whisk. Stir in mushrooms and parsley. Reduce heat and simmer until thickened, stirring constantly. **Yields 2 2/3 cups or about 10 servings.**

Per 1/4 cup serving: 35 calories; 2.2 g protein (23%); 4.9 g carbohydrate (52%); 1.1 g fat (25%); 189 mg sodium; 9 mg calcium; 0 mg cholesterol.

ONION GRAVY

2	onions, chopped
2	tablespoons water
1/4	cup whole wheat flour
2	cups water
1/3	cup clean, raw cashews
1/2	teaspoon salt

Simmer onions in 2 tablespoons water until tender. Meanwhile, brown flour in a dry skillet. Process cashews in about 1 cup of the water in a blender until very smooth. Add browned flour and salt and continue blending until smooth. Add to onions. Stir in remaining water and cook over medium heat until thickened, stirring constantly. Adjust water to desired consistency. Serve over baked potatoes, brown rice, vegetables, or toast. **Yields 22/3 cups or about 10 servings.**

VARIATIONS: (1) Add 1 clove garlic, minced; (2) Add Bernard Jensen's Protein Seasoning, to taste.

Per 1/4 cup serving: 47 calories; 1.5 g protein (12%); 5.9 g carbohydrate (48%); 2.2 g fat (40%); 101 mg sodium; 13 mg calcium; 0 mg cholesterol.

VEGETABLE GRAVY

11/2	cups water
3	tomatoes, chopped fine
11/2	onions, chopped coarse
1/2	green bell pepper, chopped coarse
1/2	teaspoon salt
	garlic salt, oregano, savory, to taste
2	tablespoons cold water
2	tablespoons cornstarch or arrowroot

Bring all ingredients, except cold water and cornstarch, to a boil, then simmer for 15 minutes. Mix cold water and cornstarch and stir in. Continue simmering until thickened, stirring constantly. Serve over vegetables, brown rice, or potatoes. **Yields 2 cups or 8 servings.**

Per 1/4 cup serving: 27 calories; 0.8 g protein (11%); 6.2 g carbohydrate (83%); 0.2 g fat (6%); 131 mg sodium; 13 mg calcium; 0 mg cholesterol.

CREAMY TOMATO GRAVY

1	quart canned tomatoes
1/2	cup clean, raw cashews
1/2	cup well-cooked brown rice
1	large onion, chopped
2	teaspoons honey (opt.)
1/4	teaspoon garlic powder
1/4	teaspoon oregano
1/4	teaspoon salt
1/2	cup water

Process cashews and rice with about 1 cup of the tomatoes in a blender until very smooth. Add remaining tomatoes and other ingredients, except water, and continue blending until smooth. Pour into a saucepan. Rinse blender with 1/2 cup water, then pour into saucepan. Simmer for 10 minutes, stirring frequently. If necessary, thicken with cornstarch mixed with a little cold water. **Yields 51/2 cups or 22 servings.**

Per 1/4 cup serving: 34 calories; 1.1 g protein (12%); 4.6 g carbohydrate (49%); 1.6 g fat (39%); 94 mg sodium; 16 mg calcium; 0 mg cholesterol.

SESAME ALMOND SAUCE

1	onion, chopped
13/4	cups roasted almonds
3/4	cup sesame seeds
2	cups water
21/2	tablespoons fresh lemon juice
1	teaspoon salt

Simmer onion in a small amount of water until tender. Process almonds and sesame seeds until fine. Process all ingredients in a blender until very smooth. Heat over medium-low heat until warmed, stirring frequently. Pour over vegetables, potatoes, etc. **Yields 1 quart or 32 servings.**

Per 2 tablespoon serving: 63 calories; 2.1 g protein (12%); 2.7 g carbohydrate (16%); 5.4 g fat (72%); 63 mg sodium; 54 mg calcium; 0 mg cholesterol.

MELTED "CHEESE" SAUCE

2	cups water
1/4	cup clean, raw cashews
4	ounce jar pimientos
3	tablespoons food yeast flakes
2	tablespoons cornstarch or arrowroot
1	tablespoon fresh lemon juice
11/2	teaspoons salt
1/2	teaspoon onion flakes or powder
1/4	teaspoon garlic powder

Process cashews in about 1/2 cup of the water in a blender until very smooth. Add remaining water and other ingredients and continue blending until very smooth. Simmer in a heavy saucepan until thickened, stirring constantly (5-6 minutes). Pour over vegetables, potatoes, tortilla chips, etc. **Yields 2 1/2 cups or 10 servings.**

VARIATIONS: For **"Cheese" Fondue** or **"Cheese" Spread**, increase corn-starch to 3 tablespoons.

Per 1/4 cup serving: 37 calories; 1.6 g protein (16%); 4.4 g carbohydrate (46%); 1.6 g fat (38%); 328 mg sodium; 11 mg calcium; 0 mg cholesterol.

GOLDEN SAUCE

1	small potato, diced
1/2	small carrot, diced
11/3	cups water
2	tablespoons clean, raw cashews
11/2	tablespoons fresh lemon juice
3/4	teaspoon salt
1/8	teaspoon celery salt

Simmer potato and carrot in water. When cooked, process with remaining ingredients (including cooking water) in a blender, until very smooth. Serve over vegetables or potatoes. **Yields 2 cups or 8 servings.**

VARIATION: For **Hollandaise Sauce**, increase lemon juice to 2 tablespoons.

Per 1/4 cup serving: 30 calories; 0.7 g protein (9%); 4.8 g carbohydrate (62%); 1 g fat (29%); 187 mg sodium; 6 mg calcium; 0 mg cholesterol.

WHITE SAUCE

2	cups hot water
1/2	cup clean, raw cashews
2	tablespoons cornstarch or arrowroot
2	teaspoons onion powder
1/2	teaspoon salt

Process cashews with about 1 cup of the hot water in a blender until very smooth. Add remaining hot water and other ingredients and continue blending until smooth. Pour into small saucepan and simmer, stirring constantly, until thickened. **Yields 2 cups or 8 servings.**

VARIATION: For **"Cheese"** Sauce, process in: 4 ounce jar pimientos, 2 tablespoons fresh lemon juice, and 1 teaspoon paprika.

Per 1/4 cup serving: 58 calories; 1.4 g protein (9%); 5 g carbohydrate (33%); 4 g fat (58%); 125 mg sodium; 8 mg calcium; 0 mg cholesterol.

TOMATO SAUCE

1	cup fresh or canned tomatoes
1	carrot, scrubbed, cut in chunks
1	teaspoon honey, *or* 2 pitted dates, minced
1	small onion, chopped
pinch	sweet basil
pinch	oregano
pinch	salt

Process first 3 ingredients in a blender until desired consistency is obtained. Pour into a saucepan and add remaining ingredients. Simmer 15 minutes. **Yields 1 1/2 cups or 6 servings.**

Per 1/4 cup serving: 27 calories; 0.8 g protein (10%); 6.2 g carbohydrate (83%); 0.2 g fat (7%); 54 mg sodium; 10 mg calcium; 0 mg cholesterol.

TOMATO PEANUT SAUCE

1/2   cup chopped onion
1/2   cup diced green bell pepper
2   small tomatoes, diced
1   cup hot "V8"
6   tablespoons smooth peanut butter
2   tablespoons Liquid Aminos
1/2   teaspoon garlic powder
1/2   teaspoon oregano

Brown onion and bell pepper over medium high heat in a nonstick pan or skillet. Add tomatoes and 1/2 cup of the "V8" and simmer. In a small bowl, gradually add the remaining "V8" to the peanut butter and mix well. Add to pan with remaining ingredients and continue simmering and stirring until thoroughly heated. Serve over pasta, rice, or vegetables. **Yields about 2 cups or 4 servings.**

Per 1/2 cup serving: 174 calories; 7.9 g protein (17%); 13.9 g carbohydrate (30%); 10.8 g fat (53%); 588 mg sodium; 27 mg calcium; 0 mg cholesterol.

TARTAR SAUCE

1   cup Almond Mayonnaise (p. 158)
1   tablespoon finely chopped bell pepper
1   tablespoon finely chopped black olives
1   tablespoon finely chopped onion
1   tablespoon finely chopped parsley
1/8   teaspoon salt
      paprika, to taste

Combine all ingredients and let stand in refrigerator overnight before using. **Yields 1 1/2 cups or 12 servings.**

Per 2 tablespoon serving: 21 calories; 0.7 g protein (12%); 2 g carbohydrate (34%); 1.4 g fat (53%); 66 mg sodium; 10 mg calcium; 0 mg cholesterol.

ZESTY TOMATO RELISH

4   large tomatoes, chopped
2   small onions, minced
8   pitted dates, chopped,
      or 1 tablespoon honey (opt.)
2   tablespoons fresh lemon juice
1   teaspoon sweet basil
1   teaspoon celery seed
1   teaspoon salt

Combine all ingredients and simmer, uncovered, about 30 minutes, stirring frequently. **Yields 21/2 cups or 10 servings.**

SERVING SUGGESTION: For **Zesty Sprouts over Rice**, add mung bean sprouts, and serve over cooked brown rice, then top with slivered almonds.

Per 1/4 cup serving: 38 calories; 0.9 g protein (9%); 9.2 g carbohydrate (86%); 0.2 g fat (5%); 200 mg sodium; 19 mg calcium; 0 mg cholesterol.

NACHO "CHEESE" SAUCE

1   cup clean, raw cashews
1   cup hot water
2   ounce jar pimientos
1   tablespoon fresh lemon juice
1   teaspoon onion powder
1   teaspoon salt
1/2   teaspoon garlic powder
1/2   teaspoon paprika
      Homemade "Chili" Powder, to taste (p. 171) (opt.)

Process cashews and hot water in a blender until very smooth. Add remaining ingredients and continue blending until very smooth. Pour into saucepan and heat over medium-low heat, stirring constantly, until thickened. Serve over Crispy Corn Chips (p. 11), if desired. **Yields 2 cups or 8 servings.**

Per 1/4 cup serving: 103 calories; 2.8 g protein (10%); 6.6 g carbohydrate (24%); 8 g fat (66%); 248 mg sodium; 12 mg calcium; 0 mg cholesterol.

ENCHILADA SAUCE

  3   cups cold water
  1   onion
  3   cloves garlic
1/2   cup flour
  2   tablespoons paprika
  1   teaspoon cumin
  1   teaspoon salt
1/2   teaspoon oregano
 15   ounce can tomato sauce

Process onion and garlic with 1 cup of the water in a blender until smooth. Pour mixture into a large saucepan. Blend flour with another cup of the water. Add this to saucepan with remaining water and seasonings. Bring to boil while stirring frequently. Reduce heat and simmer about 15 minutes. Stir in tomato sauce. Makes enough to cover 12 enchiladas. **Yields 5 cups or 6 servings.**

Per 1/6 recipe: 79 calories; 2.8 g protein (13%); 17.2 g carbohydrate (80%); 0.6 g fat (7%); 790 mg sodium; 34 mg calcium; 0 mg cholesterol.

ZESTY MEXICAN SAUCE

  3   cups water
  2   8 ounce cans tomato sauce
  6   ounce can tomato paste
  1   onion, chopped
  3   tablespoons bulgur wheat,
          or 6 tablespoons cooked cracked wheat (heaping)
  1   teaspoon cumin
  1   teaspoon garlic powder
  1   teaspoon Homemade "Chili" Powder (p. 171)
  1   teaspoon honey (opt.)
  1   teaspoon ground oregano
3/4   teaspoon salt

Combine all ingredients in a saucepan and bring to a boil. Reduce heat and simmer for 1 hour. May be served over burritos, enchiladas, haystacks, tostados, etc. **Yields 11/2 quarts or 12 servings.**

Per 1/2 cup serving: 38 calories; 1.6 g protein (14%); 8.6 g carbohydrate (79%); 0.3 g fat (6%); 374 mg sodium; 21 mg calcium; 0 mg cholesterol.

SALSA RANCHERA

4	cups chopped fresh tomatoes
	or mashed canned tomatoes
1	onion, chopped
1/2	cup chopped green bell pepper
4	ounce can diced green chilies (opt.)
1/4	cup chopped fresh parsley
2	tablespoons fresh cilantro,
	or 1 teaspoon dried cilantro (opt.)
1 1/2	tablespoons fresh lemon juice
2	cloves garlic, minced
1/4	teaspoon ground cumin
1/4	teaspoon ground oregano
	salt, to taste (opt.)

Combine all ingredients and mix well. Allow to stand, refrigerated, for a few hours, to let flavors blend. Keep refrigerated in an airtight container. For variation, add an 8 ounce can tomato sauce. **Yields 1 quart or 16 servings.**

Per 1/4 cup serving: 18 calories; 0.8 g protein (15%); 4.1 g carbohydrate (77%); 0.2 g fat (8%); 98 mg sodium; 21 mg calcium; 0 mg cholesterol.

ITALIAN SAUCE

1	cup water
8	ounce can tomato sauce
6	ounce can tomato paste
1/4	teaspoon garlic powder
1/4	teaspoon onion powder
1/8	teaspoon sweet basil
1/8	teaspoon oregano

Combine all ingredients and simmer 10 minutes, stirring occasionally. **Yields 2 1/2 cups or 10 servings.**

Per 1/4 cup serving: 22 calories; 1 g protein (15%); 4.9 g carbohydrate (78%); 0.2 g fat (7%); 272 mg sodium; 10 mg calcium; 0 mg cholesterol.

SPAGHETTI SAUCE

1 onion, chopped
1/4 cup chopped green bell pepper
2 cloves garlic, minced
15 ounce can tomato sauce
1 cup water
3/4 cup tomato paste
4 ounce can mushrooms (opt.)
2 tablespoons parsley flakes,
    or 1/4 cup fresh, chopped
2 tablespoons fresh lemon juice
1 1/2 tablespoons honey, *or* 3 tablespoons date butter
1 1/2 teaspoons sweet basil
1 teaspoon oregano
1/2 teaspoon onion powder
1/2 teaspoon salt
1/4 teaspoon thyme

Simmer first 3 ingredients in a small amount of water. Add remaining ingredients and simmer for 30 minutes, stirring occasionally. **Yields 1 quart or 8 servings.**

Per 1/2 cup serving: 62 calories; 2.1 g protein (12%); 14.7 g carbohydrate (83%); 0.4 g fat (5%); 474 mg sodium; 33 mg calcium; 0 mg cholesterol.

QUICK PIZZA SAUCE

8 ounce can tomato sauce
6 ounce can tomato paste
1/4 cup water
1/2 tablespoon date butter
1 clove garlic, crushed
1 teaspoon oregano
3/4 teaspoon sweet basil
1/2 teaspoon onion powder

Mix all ingredients in a small bowl, then spread over pizza dough. Add toppings and bake as directed. **Yields sauce for 2 large pizzas or 6 servings.**

Per 1/6 recipe: 40 calories; 1.7 g protein (14%); 9.3 g carbohydrate (79%); 0.4 g fat (7%); 248 mg sodium; 25 mg calcium; 0 mg cholesterol.

PESTO SAUCE

3	cups fresh basil leaves
1/2	cup chopped green ripe olives (not Spanish olives), with broth (opt.)
1/4	cup packed fresh parsley
1/4	cup toasted pine nuts or clean, raw cashews
1	tablespoon fresh lemon juice
2	cloves garlic
1/4	teaspoon salt
	food yeast flakes, to taste (opt.)

Process all ingredients in a blender until very smooth. If not using the olives, add about 1/4 cup of water, to aid blending. Serve over salad or pasta or as dip for fresh vegetables. Keep refrigerated in an airtight container. **Yields 9 tablespoons or 41/2 servings.**

Per 2 tablespoon serving: 63 calories; 2.2 g protein (14%); 5.1 g carbohydrate (32%); 3.9 g fat (54%); 122 mg sodium; 71 mg calcium; 0 mg cholesterol.

MAIN DISHES

Pictured at left: Mazidra, and Tofu Walnut Loaf with asparagus and corn.

MAIN DISHES

GETTING ENOUGH PROTEIN

Meatless main dishes can be delicious as well as nutritious, supplying a good quality of protein and generous amounts of B vitamins. The ultimate sources of protein are plant foods. We obtain protein either firsthand when we eat plant foods, or secondhand when we eat animal foods. Our Creator has put protein in whole grains, legumes, vegetables, fruits, nuts, and seeds—it is found in every plant food. Beans, peas, and lentils contain about the same percentage of protein, weight-for-weight, as does meat. Soybean flour and peanuts contain more than meat. Whole plant foods individually provide complete protein for the body. Using a variety of whole plant foods enables a more generous supply of complete protein without the need to eat as many calories. Animal proteins are also complete proteins, but the amount of protein is excessive in ratio to the amount of calories eaten. This excess protein burdens the body and can cause disease.

We need not worry about getting enough protein. If we are getting enough calories, we are getting enough protein. Rather, we should be careful about not getting too much. Excess protein increases risk of cancer and kidney disease. Osteoporosis is a disease which is widely publicized as being caused by inadequate calcium in the diet. This is only partially correct. The real culprit is excess protein in the diet, which requires the leaching of calcium from our bones to neutralize the acidic overload thus caused. Taking more calcium in the diet or in pill form does not alter this process. A high protein diet is also responsible for accelerated maturation and aging.

About 10-12% of our total calorie intake should come from protein. If the daily intake of calories is over 1500, an even lower percentage is adequate.

The U.S. government has set the adult daily requirement for protein at about 0.3 grams per pound of body weight, per day. Drs. Hardinge and Stare conducted studies in the U.S. and found the following average consumption per day. You can see that even vegans get more protein than they actually need:

	RDA	Non-vegetarians	Lacto-Ovo Veg.	Vegans
Women (25-50)	50 gm	94 gm	82 gm	61 gm
Men (25-50)	63 gm	125 gm	90 gm	83 gm

HEALTH ADVANTAGES OF THE VEGAN DIET

Cholesterol is found only in meat and other animal products, such as poultry, seafood, eggs, and dairy products. A diet that is strictly vegan (no animal products), is naturally free of cholesterol.

Using a plant-based diet makes it easier to avoid excess protein and fat, and such a diet is free of long-chain saturated fats, which are the most harmful fats. There is also a reduced intake of pesticide residues and decreased risk of infectious disease.

The American Dietetic Association states, "A considerable body of scientific data suggests positive relationships between vegetarian lifestyles and risk reduction for several chronic degenerative diseases and conditions, such as obesity, coronary artery disease, hypertension, diabetes mellitus, colon cancer, and others."[15] Numerous studies show that plant foods can even reverse the growth of some cancer cells that have already formed malignant tumors.[16]

BENEFITS:
- Decreased risk of infectious and degenerative disease
- Lowered risk of coronary occlusions and thrombotic disease
- Increased strength and endurance
- Increased length of life
- More economical
- Wiser use of land:
  —A cow consumes 110 grams of protein to return
    10 grams of protein to man.
  —A cow consumes 100 calories to return 4 calories to man.
  —One acre of land produces 165 pounds of beef.
  —One acre of land produces 450 pounds of soy protein.
  —4,000,000 acres of U.S. cropland is lost each year to soil erosion.
    85% of this loss is directly associated with livestock raising.[17]
- Less extravagant:
  —1,300,000,000 people could be fed by the grain and soybeans
    that are eaten by U.S. livestock![18]
  —60,000,000 people could be fed by the grain saved, if Americans
    reduced their intake of meat by only 10%![19]
- Humane: killing of animals is not required

"Grains, fruits, nuts, and vegetables constitute the diet chosen for us by our Creator. These foods, prepared in as simple and natural a manner as possible, are the most healthful and nourishing. They impart a strength, a power of endurance, and a vigor of intellect that are not afforded by a more complex and stimulating diet." Ellen G. White, *The Ministry of Healing*, page 296.

ANIMAL FOODS

CONSIDERATIONS:
• Animal fats (including dairy and eggs) are saturated fats and are recognized as a factor in the cause of heart and artery disease.
• Animal products contain cholesterol and increase serum cholesterol and other blood fats.
• A high intake of animal protein increases the risk for breast cancer.[20]
• Dairy products are the most common food sensitivity in America.[21] Chronic runny noses, recurrent ear and bronchial infections, and other inflammations are often caused by casein (milk protein). Numerous studies have implicated cow's milk in the cause of juvenile (Type I) diabetes.
• At least 60% of the world's adults cannot properly digest lactose (milk sugar).[22]
• The great incidence of disease in cattle is a major concern. Leukemia in dairy cattle is common and seems to be linked with leukemia in children.[23] Suspicious virus-like particles are often present in milk.[24] Salmonella is a microorganism often found in milk and eggs.[25] E. coli is transferable to humans through animal foods. "Mad Cow" Disease seems to have this ability as well.[26]
• Dairy products are not ideal sources of calcium. The excessive protein and phosphate content of dairy products actually contributes to the loss of calcium from the skeleton.[27] Those countries with the highest incidence of osteoporosis have the highest intake of dairy products![28] Compare the protein, calcium, and sodium in human milk and dairy milk. Cow's milk is the perfect food for calves, but not for humans.

Milk	Quantity	Protein	CHO*	Sodium	Calcium
Human breast milk	1 cup	2.4 gm	22.4 gm	40 mg	80 mg
Cow's milk	1 cup	8.5 gm	12.0 gm	122 mg	288 mg

*Carbohydrate

Comparison of the Milks of Different Species[29]		
	% of cal. as protein	Time required to double birth weight
Human	5%	180 days
Mare	11%	60 days
Cow	15%	47 days
Goat	17%	19 days
Dog	30%	8 days
Cat	40%	7 days
Rat	49%	4 days

LEGUMES

Legumes are seeds found in pods, and have two halves. They are nutrient powerhouses and inexpensive as well. You get 3 times as much protein yield for your dollar when you choose peas or beans as protein sources rather than meats, fish, and fowl. In addition, legumes are high in complex carbohydrates, water soluble fiber, B vitamins, iron, calcium, and phosphorous. With dozens of varieties to choose from, each with a unique flavor all its own, there's something for everybody! Try them in ethnic dishes, patties, loaves, salads, soups, casseroles, spreads, dips, sauces, and gravies.

COOKING DRIED LEGUMES: Sort carefully, removing pebbles, debris, and discolored legumes. Rinse well. All dried legumes (except lentils, split peas, and black-eyed peas) should be soaked ahead of cooking time. This shortens cooking time and lowers the risk of developing intestinal gas. To further reduce risk, freeze beans after soaking. (Also, be sure to chew beans thoroughly.) There are two methods for soaking:
(1) Place legumes in a large bowl and cover with 3 times as much cool water. Soak overnight at room temperature. Drain, rinse, and cook in fresh water.
(2) Place legumes in a large kettle with 3 times as much water. Boil for five minutes. Turn off heat and soak for one hour. Drain, rinse, and cook in fresh water.

To cook—bring fresh water to a boil in a large, covered kettle. Add legumes and bring to boil again. Reduce heat to low and simmer until the beans are very soft. Do not add salt until after they have softened, otherwise they may not soften properly.

Legume - 1 Cup Soaked	Water	Cooking Times	Yield
Black beans	1 quart	1 1/2 hours	2 cups
Black-eyed peas	3 cups	1 hour	2 cups
Garbanzos	1 quart	5 hours	2 cups
Great Northern beans	3 1/2 cups	2 hours	2 cups
Kidney beans	3 cups	1 1/2 hours	2 cups
Lentils & split peas	3 cups	1 hour	2 1/4 cups
Lima beans	2 cups	1 1/2 hours	1 1/4 cups
Pinto beans	3 cups	2 1/4 hours	2 cups
Red beans	3 cups	3 hours	2 cups
Soybeans	1 quart	5 hours	2 cups
Small white beans	3 cups	1 1/2 hours	2 cups

ONE OF A KIND LOAF

Create your own meat-free loaf! Simply select one ingredient from each category, except Seasonings and Vegetable Seasonings, of which several can be used.

LEGUMES — *2 cups*
cooked legumes of any variety, such as: lentils, kidney beans, garbanzos, pinto beans, soybeans, or tofu, etc.

GRAINS — *1-2 cups*
whole grain bread crumbs, rolled or quick oats, cooked brown rice or millet, Grape-Nuts cereal, crushed whole grain cereal flakes, whole grain cracker crumbs, whole grain croutons, etc.

NUTS — *1/2 cup, chopped*
   or ground:
almonds, cashews, pecans, pumpkin seeds, sunflower seeds, walnuts, etc.

LIQUID — *1-1 1/2 cups*
broth from cooked vegetables, plain soy, nut, or grain milk, tomato juice or sauce, "V8," etc.

BINDER—*1*
2 tablespoons soy flour,
2 tablespoons whole wheat flour,
2-3 tablespoons gluten flour,
3 tablespoons potato flour,
3 tablespoons minute tapioca,
1/2 cup cooked oatmeal,
1/2 cup cooked "cream of wheat"
2 tablespoons soaked mung beans,
   blended, etc.

SEASONINGS — *1/2-1 teaspoon*
   of one or several, as desired:
cumin, sweet basil, Italian seasoning, oregano, parsley flakes, rosemary, sage, All-Purpose Seasoning (p. 167), celery salt, garlic or onion salt or powder, food yeast flakes, salt, Vegex, Liquid Aminos, etc.

VEGETABLE SEASONINGS —
   1 or more
1 onion, chopped,
1-2 cloves garlic, minced,
2-3 tablespoons chopped pimiento, etc.

GENERAL DIRECTIONS: Mix all selected ingredients together. Press into a sprayed loaf pan and bake at 350° F for 45 minutes. Serve with a light gravy, if desired. Can also be sliced and used as a sandwich filling. Freezes well.

FOR PATTIES: Mix selected ingredients together. Form into patties and bake, or brown in a sprayed nonstick griddle. For uniform shape and size of patties, use a canning jar ring and lid. Place lid inside ring and fill with loaf mixture. Invert over prepared pan, push lid and mixture through ring. If lid sticks to patty, slide a table knife between mixture and lid.

GARBANZOS A LA KING

1	cup chopped celery
1	cup sliced fresh or canned mushrooms
1/2	cup minced onion
1/4	cup chopped red bell pepper or pimiento
2	tablespoons water
1/2	cup clean, raw cashews
3	cups water
1	onion, quartered
2	tablespoons All-Purpose Seasoning (p. 167)
1	tablespoon Liquid Aminos
1/4	cup whole wheat flour
1	tablespoon toasted sesame seeds (opt.)
13/4	cups cooked garbanzos, *or* 15 ounce can, drained
11/2	cups frozen peas

In a large saucepan, simmer first 5 ingredients. Meanwhile, process cashews in about 1 cup of the water in a blender, until smooth, then add remaining water and next 4 ingredients and continue blending until smooth. Combine with simmering vegetables and bring to boil, stirring frequently, until thickened. Stir in remaining ingredients and continue cooking until well heated. Serve over brown rice, noodles, or toast, if desired. **Serves 12.**

Per 1/2 cup serving: 143 calories; 5.9 g protein (16%); 20 g carbohydrate (53%); 5.3 g fat (31%); 379 mg sodium; 44 mg calcium; 0 mg cholesterol.

GARBANZO RICE CASSEROLE

1/2	cup chopped celery
1/2	onion, chopped
3	cups cooked brown rice
15	ounce can garbanzos, with broth
1/4	cup chopped fresh parsley
11/2	teaspoons All-Purpose Seasoning (p. 167)
1/4	teaspoon sweet basil
1/4	teaspoon oregano

Simmer celery and onion in garbanzo broth, until tender. Combine with remaining ingredients and mix together well. Press into a sprayed, 2 quart casserole dish and bake at 350° F for 35-45 minutes, uncovered. **Serves 5.**

Per 1 cup serving: 199 calories; 6.2 g protein (12%); 39.1 g carbohydrate (78%); 2.2 g fat (10%); 365 mg sodium; 53 mg calcium; 0 mg cholesterol.

MACARONI & "CHEESE"

2	quarts water
1	teaspoon salt (opt.)
2	cups whole wheat macaroni
1	cup clean, raw cashews
2	cups water
2	ounce jar pimientos
2	tablespoons fresh lemon juice
2	teaspoons onion powder
2	teaspoons salt
1	teaspoon garlic powder
11/2	cups soft whole wheat bread crumbs

Bring 2 quarts water and 1 teaspoon salt to a boil, then add macaroni. Bring to a second boil, then reduce heat and simmer, covered, until tender. Process cashews with 1 cup of the water in a blender, until very smooth. Add remaining water and other ingredients, except bread crumbs, and continue blending until smooth. Drain macaroni and place in a casserole dish. Pour sauce over top and stir in. Cover and bake at 350° F for 30 minutes. Uncover and top with bread crumbs. Bake for an additional 15 minutes. For variation, add 1 cup of a colorful vegetable, such as green peas. **Serves 7.**

Per 1 cup serving: 247 calories; 8.4 g protein (13%); 34.6 g carbohydrate (53%); 10.2 g fat (35%); 654 mg sodium; 36 mg calcium; 0 mg cholesterol.

RICE RING

6   cups cooked brown rice
2   cups frozen peas or mixed vegetables
1   cup mushroom pieces (opt.)
1/4   cup grated onion
2   tablespoons Liquid Aminos,
        or 1 tablespoon Bernard Jensen's Protein Seasoning
2   tablespoons chopped, fresh parsley
2   tablespoons chopped pimientos (opt.)
1   recipe White Sauce (p. 91)

Mix all ingredients together, reserving half of White Sauce recipe, and press into a sprayed Bundt pan or other circular mold. Place in a shallow pan of water and bake at 350° F for 30 minutes. Release onto a platter and top with remaining White Sauce. Fill center with cooked carrots or other colorful vegetables, if desired. Garnish with fresh parsley, if desired. **Serves 10.**

Per 1/10 ring: 214 calories; 6.1 g protein (11%); 38.8 g carbohydrate (72%); 4 g fat (17%); 279 mg sodium; 30 mg calcium; 0 mg cholesterol.

BROCCOLI AMANDINE

1   onion, chopped
41/2   cups chopped broccoli, slightly steamed
31/2   cups cooked brown rice (dextrinize first)
21/2   cups Mushroom Gravy (p. 87)
2   teaspoons onion powder
1/2   teaspoon garlic powder
2   cups Sesame Almond Sauce (p. 89)

Simmer chopped onion in a small amount of water until translucent. Combine with remaining ingredients, except Sauce, and mix well. Place in a casserole dish and spread Sauce over the top. Bake at 350° F until thoroughly heated and slightly brown on top (about 20-25 minutes). **Serves 8.**

Per 1/8 recipe: 289 calories; 10.9 g protein (14%); 36.2 g carbohydrate (47%); 13.1 g fat (38%); 391 mg sodium; 158 mg calcium; 0 mg cholesterol.

BREAD DRESSING

1/2	cup chopped celery
1/2	cup chopped onion
6	cups dry whole wheat bread cubes
2	tablespoons parsley
1	teaspoon sage
1/2	teaspoon sweet basil
1/2	teaspoon onion powder
1/2	teaspoon savory
1/2	teaspoon thyme
1 1/2	cups water
2	tablespoons All-Purpose Seasoning (p. 167)

Simmer celery and onion with a small amount of water in a 2 quart saucepan. Add remaining ingredients, except last two, and mix well. Dissolve seasoning in water and stir into other ingredients. Mixture should be quite moist—add more water, if necessary. Place on sprayed cookie sheets and bake at 350° F for about 45 minutes. For a more moist dressing, place in a casserole dish and bake. Serve with gravy of your choice. **Serves 14.**

Per 1/2 cup serving: 71 calories; 2.3 g protein (13%); 13.4 g carbohydrate (76%); 0.8 g fat (11%); 285 mg sodium; 42 mg calcium; 0 mg cholesterol.

STUFFED GREEN PEPPERS

6	whole green peppers
2	stalks celery, diced
1/2	onion, chopped
1/4	cup diced green bell pepper
2	cups chopped tomatoes
1/3	cup tomato sauce
3	cups cooked brown rice
1	teaspoon food yeast flakes
1	teaspoon honey or date sugar (opt.)
1	teaspoon salt
1	teaspoon Vegex
1/4	teaspoon sweet basil
1/4	teaspoon oregano
1/8	teaspoon marjoram
1/8	teaspoon sage
1/8	teaspoon thyme

Remove centers of green peppers and cut in half, width-wise, if desired. Steam about 8 minutes. Meanwhile, simmer next 3 ingredients in a small amount of water. Add tomatoes and tomato sauce and simmer. Add remaining ingredients and mix well. Spoon filling into peppers and place in a baking dish, with 1/4" inch of water, and bake at 350° F for 30 minutes. Serve with a tomato sauce, if desired, or top with grated American "Cheese" (p. 155). **Serves 6.**

Per stuffed pepper: 162 calories; 4.8 g protein (11%); 34.7 g carbohydrate (82%); 1.2 g fat (6%); 497 mg sodium; 38 mg calcium; 0 mg cholesterol.

POTATO POT PIE

1	cup sliced carrots
1	cup cubed potatoes
1	cup water
3/4	cup peas
1/2	cup chopped celery
1/2	cup clean, raw cashews
1 1/2	teaspoons garlic powder
1 1/2	teaspoons onion powder
1	teaspoon salt
2	recipes Basic Pie Crust (p. 58), uncooked

Simmer first 5 ingredients for about 10 minutes. Drain well and save water. Add enough hot water to equal 1 cup. Process this water with cashews and seasonings in a blender until very smooth. Pour over vegetables and stir together. Pour into unbaked 9" pie crust and place remaining uncooked pie crust over top and flute edges together. Prick top crust with fork to allow steam to escape. Bake at 400° F for 30 minutes, or until crust is lightly browned. **Serves 6.**

Per 1/6 pie: 399 calories; 10.9 g protein (10%); 43.3 g carbohydrate (41%); 22.6 g fat (48%); 642 mg sodium; 107 mg calcium; 0 mg cholesterol.

BULGUR BURGER

2	cups bulgur wheat
2	cups water
1	cup walnuts
1/2	onion, quartered
1	clove garlic
1	tablespoon All-Purpose Seasoning (p. 167)
1	teaspoon salt

Place bulgur wheat in a saucepan. Process remaining ingredients in a blender until smooth, then pour over bulgur wheat. Cook over low heat for about 5 minutes, stirring frequently. Turn off heat and let stand about 20 minutes. Spread evenly on a cookie sheet and bake at 250° F for about 1 hour, or until mostly dry. Freezes well. Use for tacos, enchiladas, soups, pizza, etc. **Yields about 6 cups or 12 servings.**

Per 1/2 cup serving: 148 calories; 4.4 g protein (11%); 20.4 g carbohydrate (52%); 6.5 g fat (37%); 276 mg sodium; 24 mg calcium; 0 mg cholesterol.

LENTIL LINKS

1/2	cup chopped celery
1/4	cup chopped onion
1	clove garlic, minced
3	cups Seasoned Bread Crumbs (p. 13)
2	cups cooked lentils*
1/2	cup chopped walnuts or pecans

Simmer first 3 ingredients in a small amount of water until tender. Stir in remaining ingredients, reserving 1 cup of bread crumbs, and let stand for 5 minutes. Add water (or nut milk) to obtain good consistency for forming links. Form into 3" links and roll in reserved bread crumbs. Bake at 350° F for about 15 minutes. Turn and bake an additional 15 minutes. **Yields 21/2 dozen or 15 servings.**

*Simmer 1 cup dried lentils in 2 cups salted water for 1 hour, or until tender.

VARIATIONS: (1) Add smoked yeast, to taste; (2) Add sesame seeds to reserved bread crumbs; (3) Form into patties or balls instead of links; (4) Substitute packaged stuffing mix for the Seasoned Bread Crumbs.

Per two links: 96 calories; 4.5 g protein (18%); 13.4 g carbohydrate (52%); 3.4 g fat (30%); 374 mg sodium; 27 mg calcium; 0 mg cholesterol.

ALMOND RICE LOAF

1/2	cup soaked, raw mung beans or garbanzos*
1/2	cup water
1	cup Seasoned Bread Crumbs (p. 13) or plain dry bread crumbs
1	cup cooked brown rice
1	onion, chopped
1/2	cup hot water
1/2	cup chopped almonds
1/2	cup chopped celery
1/2	cup sunflower seeds
1	teaspoon marjoram
1	teaspoon thyme
1/2	teaspoon salt
1	cup Country-style Gravy (p. 86)

Process mung beans and 1/2 cup water in a blender until smooth. Combine all ingredients, except Gravy and mix well. Let stand for 5 minutes. Press into a sprayed loaf pan. Bake at 350° F for 45-60 minutes. May also be baked in a Bundt pan. Release from pan onto serving dish and pour Gravy over the top, just before serving. Freezes and slices well. For variation, slice and use as a sandwich filling. **Serves 6.**

*Soak overnight in refrigerator.

Per 1/6 loaf: 260 calories; 9.9 g protein (14%); 26.4 g carbohydrate (38%); 14.5 g fat (47%); 698 mg sodium; 85 mg calcium; 0 mg cholesterol.

TOFU LOAF

2	cups rolled oats
1	pound tofu, mashed
1	onion, chopped fine
1/2	cup chopped parsley
1/2	cup tomato sauce
1/3	cup Liquid Aminos
2	cloves garlic, minced
1	teaspoon Vegex or Bernard Jensen's Protein Seasoning

Mix all ingredients together. Press into a sprayed loaf pan and bake at 350° F for about 1 hour. Let cool 10-15 minutes before removing from pan. Garnish with parsley and tomato slices, if desired. For variation, slice and use as a sandwich filling. **Serves 8.**

Per 1/8 loaf (1/2 cup): 182 calories; 14.3 g protein (30%); 19.6 g carbohydrate (41%); 6.3 g fat (30%); 647 mg sodium; 139 mg calcium; 0 mg cholesterol.

TOFU WALNUT LOAF

1	cup hot water
1	tablespoon Vegex
2	cloves garlic, minced
1	teaspoon Italian seasoning
1	teaspoon paprika
1	teaspoon salt
1	pound soft tofu, mashed
1	cup dry whole wheat bread crumbs
1	cup rolled oats
1	cup finely chopped walnuts
1	large onion, chopped
1/4	cup gluten flour

Dissolve Vegex in hot water. Stir in garlic and seasonings. Mix remaining ingredients together. Add Vegex mixture and mix well (it will be stiff). Place in a sprayed 1 1/2 quart casserole dish and bake uncovered at 375° F for 1 hour or until set in the middle. Will hold its shape if turned out on a platter. Garnish with cherry tomatoes and parsley, if desired. **Serves 10.**

Per 1/10 loaf (1/2 cup): 203 calories; 10.5 g protein (20%); 19.5 g carbohydrate (36%); 10.5 g fat (44%); 390 mg sodium; 97 mg calcium; 0 mg cholesterol.

MILLET PEANUT BALLS

2	cups cooked millet*
1	onion, chopped fine
1/2	cup peanut or almond butter
1/2	teaspoon celery salt
1/2	teaspoon garlic powder
1/2	teaspoon salt

Combine all ingredients and mix well. Chill for about 20 minutes, then form into 1" balls and bake on a sprayed cookie sheet at 375° F for about 30 minutes, until browned. May also be formed into patties. Serve with Zesty Tomato Relish (p. 93), if desired. For a chewier texture, substitute 1/2 cup cooked bulgur for 1/2 cup of the cooked millet. **Yields 24 balls or 8 servings.**

*Simmer 1/2 cup millet grain in 2 cups salted water for 45-60 minutes.

Per three 1" balls: 165 calories; 6.4 g protein (15%); 19.1 g carbohydrate (45%); 7.6 g fat (40%); 236 mg sodium; 13 mg calcium; 0 mg cholesterol.

BETTER BURGERS

1	cup water
1	onion, chopped
3	tablespoons Liquid Aminos
1	tablespoon food yeast flakes
1	clove garlic, minced
1 1/2	cups rolled oats
1/4	cup chopped walnuts
1/2	teaspoon salt
1/4	teaspoon sage
1/8	teaspoon marjoram
1/8	teaspoon thyme

Bring first 5 ingredients to a boil. Stir in remaining ingredients and let stand for 10 minutes. Drop by 1/4 cup scoop onto a sprayed cookie sheet. Flatten and bake at 350° F for 25 minutes, then turn and bake an additional 15 minutes. Can also be browned in a covered, nonstick skillet, or in a waffle iron, using the flat grills. **Serves 8.**

Per burger: 96 calories; 4.2 g protein (17%); 12.9 g carbohydrate (52%); 3.3 g fat (30%); 407 mg sodium; 22 mg calcium; 0 mg cholesterol.

KING BURGERS

1 cup soaked garbanzos*
1/4 cup soy or nut milk
1 cup rolled oats
1 onion, minced
1/2 cup walnuts, chopped fine
1 tablespoon Liquid Aminos
2 teaspoons McKay's Beef Style Seasoning (MSG Free)
1 teaspoon sage or Italian seasoning

Process garbanzos and soy milk in a blender until smooth, adding more soy milk if necessary for blending. Pour into a bowl and stir in remaining ingredients. Drop by spoonful or ice cream scoop onto a sprayed skillet. Flatten with back of spoon. Cover and brown slowly (about 20 minutes on each side) over low heat. **Serves 8.**

*Soak overnight or substitute canned garbanzos.

VARIATION: For **King Burger Bake**, place browned burgers in a covered casserole dish and spread gravy over top. Bake at 350° F for 30 minutes.

Per burger: 136 calories; 5.5 g protein (16%); 16.6 g carbohydrate (47%); 6 g fat (38%); 147 mg sodium; 33 mg calcium; 0 mg cholesterol.

SUNBURGERS

1/2 cup chopped onion
2 tablespoons water
2 cups sunflower seeds
3 tablespoons whole wheat flour
1 tablespoon onion powder
1 teaspoon salt
2 cups finely grated carrots
11/2 cups tomato juice

Simmer onion in 2 tablespoons water until tender. Process next 4 ingredients in a blender until seeds are well ground. Toss with onions and grated carrots. Add tomato juice and mix together well. Form into burgers (1/3 cup per burger), and place on a sprayed cookie sheet. Bake at 400° F for 20-25 minutes. Turn and bake an additional 20 minutes. **Serves 11.**

Per burger: 175 calories; 6.8 g protein (14%); 10.9 g carbohydrate (23%); 13.1 g fat (62%); 322 mg sodium; 45 mg calcium; 0 mg cholesterol.

TOFU MILLET BURGERS

2	cups cooked millet*
1	cup mashed, firm tofu
1	onion, chopped, steamed
1/2	cup soft whole wheat bread crumbs
1/4	cup chopped nuts or nut butter
31/2	tablespoons Liquid Aminos
3	tablespoons whole wheat or oat flour
1	clove garlic, minced
1/4	teaspoon sage

Mix all ingredients together. Form into burgers and brown in a covered, sprayed or nonstick skillet. **Serves 10.**

*Simmer 1/2 cup millet grain in 2 cups salted water for 45-60 minutes.

Per burger: 101 calories; 6.3 g protein (24%); 10.1 g carbohydrate (38%); 4.5 g fat (38%); 276 mg sodium; 63 mg calcium; 0 mg cholesterol.

TOFU OAT BURGERS

2	cups quick oats
1	pound soft tofu
1	cup finely chopped onion
1	cup walnuts or pecans, ground
1/2	cup soy or gluten flour
1	tablespoon Vegex
1	teaspoon Italian seasoning
1	teaspoon paprika
1	teaspoon salt

Mix all ingredients together well and form into burgers. Cover and brown slowly on both sides in a sprayed, nonstick skillet. Be sure to cook thoroughly. **Serves 16.**

Per burger: 123 calories; 6.8 g protein (21%); 10.8 g carbohydrate (33%); 6.7 g fat (46%); 197 mg sodium; 59 mg calcium; 0 mg cholesterol.

TOFU CUTLETS

1	pound firm tofu
1	large onion, chopped
2	cloves garlic, minced
1/2	cup water
1/4	cup Liquid Aminos
1/4	teaspoon sweet basil
1/4	teaspoon oregano
1	cup food yeast flakes

Drain tofu well. Cut into 1/4" thick slices. Steam onion and garlic in water. Pour into a bowl and add next 3 ingredients. Marinate tofu slices in this mixture for about 1 hour. Place yeast flakes in a shallow bowl and dip marinated tofu into flakes and coat thoroughly. Place on a sprayed cookie sheet and bake at 325° F for 5-7 minutes on each side, then broil until crispy. May also be pan-fried in a nonstick skillet. For variation, add 2 tablespoons fresh lemon juice to marinade mixture. **Serves 5.**

Per 1/4" slice: 197 calories; 21.6 g protein (42%); 12.3 g carbohydrate (24%); 8 g fat (35%); 630 mg sodium; 230 mg calcium; 0 mg cholesterol.

BAKED BEANS

3	cups dried navy beans
21/2	quarts water
1	cup tomato sauce
1/2	cup chopped dates
1/3	cup chopped onion
1	tablespoon fresh lemon juice
2	teaspoons salt
1/2	teaspoon garlic powder

Soak beans overnight. Drain, then simmer beans in 21/2 quarts fresh water in a large, covered kettle for 1 hour. Place beans and liquid in a sprayed crockpot. Process tomato sauce and dates in a blender until smooth. Add to beans and stir in, along with remaining ingredients. Cook for 6-8 hours, covered, stirring occasionally. Add more water, if necessary. Can also be baked, covered, at 300° F for 30 minutes, then 250° F for 6-8 hours. **Serves 13.**

Per 1/2 cup serving: 139 calories; 7.9 g protein (22%); 26.9 g carbohydrate (74%); 0.6 g fat (4%); 450 mg sodium; 56 mg calcium; 0 mg cholesterol.

ADZUKI BEANS

1	cup dried Adzuki beans
1 1/2	quarts water
1	onion, chopped
1	tablespoon All-Purpose Seasoning (p. 167)
2	teaspoons Liquid Aminos
2	teaspoons Vegex or Bernard Jensen's Protein Seasoning
1	clove garlic, minced
1/2	teaspoon dried parsley
1/2	teaspoon savory
1/4	teaspoon grated lemon peel
1/2	teaspoon sweet basil (opt.)
1/4	teaspoon marjoram (opt.)

Soak beans overnight in 3 cups of the water. Drain and place soaked beans in a large saucepan with remaining 3 cups water. Add onion and cook until beans are softened. Add remaining ingredients and continue cooking for another 20-30 minutes. **Serves 6.**

Per 1/2 cup serving: 141 calories; 8.8 g protein (24%); 26.9 g carbohydrate (74%); 0.2 g fat (1%); 406 mg sodium; 42 mg calcium; 0 mg cholesterol.

SEASONED BEANS

3	cups water
2 1/2	cups soaked pinto beans*
1/2	cup chopped onion
1/3	cup chopped green bell pepper
2	cloves garlic, minced
1/2	teaspoon cumin
1	teaspoon salt

Combine water and beans and simmer until beans are tender (about 2 hours), stirring occasionally. Add remaining ingredients and simmer another 20 minutes. **Serves 6.**

*Soak 1 cup dried pinto beans overnight in water, then drain.

Per 1/2 cup serving: 107 calories; 6.2 g protein (22%); 20.4 g carbohydrate (74%); 0.4 g fat (4%); 358 mg sodium; 43 mg calcium; 0 mg cholesterol.

REFRIED BEANS

1   small onion, chopped
1   clove garlic, minced
2   cups cooked pinto beans (save broth)
1/2   cup tomato sauce
1/2   teaspoon oregano
1/4   teaspoon cumin
1/2   teaspoon salt
    cilantro, to taste (opt.)

Simmer onion and garlic in a little water until soft. Process all ingredients in a blender to desired consistency, using broth as necessary. Bake in a sprayed casserole dish at 325° F for 20-30 minutes, or simmer in a skillet, stirring frequently. **Serves 6.**

Per 1/2 cup serving: 91 calories; 5.1 g protein (22%); 17.5 g carbohydrate (74%); 0.4 g fat (4%); 303 mg sodium; 38 mg calcium; 0 mg cholesterol.

HAYSTACKS AND TOSTADOS

3   dozen Crispy Corn Chips (p. 11),
    or 6 Maria's Tortillas (p. 10)
3   cups Seasoned Beans (p. 118)
3   cups chopped or shredded lettuce
11/2   cups diced tomato
6   tablespoons chopped green onions
6   tablespoons finely diced onion
11/2   cups Salsa Ranchera (p. 95) **or** Tomato Sauce (p. 91)
3/4   cup Guacamole (p. 150)
6   tablespoons chopped black olives

For **Haystacks**, place Crispy Corn Chips on plates, then place remaining ingredients on top of chips, in the order given. **Serves 6.**

For **Tostados**, bake Maria's Tortillas at 250° F for about 15 minutes, or until crisp. Watch closely to prevent burning. Place remaining ingredients on top of tortillas, in the order given. **Serves 6.**

Per 1/6 recipe: 267 calories; 11.1 g protein (15%); 42.5 g carbohydrate (59%); 8.3 g fat (26%); 745 mg sodium; 146 mg calcium; 0 mg cholesterol.

LAYERED BEAN CHIP CASSEROLE

2	dozen warmed tortilla chips (4 tortillas)
1	cup Nacho "Cheese" Sauce (p. 93)
2	cups hot Refried Beans (p. 119)
2	cups finely shredded lettuce
1/4	cup finely shredded cilantro (opt.)
1	cup diced tomato
1/2	cup Nacho "Cheese" Sauce (p. 93)
1/4	cup chopped black olives
1/4	cup chopped green onions

Layer all ingredients in a deep, clear, serving bowl, in the order given above. Serve immediately, with Guacamole, if desired. **Serves 4.**

Per 1/4 recipe: 346 calories; 12.9 g protein (14%); 45.7 g carbohydrate (50%); 14.7 g fat (36%); 963 mg sodium; 132 mg calcium; 0 mg cholesterol.

TACO FILLING

1	recipe Bulgur Burger (p. 111)
1	onion, chopped
1	green bell pepper, chopped
2	cloves garlic, minced
1	tablespoon water
8	ounce can tomato sauce
1	cup cooked or fresh chopped tomatoes
1	teaspoon paprika
1/2	teaspoon cumin

Cover Bulgur Burger with water to soften, if it has been crisp-dried. Meanwhile, simmer onion, bell pepper, and garlic in water until tender. Add remaining ingredients, including drained Bulgur Burger and heat thoroughly, stirring occasionally. Serve in soft or crispy warmed corn tortillas, stuffed with salad greens and salsa, if desired. **Serves 12.**

Per 1/12 recipe: 166 calories; 5.2 g protein (12%); 24.5 g carbohydrate (55%); 6.7 g fat (34%); 424 mg sodium; 38 mg calcium; 0 mg cholesterol.

SUMMER VEGETABLE ENCHILADAS

Sauce:
- 1 large onion, chopped
- 3 tablespoons water
- 2 large tomatoes, peeled and chopped
- 2 canned green chilies, chopped
- 1/2 cup tomato juice
- 1 clove garlic, minced
- 1/2 teaspoon salt
- 1/4 teaspoon coriander
- 1/4 teaspoon cumin

Filling:
- 4 small zucchini, cubed
- 1/4 cup water
- 1 cup whole kernel corn
- 1 green bell pepper, diced
- 1 red bell pepper, diced
- 1 onion, chopped fine
- 2 cloves garlic, minced
- salt, to taste (opt.)

Miscellaneous:
- 1 cup rich soy or nut cream
- 1 dozen 6" corn tortillas
- 1/2 cup Melted "Cheese" Sauce (p. 90)
- 1/4 cup sliced black olives
- 2 green onions, chopped

Prepare sauce first. Simmer onion in water in a large skillet over medium heat. Add remaining sauce ingredients and bring to a boil over high heat. Cover, reduce heat, and simmer for 15 minutes. Uncover and return to a boil over medium-high heat, stirring often, until sauce is reduced to about 11/2 cups. Spread sauce in a 9 x 13" baking dish.

Prepare filling next. In a large skillet, simmer zucchini in water. Add remaining filling ingredients and continue cooking, stirring often, until liquid evaporates and vegetables are tender-crisp (about 5 minutes). Add salt, to taste.

Heat soy or nut cream in a small pan over medium-low heat. Dip each tortilla, one at a time, in hot cream, to soften. Spoon an equal amount of filling down the center of each tortilla. Roll tortillas up and place seam-side down in baking dish with sauce. Make only one layer of tortillas. Pour Melted "Cheese"

Sauce over the top and bake, uncovered, at 375° F for 20-30 minutes. Sprinkle with olives and green onions just before serving. **Serves 12.**

Per enchilada: 239 calories; 9 g protein (14%); 43.5 g carbohydrate (67%); 5.5 g fat (19%); 558 mg sodium; 131 mg calcium; 0 mg cholesterol.

PINTO ENCHILADAS

2	onions, chopped
1	carrot, grated fine
1	celery stalk, chopped fine
3	cups cooked pinto beans, drained
1	cup cooked brown rice
1	teaspoon cumin
1	teaspoon garlic powder
1	teaspoon salt
1	dozen corn tortillas
1	recipe Italian Sauce (p. 95)
1 1/2	cups Melted "Cheese" Sauce (p. 90)

Simmer first 3 ingredients in a skillet in a small amount of water. Add beans, rice, and seasonings. Mash beans slightly and heat thoroughly. Pour a layer of Italian Sauce in bottom of a deep, flat casserole dish. Lightly steam tortillas, or dip in sauce to soften, then fill each tortilla with 1/4 cup of rice/bean filling and roll up. Place in casserole dish, seam-side down, and pour remaining Italian Sauce over the top. Top with "Cheese" Sauce and bake at 350° F for 30 minutes. Baste occasionally during baking, or cover to prevent drying out. **Serves 12.**

Per enchilada: 195 calories; 8.1 g protein (16%); 37.1 g carbohydrate (73%); 2.6 g fat (11%); 527 mg sodium; 90 mg calcium; 0 mg cholesterol.

FIESTA ENCHILADAS

1/2	recipe Bulgur Burger (p. 111), unbaked
1/2	cup grated American "Cheese" (p. 155)
1/2	cup sliced black olives
6	green onions, chopped
1	dozen 6" corn tortillas
1	recipe Enchilada Sauce (p. 94)
1	cup grated American "Cheese" (p. 155)

Mix first 4 ingredients and set aside. Dip tortillas in Enchilada Sauce to soften, then place 2 heaping tablespoons of burger filling in each tortilla. Roll up and place in a 9 x 12" baking dish, seam-side down. Cover with Sauce, then sprinkle grated "Cheese" over the top. Bake at 350° F for 45 minutes. **Serves 12.**

Per enchilada: 198 calories; 6.2 g protein (12%); 32.6 g carbohydrate (61%); 6.5 g fat (27%); 654 mg sodium; 79 mg calcium; 0 mg cholesterol.

TAMALE PIE

2 1/4	ounce can sliced olives
2	tablespoons water or olive broth
1	small onion, chopped
1	clove garlic, minced
3	cups chopped, stewed tomatoes
1	cup lightly blended, whole kernel corn
3/4	teaspoon ground cumin
3/4	teaspoon oregano
1/2	teaspoon garlic powder
1/2	teaspoon salt
2/3	cup fine yellow cornmeal

Simmer first 4 ingredients 2-3 minutes. Stir in remaining ingredients, except cornmeal, and cook for 5 minutes. Stir in cornmeal and simmer over low heat for 10 minutes. Place in a 9" pie plate and bake at 325° F for 30-45 minutes. Watch to avoid drying out. **Serves 9.**

Per 1/9 pie (1/2 cup): 91 calories; 2.4 g protein (9%); 16.4 g carbohydrate (65%); 2.9 g fat (26%); 322 mg sodium; 23 mg calcium; 0 mg cholesterol.

SPANISH RICE

1	cup uncooked brown rice
13/4	cups water
11/2	cups blended, stewed tomatoes
1	clove garlic, whole
1	bay leaf
1	teaspoon All-Purpose Seasoning (p. 167)
1/4	teaspoon cumin
1/4	teaspoon onion powder
1/4	teaspoon paprika

Lightly brown rice in a dry skillet over medium heat, stirring constantly. Add remaining ingredients and bring to a boil. Reduce heat to low, cover, and simmer for 50 minutes, stirring occasionally. Remove bay leaf and garlic clove before serving. For variation, add 1/2 cup chopped onion and/or green bell pepper. **Serves 6.**

Per 2/3 cup serving: 137 calories; 3 g protein (9%); 26.7 g carbohydrate (80%); 1.6 g fat (11%); 181 mg sodium; 19 mg calcium; 0 mg cholesterol.

CUBAN BLACK BEANS ON RICE

5	cups boiling water
1	pound dried black beans
1	large onion, chopped
1	green bell pepper, chopped
2	cloves garlic, minced
1	bay leaf
11/2	teaspoons cumin
11/2	teaspoons oregano leaves
1	teaspoon salt
1	pound brown rice, cooked
1	cup chopped tomato
2	green onions, chopped

Combine first 6 ingredients a large saucepan. Cook until beans are tender and liquid is thickened (about 11/2 hours). Remove bay leaf, add seasonings, and simmer a few more minutes. Serve over rice and garnish with tomato and green onions. **Serves 8.**

Per 1 cup serving: 241 calories; 10.9 g protein (18%); 47.1 g carbohydrate (77%); 1.6 g fat (6%); 322 mg sodium; 58 mg calcium; 0 mg cholesterol.

BRITISH LENTIL CASSEROLE

1	cup chopped celery
1	cup chopped onion
2	tablespoons finely chopped green bell pepper
1	clove garlic, minced
2 1/2	cups cooked lentils
1 1/2	cups soft whole wheat bread crumbs
1	cup tomato puree
2/3	cup chopped or ground walnuts or almonds
1/2	cup soy or nut milk
3	tablespoons whole wheat flour
1	teaspoon onion powder
1	teaspoon salt
1/2	teaspoon sage leaves
1	cup Creamy Tomato Gravy (p. 89)

Simmer first 4 ingredients in a small amount of water until just tender. Combine with remaining ingredients, except Gravy, and mix well. Place in a 9 x 9" casserole dish and bake at 325° F for 30 minutes. Spread Gravy over the top and bake an additional 15 minutes. For variation, add 1/2 cup chopped pecans before baking, or sprinkle on top before serving. **Serves 10.**

Per 1/2 cup serving: 164 calories; 7.6 g protein (17%); 22.4 g carbohydrate (51%); 6.2 g fat (32%); 405 mg sodium; 48 mg calcium; 0 mg cholesterol.

MINI FRENCH PIZZAS

10	whole wheat buns
1	cup grated American "Cheese" (p. 155)
8	ounce can tomato sauce
6	ounce can black olives, drained, sliced
5	ounce jar Spanish olives, drained, rinsed, sliced
1/4	cup tomato paste
1/8	teaspoon sweet basil (opt.)
1/8	teaspoon oregano (opt.)

Cut buns in halves and toast. Mix remaining ingredients together and spread over each half. Broil until bubbly. These can be made ahead and frozen— freeze on cookie sheets until firm, then place wax paper over top of half of the pizzas. Place the other pizzas over top (face to face). Place all in a freezer bag or container. **Yields 20 mini pizzas or 10 servings.**

Per two mini pizzas: 165 calories; 5.7 g protein (12%); 25.4 g carbohydrate (53%); 7.3 g fat (35%); 799 mg sodium; 73 mg calcium; 0 mg cholesterol.

FRENCH ONION QUICHE

1	onion, sliced thin
1/4	cup clean, raw cashews
1	cup water
14	ounce package firm tofu, rinsed and drained
1/4	onion
2	tablespoons cornstarch or arrowroot
1	tablespoon fresh lemon juice
11/2	teaspoons salt
1	teaspoon sweet basil
1/4	teaspoon oregano
1/8	teaspoon garlic powder, *or* 1/2 clove fresh garlic
2	green onions, chopped
2	cups fresh or frozen vegetables, shredded, or cut in bite-size pieces
1	Basic Pie Crust (p. 58), unbaked

Prepare onion as described in the Braised-Deglazed Onions recipe (p. 177). Meanwhile, process cashews with 1 cup water in a blender until very smooth. Add remaining ingredients, except last 3, and continue blending until smooth. Combine all filling ingredients and pour into pie crust. Cover and bake at 350° F for 1 hour. Remove cover and continue baking until set in the middle, about 20 minutes Let stand for a few minutes before serving. Sprinkle with paprika, if desired. For variation, use filling for manicotti or crepes. **Serves 10.**

Per 1/10 pie: 198 calories; 10.3 g protein (19%); 19.3 g carbohydrate (36%); 10.4 g fat (44%); 414 mg sodium; 131 mg calcium; 0 mg cholesterol.

PASTA ITALIANA

1/2	pound whole wheat macaroni noodles
2	16 ounce cans tomatoes, drained
2	15 ounce cans red kidney beans, drained
1	cup tomato sauce
4	ounce can mushroom pieces, drained (opt.)
1	clove garlic, minced
1	bay leaf
1	teaspoon onion powder
1	teaspoon chopped parsley
1/2	teaspoon sweet basil
1/2	teaspoon oregano

Cook macaroni as directed on package. Meanwhile, bring remaining ingredients to a boil, then simmer for 20 minutes. Remove bay leaf, and pour over macaroni. May be baked as a casserole, or served immediately. For variation, substitute cooked brown rice for macaroni. **Serves 8.**

Per 1 cup serving: 171 calories; 9.5 g protein (21%); 33.5 g carbohydrate (74%); 0.9 g fat (4%); 926 mg sodium; 90 mg calcium; 0 mg cholesterol.

RATATOULLE

1/2	cup sliced black olives
1	large eggplant, cubed
2	green peppers, cut in wide strips
1	onion, chopped coarse
2	cloves garlic, minced
4	tomatoes, quartered
1	teaspoon salt
1/4	teaspoon sweet basil
1/4	teaspoon marjoram
1/4	teaspoon thyme
pinch	rosemary
41/2	cups cooked noodles, brown rice, or millet (opt.)

Drain olives and save broth. Combine broth with next 4 ingredients and simmer briefly. Add remaining ingredients, except noodles, and cook, covered, over low heat until vegetables are tender. May be served with noodles, rice, or millet, if desired. **Serves 9.**

Per 1/2 cup serving: 42 calories; 1.3 g protein (10%); 7.1 g carbohydrate (55%); 1.9 g fat (34%); 291 mg sodium; 21 mg calcium; 0 mg cholesterol.

ZUCCHINI SPINACH LASAGNE

1 cup chopped onion
1/2 cup chopped green bell pepper
2 zucchini squash, sliced
16 ounce can stewed tomatoes, drained
8 ounce can tomato sauce
1 teaspoon salt (opt.)
1/4 teaspoon sweet basil
1/4 teaspoon oregano
9 whole wheat lasagne noodles, cooked *al dente*
1 cup chopped spinach or other greens
1 recipe Melted "Cheese" Sauce (p. 90)

Simmer onion and green bell pepper in a small amount of water until tender. Add next 6 ingredients and simmer for 20 minutes. Alternate layers of tomato sauce, noodles (cooked al dente), spinach, and "Cheese" Sauce in a large baking dish. Bake at 350° F for 45 minutes. **Serves 12.**

Per 1/12 recipe: 238 calories; 10.3 g protein (16%); 48.8 g carbohydrate (76%); 2.3 g fat (8%); 499 mg sodium; 73 mg calcium; 0 mg cholesterol.

SPINACH-STUFFED MANICOTTI

14 ounce package firm tofu
10 ounce package frozen chopped spinach,
     or 1 bunch fresh spinach, chopped fine
2 cloves garlic, minced
1 tablespoon fresh lemon juice
1 tablespoon food yeast flakes
1/2 teaspoon salt
6 large manicotti shells, cooked *al dente*
2 cups Spaghetti Sauce (p. 96)

Drain tofu well. Mash until it is similar to cottage cheese. Simmer spinach and garlic in a small amount of water. Do not overcook. Combine with tofu and seasonings and mix well. Fill manicotti shells with mixture and place in a baking dish. Pour Spaghetti Sauce over the top and bake at 350° F until heated through. For variation, use filling for crepes. **Serves 6.**

Per two manicotti: 218 calories; 16 g protein (27%); 28.5 g carbohydrate (48%); 6.4 g fat (24%); 546 mg sodium; 235 mg calcium; 0 mg cholesterol.

VEGETABLE CACCIATORE

2	carrots, diced
1	onion, chopped
1/4	cup chopped green bell pepper
1/4	cup chopped fresh parsley
1	clove garlic, minced
4	cups diced, canned tomatoes with juice
8	ounce can low sodium tomato sauce
2	teaspoons All-Purpose Seasoning (p. 167)
1	bay leaf
1/2	teaspoon sweet basil
31/2	cups cooked brown rice or whole grain pasta

Simmer first 5 ingredients in a small amount of water until tender. Add remaining ingredients, except rice, and simmer 30-60 minutes. Remove bay leaf and serve over brown rice or pasta. **Serves 7.**

VARIATIONS: (1) For **"Sloppy Joes,"** add Bulgur Burger (p. 110) to sauce and serve over open-faced buns; (2) Add other vegetables in season and/or cubed tofu.

Per 1 cup serving: 173 calories; 5 g protein (11%); 36.2 g carbohydrate (82%); 1.3 g fat (6%); 586 mg sodium; 88 mg calcium; 0 mg cholesterol.

MAZIDRA

3	cups water
1	cup dried lentils
1	onion, chopped
1	clove garlic, minced
1	teaspoon salt
1	bay leaf
1/8	teaspoon thyme (opt.)
31/2	cups cooked brown rice
13/4	cups shredded lettuce
13/4	cups diced tomatoes
7	tablespoons chopped green onions
7	tablespoons sliced black olives

Bring first 7 ingredients to a boil, then reduce heat and simmer for 45-60 minutes, or until thickened and lentils are tender. Remove bay leaf. Place in a serving bowl and place remaining ingredients in individual serving bowls. Let each person make their own "haystack." **Serves 7.**

SERVING SUGGESTIONS: Top with tomato sauce, guacamole, or fresh lemon juice and garlic salt.

Per 1 cup serving: 261 calories; 12.8 g protein (19%); 47.7 g carbohydrate (70%); 3.3 g fat (11%); 465 mg sodium; 64 mg calcium; 0 mg cholesterol.

MUSHROOM STROGANOFF

8	ounces spinach ribbon noodles
1	pound fresh mushrooms, sliced,
	or three 4 ounce cans mushroom pieces
1	onion, chopped
1	clove garlic, minced
3	tablespoons water
2	tablespoons Liquid Aminos
2	tablespoons tomato sauce or ketchup
1	tablespoon McKay's Beef Style Seasoning (MSG Free)
5	tablespoons whole wheat pastry flour
1	cup water
1/4	cup apple or white grape juice
1/2	teaspoon dried dill weed,
	or 1 tablespoon chopped fresh dill weed
3/4	cup tofu yogurt or Sour Cream variation of Tofu Mayonnaise (p. 158) (opt.)

Prepare noodles as directed. Simmer mushrooms, onion, and garlic, in 3 tablespoons water for 3-5 minutes until tender. Stir in next 3 ingredients. Mix flour and 1 cup water until smooth and gradually add to vegetables while stirring. Bring to a boil, stirring constantly. Reduce heat and simmer for 5 minutes. Stir in remaining ingredients and heat thoroughly. Pour over cooked and drained noodles and serve. May also be served over brown rice. **Serves 8.**

Per 1 cup serving: 133 calories; 7.2 g protein (21%); 25.7 g carbohydrate (74%); 0.9 g fat (6%); 291 mg sodium; 22 mg calcium; 0 mg cholesterol.

RUSSIAN-STYLE PASTIES

1/4	head cabbage, diced
1/2	cup sliced mushrooms
1	small onion, diced
1	tablespoon Liquid Aminos
2/3	recipe Whole Wheat Bread dough (p. 5)

Simmer all ingredients, except dough, until vegetables are softened. Roll out bread dough onto floured board to 1/4" thickness or less. Cut out circles with a largemouth canning ring. Place a tablespoon of cabbage mixture on one side of each circle. Fold dough over and pinch edges to seal. Allow to rise in the oven on the lowest heat setting until double in size. Bake at 350° F for 15-20 minutes. Serve hot or cold. Good with soup. **Yields about 2 dozen pasties.**

VARIATIONS: (1) For **Potato Pasties**, fill with seasoned, mashed potatoes; (2) For **Fruit Pasties**, fill with a mixture of dried fruit.

Per pastie: 79 calories; 3.7 g protein (18%); 16.2 g carbohydrate (77%); 0.4 g fat (5%); 94 mg sodium; 14 mg calcium; 0 mg cholesterol.

RED LENTIL DAL

2	cups red lentils
3	cups hot water
1	teaspoon cumin seed
1/4	cup chopped onion
2	cloves garlic
2	bay leaves
1/2	tablespoon salt, or to taste
1/2	teaspoon turmeric
1	quart hot water

Rinse lentils well and soak in 3 cups hot water for 5 minutes. Drain. Lightly spray a large pot or skillet with pan spray. Heat pot and add cumin seed. Stir briefly and add onion and garlic. Heat for a few minutes, stirring occasionally. Add lentils and remaining seasonings and stir briefly. Add 1 quart hot water and mix well. Cover and cook until lentils are tender. Serve over brown rice, if desired. **Serves 10.**

Per 1/2 cup serving: 119 calories; 9.1 g protein (30%); 20.7 g carbohydrate (67%); 0.4 g fat (3%); 327 mg sodium; 28 mg calcium; 0 mg cholesterol.

ORIENTAL RICE

1	cup uncooked brown rice
2	cups water
1/2	pound firm tofu, drained, mashed
1	carrot, grated
2	green onions, chopped
1/2	teaspoon garlic powder
1/2	teaspoon onion powder
1/4	teaspoon turmeric (opt.)
2	tablespoons Liquid Aminos

Lightly brown rice in a dry skillet over medium heat, stirring constantly. Bring water to boil, then add rice. Bring to boil again, reduce heat, cover, and simmer for 35 minutes. Do not uncover or stir. While rice is cooking, simmer remaining ingredients, except Liquid Aminos. When rice is cooked, combine all ingredients and toss. **Serves 6.**

Per 1/2 cup serving: 176 calories; 9.1 g protein (20%); 27.2 g carbohydrate (60%); 3.9 g fat (20%); 265 mg sodium; 94 mg calcium; 0 mg cholesterol.

"FRIED" RICE

2	cups uncooked brown rice
1	quart water
2	tablespoons McKay's Chicken Style Seasoning (MSG Free)
1	pound broccoli slaw* or frozen mixed vegetables
1	large onion, chopped
4	cloves garlic, minced
2	tablespoons Liquid Aminos
	salt, to taste (opt.)
1/2	cup ground, toasted sesame seeds

Cook rice with water and McKay's Seasoning. Meanwhile, in a large, uncovered skillet, steam remaining ingredients, except sesame seeds, on highest heat setting. Stirring constantly, cook 3-5 minutes, adding a little water if necessary. Add hot, cooked rice and ground sesame seeds. Toss gently. **Serves 10.**

*Prepackaged grated broccoli hearts, carrots and cabbage.

Per appr. 1 cup serving: 196 calories; 5.4 g protein (11%); 36 g carbohydrate (72%); 3.7 g fat (17%); 289 mg sodium; 81 mg calcium; 0 mg cholesterol.

SWEET & SOUR TOFU

2	stalks celery, sliced diagonally
1	onion, sliced vertically
1	green bell pepper, sliced in chunks or strips
1	clove garlic, minced
1/4	cup water
2	tablespoons cornstarch or arrowroot
1	cup pineapple juice
1	cup pineapple chunks
2	tablespoons date butter
1/4	cup tomato sauce
1	tablespoon lemon juice
1	cup cubed firm tofu
1	cup tomato wedges
4	cups cooked brown rice or noodles (opt.)

Steam celery, onion, and garlic in water until just tender. Meanwhile, dissolve cornstarch in pineapple juice and add to steaming vegetables. Add green peppers and remaining ingredients, except last three. Bring to a boil, stirring constantly, until thickened. Fold in tofu carefully. Garnish with tomatoes. Serve over brown rice or noodles, if desired. **Serves 8.**

Per 1/2 cup serving: 119 calories; 6.1 g protein (19%); 19.3 g carbohydrate (60%); 3 g fat (21%); 64 mg sodium; 88 mg calcium; 0 mg cholesterol.

TOFU BALLS

11/2	pounds firm tofu, mashed
5	ounce can water chestnuts, drained, chopped fine
1	green bell pepper, chopped fine
8	green onions, chopped fine
1/4	cup chopped parsley
3	tablespoons Liquid Aminos
11/2	tablespoons almond butter
1	cup fine, dry bread crumbs

Combine all ingredients, except bread crumbs, and mix together well. Form into 2" balls and roll in bread crumbs. Place on a cookie sheet and bake at 350° F for 45-60 minutes. **Yields 11/2 dozen 2" balls or 9 servings.**

Per two 2" balls: 184 calories; 14.7 g protein (30%); 14.9 g carbohydrate (30%); 8.8 g fat (40%); 345 mg sodium; 182 mg calcium; 0 mg cholesterol.

KOREAN JHAPCHAE

4-5	ounce package mung bean noodles (bean threads)*
2	tablespoons water
5	cloves garlic, minced
1/2	teaspoon salt
3	medium carrots, cut into tiny strips
1	medium onion, cut into tiny strips
1	cup sliced, fresh mushrooms
1	small green or yellow zucchini, cut into tiny strips
1/2	red bell pepper, cut into tiny strips
1	bunch fresh spinach
2	cups bean sprouts
1/2	cup Liquid Aminos
1/4	cup toasted sesame seeds

Cook and drain noodles, then rinse in cold water. Place water in a wok or large skillet with minced garlic and salt. Add vegetables in order given, cooking each about a minute before adding the next. When bean sprouts are just tender, toss vegetables with noodles, Liquid Aminos, and sesame seeds. Serve immediately. **Serves 6.**

Nutrient analysis for mung bean noodles is unavailable.

HAWAIIAN CHESTNUT BALLS

1	pound firm tofu, well-drained
1	cup cooked brown rice
1	cup shredded carrots
1	cup water chestnuts, chopped
1/2	cup finely chopped green onion
1/4	cup finely chopped celery
1/4	cup finely chopped green bell pepper
2	tablespoons food yeast flakes
1 1/2	teaspoons salt
1	clove garlic, minced

Mash tofu and combine with remaining ingredients. Mix well and form into balls. Bake on a sprayed cookie sheet at 350° F for 30 minutes. Serve with Tomato Sauce (p. 91) or Tartar Sauce (p. 92), if desired. **Serves 8.**

Per 1/2 cup serving: 130 calories; 10.4 g protein (30%); 12.7 g carbohydrate (37%); 5.2 g fat (34%); 420 mg sodium; 133 mg calcium; 0 mg cholesterol.

QUICK HAWAIIAN DINNER

20	ounce can pineapple tidbits
2	carrots, sliced thin
1	large onion, sliced thin
1	green bell pepper, sliced thin
1/8	teaspoon salt, or to taste
2	tomatoes, chopped
20	snow pea pods (opt.)
11/2	tablespoons cornstarch or arrowroot
1	tablespoon water
5	cups cooked brown rice

Drain pineapple tidbits and save juice. Simmer next 4 ingredients in juice. Add tidbits, tomatoes, and pea pods and simmer briefly. Mix cornstarch and water, then add to mixture, stirring constantly until thickened. Serve over brown rice. Top with toasted sliced almonds, if desired. **Serves 10.**

Per 1 cup serving: 166 calories; 3.4 g protein (8%); 36.9 g carbohydrate (86%); 1.1 g fat (6%); 16 mg sodium; 27 mg calcium; 0 mg cholesterol.

SAVORY SEED MIX

1	quart water
1	cup dried soybeans
1	cup pumpkin seeds
1	cup sunflower seeds
1	tablespoon Liquid Aminos
1/2	teaspoon sweet Hungarian paprika
1/8	teaspoon garlic powder

Soak soybeans in 1 quart water for 8-12 hours. Drain and mix with remaining ingredients. Spread on a cookie sheet and bake at 275° F for about 1 hour, stirring occasionally, until golden. **Serves 14.**

Per 1/4 cup serving: 168 calories; 9.7 g protein (22%); 7.8 g carbohydrate (17%); 12.3 g fat (61%); 58 mg sodium; 55 mg calcium; 0 mg cholesterol.

SALADS & SANDWICHES

Pictured at left: Spinach Salad, and Pocket Sandwich made with Hummus, alfalfa sprouts, tomato, cucumber, avocado, and lettuce.

SALADS & SANDWICHES

PACKED LUNCHES

Lunch is the second most important meal of the day. If you prepare packed lunches for your family, a thoughtfully prepared lunch can say, "I love you; I cared enough to plan." Avoid refined foods and junk foods. Instead, fill the lunch box with tasty, naturally nutritious, wholesome treats.

BE CREATIVE!
Variety: Vary your breads — raisin, rye, pita, bagels, tortillas, etc.
Variety: Vary the routine sandwich with chili, soup, leftover casserole,
    fruit crisp or pie, etc.
Variety: Vary sandwich fillings —
* Leftover loaf or patty with sprouts and mashed avocado
* Almond or peanut butter with crushed pineapple, dates, or
    a banana, mashed when ready to eat, and topped with raisins
* Seasoned tofu combined with one or more of the following:
    sliced black olives, chopped celery, minced onion;
    or chopped figs, dates, and crushed pineapple
* Mashed beans with minced onions.

THEN ADD:
* A fresh, juicy apple, strawberries, dried fruit; or carrot sticks and
    celery stuffed with almond or peanut butter
* Homemade trail mix
* A special touch, such as a homemade card or note that
    expresses your love

Packed lunches can travel almost anywhere — to school, to work, on trips, on hikes, etc. The secret is planning ahead. If you're making trail mix, cookies, or other packable foods, double or triple the recipe. Store in the freezer, handy for lunch packing. Having the right supplies and equipment makes lunches easy to put together, such as:
* A good quality lunch box, or insulated lunch tote
* Thermos bottles to keep hot foods hot and cold foods cold
* Assorted plastic containers or small jars
* Sandwich bags, plastic wrap, and foil

SAMPLE LUNCH BOX MENUS

LUNCH #1
- Sandwich with Guacamole (p. 150), sliced tomato, lettuce, and onion on a whole grain bun
- Coconut Crackers (p. 12)
- Tapioca Pudding (p. 63)

LUNCH #2
- Hot Lentil Vegetable Soup (p. 169) in a thermos
- Oven Toasties (p. 33)
- Oatmeal Cookies (p. 75)
- Carrot and celery sticks

LUNCH #3
- Sandwich with nut butter and fruit spread (See Index for Jams/Sweet Toppings) on whole grain raisin bread
- Crispy Corn Chips (p. 11)
- Fresh fruits

GREAT FOOD IDEAS FOR BACKPACKING

- Home-dry fruit and sauces for camp recipes. For sauces, dry fruit, then process in a food grinder until a coarse powder. Reconstitute with hot water.
  — Dry apples for applesauce, peaches, pears, or apricots for making fruit sauces to serve over granola or cooked cereals.
  — Dry tomato sauce and gravies for pasta or rice dishes.
- Make your own dry soup mixes by pouring a thin layer of soup onto cookie sheets and drying in the oven at a low temperature. When dry, process in a food grinder until a coarse powder. Reconstitute by adding water and heating over a camp stove. Or, dry diced, cooked vegetables and add soup seasonings. Reconstitute with boiling water.
- Pack homemade trail mix: nuts, seeds, dried fruit, ready-to-eat cereal, etc.
- Package dry ingredients in re-closable bags with instructions attached:
  —Rice dishes, such as rice pilaf or Spanish rice, using quick-cooking brown rice
  —Spaghetti or noodle dishes,
  —Oats or cracked wheat, with dried fruit and chopped nuts.
- Coconut Crackers or Oven Toasties are the kind of goodies that help to make a meal special. Before making cookies or crackers, be sure they have a low moisture content. Moist foods will generally spoil more quickly than dry foods.
- Commercially freeze-dried, vegetarian foods are also available.

TOFU COTTAGE "CHEESE"

1   pound firm tofu, drained
11/4   tablespoons minced fresh chives
1   teaspoon minced fresh parsley
1/4   teaspoon dill weed
1/4   cup water
11/2   teaspoons fresh lemon juice
1   teaspoon onion powder
1   teaspoon salt
1/4   teaspoon garlic powder

Mash tofu and reserve 1/2 cup of mashed tofu. Combine tofu with chives, parsley, and dill. Process the 1/2 cup tofu with remaining ingredients in a blender, until smooth. Combine all ingredients and mix well. Let stand in refrigerator for a short time to let flavors blend. **Serves 4.**

Per 1/3 cup serving: 168 calories; 18 g protein (39%); 5.7 g carbohydrate (12%); 9.9 g fat (48%); 505 mg sodium; 240 mg calcium; 0 mg cholesterol.

THREE-BEAN SALAD

1   cup cooked garbanzos
1   cup cooked, sliced green beans
1   cup cooked kidney beans
1/2   cup fresh lemon juice
1/4   cup chopped green onions
1/4   cup chopped green bell pepper
1/8   teaspoon sweet basil or oregano (opt.)

Combine all ingredients and mix well. Place in an airtight container and leave in refrigerator overnight. Serve chilled on a crisp bed of lettuce or other greens, if desired. **Serves 6.**

VARIATIONS: (1) Add sliced olives or avocado just before serving; (2) Omit lemon juice and add Poppy Seed Dressing (p. 147).

Per 1/2 cup serving: 72 calories; 4.2 g protein (22%); 13.8 g carbohydrate (71%); 0.6 g fat (7%); 116 mg sodium; 24 mg calcium; 0 mg cholesterol.

CARROT SALAD

4	cups grated carrots
20	ounce can unsweetened, crushed pineapple
1	cup diced apples
1/2	cup raisins
1/2	cup chopped walnuts

Combine all ingredients and mix well. **Serves 14.**

Per 1/2 cup serving: 85 calories; 1.3 g protein (6%); 15.6 g carbohydrate (67%); 2.8 g fat (27%); 13 mg sodium; 21 mg calcium; 0 mg cholesterol.

SPINACH SALAD

1/2	bunch spinach
1	tomato, cut in wedges
1/2	cup sliced fresh mushrooms*
1/2	red onion, sliced
1	tablespoon toasted whole sesame seeds
1/2	cup toasted, ground sesame seeds
1/4	cup fresh lemon juice
1/4	cup water
2	tablespoons Liquid Aminos
1	clove garlic

Rinse spinach well and combine with tomato, mushrooms, and onion in a mixing bowl. Sprinkle with whole sesame seeds. Process remaining ingredients until smooth. Pour into a decorative cruet or individual dressing pots and serve with salad. **Serves 4.**

*See Glossary.

Per 1 cup serving: 149 calories; 6.4 g protein (16%); 11.1 g carbohydrate (27%); 10.4 g fat (57%); 414 mg sodium; 250 mg calcium; 0 mg cholesterol.

POTATO SALAD

1	quart diced, cooked potatoes
3/4	cup Tofu Mayonnaise (p. 158)
8	radishes, thinly sliced
1/2	cup chopped celery
1/2	cup olive slices, well-drained
1/4	cup chopped green onion
1	teaspoon dill weed

Combine all ingredients and mix well. Refrigerate a few hours before serving. Garnish with fresh parsley and/or paprika, if desired. **Serves 15.**

Per 1/2 cup serving: 76 calories; 2.5 g protein (12%); 14 g carbohydrate (69%); 1.7 g fat (19%); 93 mg sodium; 28 mg calcium; 0 mg cholesterol.

TABBOULI SALAD

1	cup bulgur wheat
1	cup boiling water
2	large tomatoes, diced
1	bunch Italian parsley, chopped
1/2	bunch green onions, chopped
1	small sweet onion, chopped
1	cucumber, diced
1/2	teaspoon salt, or to taste
1/2	cup fresh lemon juice
1/4	cup fresh mint leaves, chopped (opt.)
1/2	cup sliced black olives (opt.)

Rinse bulgur wheat well, using a strainer. Place in a large bowl and cover with boiling water. Let stand while chopping vegetables, then drain well. Mix with chopped tomatoes and allow bulgur to absorb tomato juices. Layer vegetables in order given and sprinkle salt over top. Allow to sit while squeezing lemons. Add lemon juice and remaining ingredients and toss well. Serve on a platter or on individual plates lined with Romaine lettuce leaves, if desired. **Serves 10.**

Per 1/2 cup serving: 65 calories; 2.4 g protein (13%); 14.9 g carbohydrate (82%); 0.4 g fat (5%); 114 mg sodium; 22 mg calcium; 0 mg cholesterol.

"KIM CHI," AMERICAN-STYLE

1	Napa (Chinese) cabbage
1/4	cup salt
1	Chinese radish, shredded fine (opt.)
1	carrot, shredded fine
1/2	sweet onion, shredded fine
2	green onions, chopped fine
3	red bell peppers, *or* 4 ounce jar pimientos
1/4	cup fresh lemon juice
1/4	cup toasted whole sesame seeds
4	cloves garlic
1	tablespoon honey (opt.)
1	teaspoon salt

Wash the cabbage leaves and sprinkle 1/4 cup salt over the leaves. Cover with plastic wrap and let stand for 30 minutes at room temperature. Wash salted leaves again, then shred into strips and squeeze in a towel to remove moisture. Place cabbage, radish, carrot, and onions in a mixing bowl and toss together well. Process red peppers, lemon juice, sesame seeds, garlic, honey, and salt in a blender until smooth and pour over salad. Toss well and serve. **Serves 8.**

Per 1 cup serving: 80 calories; 2.9 g protein (13%); 12.8 g carbohydrate (57%); 3 g fat (30%); 277 mg sodium; 113 mg calcium; 0 mg cholesterol.

KOREAN CUCUMBER SALAD

2	cucumbers
1/2	red onion
1/2	lemon peel
1/4	cup fresh lemon juice
1/4	cup toasted, ground sesame seeds
2	tablespoons water
1	teaspoon minced garlic
1/2	teaspoon salt

Peel and slice cucumbers. Shred onion and lemon peel and mix with cucumbers. Combine remaining ingredients and mix together well. Pour over cucumbers and toss together. Chill and serve. **Serves 6.**

Per 1/6 recipe: 44 calories; 1.4 g protein (12%); 6.2 g carbohydrate (51%); 2.0 g fat (38%); 181 mg sodium; 58 mg calcium; 0 mg cholesterol.

NAPA CABBAGE SALAD

1	small Napa (Chinese) cabbage
1/2	cup unsweetened, crushed pineapple
1/2	cup pineapple juice
1/4	cup clean, raw cashews
1/4	cup unsweetened coconut

Shred cabbage into a bowl. Process remaining ingredients in a blender until smooth. Let stand a few minutes and blend again until very smooth. Toss with cabbage and chill. For variation, add 3/4 cup pineapple tidbits. **Serves 7.**

Per 1 cup serving: 71 calories; 1.9 g protein (10%); 9.8 g carbohydrate (51%); 3.4 g fat (40%); 9 mg sodium; 67 mg calcium; 0 mg cholesterol.

APPLE WALNUT SALAD

1/2	cup extra-rich cold soy or nut milk
1	tablespoon cornstarch or arrowroot
1	tablespoon honey
1/2	teaspoon vanilla
pinch	salt
3	Red Delicious apples
1/2	cup raisins
1/2	cup chopped walnuts

Process first 5 ingredients in a blender just until mixed. Pour into a saucepan and simmer, stirring constantly, until thickened. Cover and refrigerate until cooled. When cool, dice apples and combine with all ingredients. Mix well. Best if served immediately. For variation, add 1/2 cup unsweetened, crushed pineapple or substitute for raisins. **Serves 7.**

Per 1/2 cup serving: 145 calories; 2.3 g protein (6%); 23.8 g carbohydrate (61%); 5.7 g fat (33%); 22 mg sodium; 21 mg calcium; 0 mg cholesterol.

FRUIT GELATIN

20	ounce can unsweetened, crushed pineapple
3	tablespoons unflavored Emes Kosher Jel
3/4	cup pineapple juice concentrate
3/4	cup water
2	cups fresh or frozen fruit in any combination, such as raspberries, diced apples, bananas, cherries

Drain crushed pineapple. Combine juice with Emes Jel in a small saucepan. Add juice concentrate and water and heat until Jel is dissolved, stirring constantly. Remove from heat and add fruit. Pour into a decorative mold and chill. To release from mold, place in pan of warm water for a few seconds, then invert onto serving platter. **Serves 12.**

Per 1/12 recipe: 76 calories; 0.6 g protein (3%); 19 g carbohydrate (95%); 0.2 g fat (2%); 2 mg sodium; 18 mg calcium; 0 mg cholesterol.

CRANBERRY RELISH

12	ounce bag cranberries
1 1/2	cups pitted dates
2	apples, cored
1	orange, peeled, seeds removed
1	tablespoon grated orange peel

Chop all ingredients in food processor or grinder. Chill and allow flavors to blend before serving. **Yields 4 1/4 cups or 17 servings.**

VARIATION: For **Holiday Fruit Ring**, make a "jello" using Emes Kosher Jel and raspberry-apple juice, combined with relish ingredients. Add chopped nuts, if desired. Pour into a decorative ring mold and chill.

Per 1/4 cup serving: 65 calories; 0.5 g protein (3%); 17.3 g carbohydrate (95%); 0.2 g fat (2%); 1 mg sodium; 11 mg calcium; 0 mg cholesterol.

POPPY SEED DRESSING

1/2	cup clean, raw cashews
1/4	cup water
3	tablespoons fresh lemon juice
3	tablespoons orange juice
1	tablespoon honey, or to taste
1	tablespoon chopped onion, or to taste
1/2	teaspoon celery salt
1/2	teaspoon paprika
1	tablespoon poppy seeds

Process all ingredients in a blender, except poppy seeds, until very smooth. Stir in poppy seeds. Keep refrigerated in an airtight container. **Serves 5.**

Per 2 tablespoon serving: 109 calories; 2.6 g protein (9%); 10.4 g carbohydrate (36%); 7.1 g fat (55%); 163 mg sodium; 35 mg calcium; 0 mg cholesterol.

GREEN DRESSING

1	cucumber, thinly peeled
1/2	cup clean, raw cashews
1	green onion
2	tablespoons fresh lemon juice
1	teaspoon onion salt

Process all ingredients in a blender until very smooth, adding a little water for blending, if necessary. Use as a dressing or dip. Keep refrigerated in an airtight container. **Yields 2 cups or 16 servings.**

Per 2 tablespoon serving: 28 calories; 0.8 g protein (10%); 2.1 g carbohydrate (29%); 2 g fat (61%); 93 mg sodium; 6 mg calcium; 0 mg cholesterol.

CREAMY CUCUMBER DRESSING

    1   avocado
  1/2   cucumber, peeled
    1   green onion, *or* 1/4 cup chopped onion
    2   tablespoons fresh lemon juice
    1   teaspoon honey (opt.)
  1/2   teaspoon salt
  1/4   teaspoon dill weed or sweet basil
  1/4   teaspoon garlic powder

Process all ingredients together in a blender. Keep refrigerated in an airtight container. May be used as a salad or sandwich dressing, or as a sauce for vegetables. **Yields 1 cup or 8 servings.**

Per 2 tablespoon serving: 42 calories; 0.6 g protein (5%); 2.5 g carbohydrate (22%); 3.8 g fat (73%); 125 mg sodium; 7 mg calcium; 0 mg cholesterol.

CREAMY ONION DRESSING

    1   cup clean, raw cashews
    1   cup water
    1   tomato, quartered
  1/4   cup onion flakes
    2   tablespoons fresh lemon juice
    1   tablespoon food yeast flakes
  1/2   teaspoon onion salt
  1/4   teaspoon garlic salt

Process cashews and water in a blender until very smooth. Add remaining ingredients and continue blending until smooth. Keep refrigerated in an airtight container. May be used as a salad or sandwich dressing, or as a sauce for vegetables. **Yields 21/2 cups or 20 servings.**

Per 2 tablespoon serving: 45 calories; 1.3 g protein (11%); 3.6 g carbohydrate (30%); 3.2 g fat (60%); 68 mg sodium; 7 mg calcium; 0 mg cholesterol.

AVOCADO DRESSING

    2   avocados
    1/2 cup water
    1/4 cup chopped onion
    1   teaspoon lemon juice
    1/8 teaspoon salt, or to taste

Process all ingredients in a blender until smooth. May also be used as guacamole topping. **Yields 11/2 cups or 12 servings.**

Per 2 tablespoon serving: 52 calories; 0.6 g protein (5%); 2.3 g carbohydrate (16%); 5 g fat (79%); 26 mg sodium; 4 mg calcium; 0 mg cholesterol.

TAHINI DRESSING

    1/2 cup water
    1/4 cup fresh lemon juice
    1/4 cup tahini (sesame seed butter)
    1   tablespoon peanut butter
    1/2 teaspoon onion powder
    1/4 teaspoon garlic powder
    1/4 teaspoon salt

Process all ingredients in a blender until very smooth. If not used at time of preparation, more water may need to be blended in before serving. Keep refrigerated in an airtight container. **Yields 1 cup or 8 servings.**

Per 2 tablespoon serving: 44 calories; 1.7 g protein (15%); 1.3 g carbohydrate (12%); 3.7 g fat (73%); 71 mg sodium; 2 mg calcium; 0 mg cholesterol.

TOASTED AVOCADO SANDWICH

  3   ounces firm tofu
  2   teaspoons Liquid Aminos
  1   slice whole wheat bread
  2   tablespoons Guacamole (p. 150)
1/2 tomato, sliced
1/4 cup alfalfa sprouts

Slice tofu thinly and soak in Liquid Aminos for at least 30 minutes, then drain. Toast bread and spread with Guacamole. Top with marinated tofu and tomato, then broil in oven or toaster oven until toppings are hot. Top with sprouts. Serve with your favorite soup. **Serves 1.**

Per recipe: 247 calories; 18.2 g protein (27%); 19 g carbohydrate (28%); 13.3 g fat (45%); 678 mg sodium; 205 mg calcium; 0 mg cholesterol.

GUACAMOLE

  2   large, ripe avocados (2 cups mashed)
  2   tablespoons finely chopped tomato
  1   tablespoon fresh lemon juice
  2   teaspoons finely chopped onion
1/2 teaspoon salt
1/8 teaspoon garlic powder, or to taste

Mash avocados until smooth. Stir in remaining ingredients. Keep refrigerated in an airtight container. Pour a thin layer of lemon juice over the surface to prevent browning. Pour off or stir in when ready to serve. Use within 24 hours. **Yields 2 cups or 8 servings**

VARIATION: For **Guacamole Dressing**, add tomato or vegetable juice until desired consistency is obtained.

Per 1/4 cup serving: 72 calories; 1.1 g protein (6%); 4.5 g carbohydrate (3%); 8.1 g fat (91%); 143 mg sodium; 9 mg calcium; 0 mg cholesterol.

HUMMUS

2	cups cooked garbanzos
1/3	cup fresh lemon juice
1/4	cup tahini (sesame seed butter)
2	cloves garlic
1	teaspoon salt
1/2	teaspoon onion powder
1/4	cup water or broth from garbanzos
	cumin, to taste (opt.)
	fresh parsley or mint, to taste (opt.)

Process all ingredients in a blender until very smooth and creamy. Add a little more water if necessary. Use as a spread or dip. **Yields 2 cups or 8 servings.**

SERVING SUGGESTION: For **Pocket Sandwiches,** fill pita bread pockets with Hummus, bean sprouts, and diced tomato.

Per 1/4 cup serving: 123 calories; 6.3 g protein (20%); 16.6 g carbohydrate (52%); 3.9 g fat (28%); 251 mg sodium; 42 mg calcium; 0 mg cholesterol.

CUCUMBER RAITA

1	package silken soft tofu
1/2	large cucumber
2	tablespoons fresh lemon juice
1	teaspoon honey
3	fresh cilantro leaves
2	fresh mint leaves
1	tablespoon finely chopped sweet onion
1/8	teaspoon ground cumin (opt.)
1/4	teaspoon salt, or to taste

Drain tofu while preparing other ingredients. Peel cucumber, remove seeds, and grate coarsely. Set aside. Combine tofu, lemon juice, honey, cilantro, and mint in a blender and process until smooth. Pour into a bowl and stir in cucumber and onion. Heat cumin briefly in a small pan, then combine with the rest of the mixture. Add salt and stir thoroughly. Chill. Serve with curried dishes, on crackers, in pita bread sandwiches, etc. **Yields 1 1/2 cups or 6 servings.**

Per 1/4 cup serving: 35 calories; 2.6 g protein (28%); 3.4 g carbohydrate (37%); 1.4 g fat (35%); 93 mg sodium; 20 mg calcium; 0 mg cholesterol.

GARBANZO PEANUT SPREAD

15	ounce can garbanzos
1/3	cup peanut butter
11/2	tablespoons tomato sauce
1/4	teaspoon fresh lemon juice
1/4	teaspoon onion powder
2/3	cup chopped black olives

Drain garbanzos and save broth. Whip peanut butter and garbanzo broth together until well mixed. Combine remaining ingredients, except olives, and blend together with garbanzos until smooth. Combine all ingredients and stir together well. **Yields 21/2 cups or 20 servings.**

SERVING SUGGESTIONS: Serve on crackers and top with sprouts and sweet onion, or use as a sandwich filling.

Per 2 tablespoon serving: 54 calories; 2.3 g protein (15%); 4.5 g carbohydrate (30%); 3.5 g fat (54%); 140 mg sodium; 14 mg calcium; 0 mg cholesterol.

MUSHROOM ALMOND PATÉ

3/4	pound fresh mushrooms, *or* 8 ounce can mushrooms
1	small onion, chopped coarse
2	tablespoons water
1	clove garlic, minced
3/4	teaspoon salt or seasoning salt (omit when using canned mushrooms)
1/2	teaspoon thyme leaves
1	cup toasted almonds*
2	tablespoons water

Slice mushrooms. Place all ingredients, except last 2, in a large skillet over medium-high heat. Simmer, stirring occasionally, until onion is tender and most of liquid has evaporated. Process almonds in a blender or food processor to form a paste. With motor running, add the last 2 tablespoons of water and blend until creamy. Add cooked ingredients and blend until smooth. **Yields 21/2 cups or 20 servings.**

*Toast raw almonds in a 350° F oven for about 8 minutes.

Per 2 tablespoon serving: 44 calories; 1.7 g protein (14%); 2.5 g carbohydrate (21%); 3.5 g fat (65%); 75 mg sodium; 21 mg calcium; 0 mg cholesterol.

NUT RAISIN SPREAD

1 cup almonds
1 cup roasted cashews
1 tablespoon fresh lemon juice
1/2 teaspoon ground coriander
1 cup orange juice
1 cup raisins

Process nuts in a blender or food processor for 3-5 minutes, or until a paste forms. Mix in lemon juice and coriander. Add orange juice and raisins and continue processing until well mixed. **Yields 21/4 cups or 18 servings.**

Per 2 tablespoon serving: 116 calories; 2.9 g protein (9%); 11.8 g carbohydrate (38%); 7.4 g fat (53%); 3 mg sodium; 28 mg calcium; 0 mg cholesterol.

DILL "CHEESE" SPREAD

1 tablespoon Minute Tapioca
1/4 cup water
1/2 pound tofu
2 tablespoons lemon juice
1/3 cup clean, raw cashews
3 tablespoons pimiento
2 tablespoons food yeast flakes
1/2 teaspoon dill weed
1/2 teaspoon onion powder
1/2 teaspoon salt
1/4 teaspoon garlic salt

Soak tapioca in water until soft. Process tofu and lemon juice in a blender, adding a little water, if necessary. Combine all ingredients and process until smooth. Cook in a double boiler until thickened all the way through (about 1 hour). No stirring is necessary. Pour into a mold (use a pan spray) or form into a ball and chill. Serve with crackers or use as sandwich filling. **Yields 2 cups or 16 servings.**

Per 2 tablespoon serving: 42 calories; 2.9 g protein (26%); 2.7 g carbohydrate (24%); 2.6 g fat (51%); 102 mg sodium; 33 mg calcium; 0 mg cholesterol.

JIFFY "CHEESE" SPREAD

3/4   cup water
1/3   cup clean, raw cashews
  1   cup cooked brown rice
  2   ounce jar pimientos
  2   tablespoons food yeast flakes
  2   tablespoons fresh lemon juice
  1   teaspoon onion powder
  1   teaspoon salt
1/4   teaspoon garlic powder
pinch   dill weed

Process cashews with about 1/2 cup of the water in a blender until very smooth. Add remaining water and cooked rice and continue blending. Add remaining ingredients and continue to blend until very smooth. Will keep in refrigerator, in an airtight container about 1 week. For variation, add caraway or chives. **Yields 2 cups or 16 servings.**

Per 2 tablespoon serving: 36 calories; 1.2 g protein (13%); 4.9 g carbohydrate (53%); 1.4 g fat (34%); 124 mg sodium; 7 mg calcium; 0 mg cholesterol.

"CHEESE" WHIZ

  1   cup clean, raw cashews
  1   cup water
  2   ounce jar pimientos
1/2   teaspoon onion powder
1/2   teaspoon salt
pinch   garlic powder
pinch   thyme (opt.)
  2   teaspoons fresh lemon juice

Process all ingredients in a blender, except lemon juice, until very smooth. Cook until thickened, stirring constantly. Remove from heat and stir in lemon juice. Use as a dip or spread. **Yields 13/4 cups or 14 servings.**

Per 2 tablespoon serving: 58 calories; 1.5 g protein (10%); 3.6 g carbohydrate (23%); 4.6 g fat (67%); 72 mg sodium; 6 mg calcium; 0 mg cholesterol.

AMERICAN "CHEESE"

21/4 cups boiling water
1/3 cup Emes Kosher Jel
1 cup clean, raw cashews
4 ounce jar pimientos
3 tablespoons food yeast flakes
2 tablespoons fresh lemon juice
2 teaspoons onion powder
2 teaspoons salt
1 teaspoon paprika
1/4 teaspoon garlic powder

Dissolve Emes Jel in boiling water. Process cashews with water and Emes Jel in a blender until very smooth. Add remaining ingredients and continue blending until very smooth. Pour into a container and refrigerate. Can be sliced when firm. For grating, freeze first, then grate while still partially frozen. Will melt when heated. **Yields 21/2 cups (11/2 pounds) or 24 servings.**

SERVING SUGGESTION: Pour into a decorative mold. When firm, release onto a platter and surround with fresh vegetables or crackers.

VARIATION: For **Jack "Cheese,"** omit pimientos and paprika, and increase other seasonings, to taste.

Per 1 ounce serving: 42 calories; 1.1 g protein (10%); 3.8 g carbohydrate (34%); 2.7 g fat (55%); 181 mg sodium; 7 mg calcium; 0 mg cholesterol.

HERB "CHEESE"

1/2 cup hot water
21/2 tablespoons Emes Kosher Jel
1 cup hot, cooked millet*
4 ounce jar pimientos
1/4 cup clean, raw cashews
1 tablespoon fresh lemon juice
11/2 teaspoons caraway, celery, or dill seed
11/2 teaspoons onion powder
1 teaspoon salt
1/8 teaspoon garlic powder

Soak Emes Jel in hot water for a few minutes. Process all ingredients in a blender until very smooth. Pour into a mold, such as a food can, and refrigerate. When firm, can be sliced (if using a can, cut other end from can and push out for slicing). For grating, freeze first, then grate while still frozen. **Yields 18 ounces or 18 servings.**

*Simmer 1/4 cup millet grain in 1 cup salted water for 45-60 minutes.

VARIATIONS: (1) For **Jack "Cheese" with Herbs**, omit pimientos and increase lemon juice and seasonings, to taste; (2) Add a 4 ounce can of chopped black olives, after blending.

Per 1 ounce serving: 23 calories; 0.7 g protein (11%); 3.2 g carbohydrate (52%); 1 g fat (37%); 110 mg sodium; 6 mg calcium; 0 mg cholesterol.

MILLET BUTTER

3/4	cup water
1/2	tablespoon Emes Kosher Jel or agar agar
1/2	cup packed, cooked, hot millet*
2	tablespoons clean, raw cashews
1	tablespoon peeled, cooked carrot
1/2	teaspoon salt
	butter flavoring, to taste (opt.)

Stir Emes Jel into water and heat, stirring constantly, until Emes Jel is dissolved and liquid is clear. Process in a blender with remaining ingredients until very smooth. Let stand a few minutes so that air bubbles can escape. Pour into a container and chill, covered. Keeps about 1 week. May be frozen and then heated in microwave to obtain smooth texture. **Yields 1 1/4 cups or 20 servings.**

*Simmer 2-3 tablespoons millet grain in 1/2 cup salted water for 45-60 minutes.

VARIATIONS: (1) For **Garlic Butter**, add garlic powder or garlic cloves, to taste; (2) For **Orange Butter**, add orange flavoring and honey, to taste; (3) Substitute cornmeal for millet—mix 1/2 cup fine cornmeal and 1/2 cup cold water. Gradually stir in 1 cup boiling water. Simmer for 20 minutes.

Per 1 tablespoon serving: 8 calories; 0.2 g protein (11%); 1 g carbohydrate (46%); 0.4 g fat (44%); 50 mg sodium; 1 mg calcium; 0 mg cholesterol.

GARLIC BUTTER

1	cup water
1/2	cup clean, raw cashews
3/4	cup warm, well-cooked cornmeal*
4	teaspoons fresh lemon juice
3	cloves garlic
1	tablespoon food yeast flakes
1	teaspoon onion powder
1	teaspoon salt
1/2	teaspoon dill weed
	butter flavoring, to taste (opt.)

Process cashews with about 1/2 cup of water in a blender until very smooth. Add remaining water and other ingredients and continue blending until very smooth.   Keep refrigerated in an airtight container. **Yields 2 cups or 32 servings.**

*1/2 cup dry fine cornmeal cooked in 2 cups salted water.

SERVING SUGGESTION: For **Garlic Bread**, spread on sliced bread and bake at 350° F for about 10-15 minutes.

Per 1 tablespoon serving: 17 calories; 0.5 g protein (12%); 1.6 g carbohydrate (37%); 1 g fat (51%); 68 mg sodium; 3 mg calcium; 0 mg cholesterol.

SUNNY SOUR CREAM

3/4	cup water
2/3	cup sunflower seeds
3	tablespoons fresh lemon juice
1/2	teaspoon onion powder
1/2	teaspoon salt
1/4	teaspoon garlic powder

Process all ingredients in a blender until very smooth. Adjust water and seasonings to taste and consistency desired. Keep refrigerated in an airtight container. For variation, blend in tomato and/or avocado for a salad or sandwich dressing. **Yields 11/4 cups or 10 servings.**

Per 2 tablespoon serving: 57 calories; 2.2 g protein (15%); 2.3 g carbohydrate (15%); 4.8 g fat (70%); 99 mg sodium; 13 mg calcium; 0 mg cholesterol.

ALMOND MAYONNAISE

2	cups water
1/2	cup blanched almonds*
3 1/2	tablespoons Instant Clear Jel
1/2	tablespoon fresh lemon juice
1/2	teaspoon onion powder
1/2	teaspoon salt
1/8	teaspoon garlic powder

Process water and almonds in a blender until very smooth. Strain and save liquid (use pulp in patties or waffles, etc.). Process liquid and remaining ingredients until thickened. Add dill or turmeric, to taste, if desired. **Yields 2 cups or 32 servings.**

*Boil raw almonds in water for 1 minute. Drain and cool, then pinch off skins.

Per 1 tablespoon serving, unstrained: 15 calories; 0.4 g protein (11%); 1.2 g carbohydrate (30%); 1.1 g fat (60%); 31 mg sodium; 6 mg calcium; 0 mg cholesterol.

TOFU MAYONNAISE

1	pound soft tofu
1/4	cup fresh lemon juice
1	tablespoon honey (opt.)
2	teaspoons onion powder
1	clove garlic
1/2	teaspoon dill weed
1	teaspoon salt

Process all ingredients in a blender until very smooth. Add a little water for blending, if necessary. Keep refrigerated in an airtight container. **Yields 2 cups or 32 servings.**

VARIATION: For **Tofu Sour Cream,** omit honey and increase lemon juice to 1/3 cup.

Per 1 tablespoon serving: 12 calories; 1.2 g protein (36%); 0.6 g carbohydrate (18%); 0.7 g fat (47%); 68 mg sodium; 16 mg calcium; 0 mg cholesterol.

"MUSTARD"

1/2	cup Almond Mayonnaise (p. 158)
1	tablespoon finely chopped parsley
2	teaspoons fresh lemon juice
1	teaspoon grated onion
1	teaspoon turmeric
1/8	teaspoon garlic salt
1/8	teaspoon onion salt
1/8	teaspoon paprika

Process all ingredients in a blender until very smooth. Keep refrigerated in an airtight container. **Yields 2/3 cup or 11 tablespoons.**

Per 1 tablespoon serving: 12 calories; 0.4 g protein (13%); 1.2 g carbohydrate (38%); 0.7 g fat (49%); 61 mg sodium; 6 mg calcium; 0 mg cholesterol.

KETCHUP

1	cup tomato sauce
1/4	cup tomato paste
2	tablespoons fresh lemon juice
1	tablespoon honey, *or* 2 tablespoons date butter
1/2	teaspoon sweet basil
1/2	teaspoon garlic powder
1/2	teaspoon onion powder
1/2	teaspoon salt

Stir all ingredients together. Keep refrigerated in an airtight container. **Yields 11/2 cups or 24 tablespoons.**

Per 1 tablespoon serving: 9 calories; 0.3 g protein (10%); 2.2 g carbohydrate (86%); .04 g fat (4%); 124 mg sodium; 4 mg calcium; 0 mg cholesterol.

SOUPS & VEGETABLES

Pictured at left: Rice Soup, Oriental Vegetables with Garlic Sauce, and Korean Vegetable Patties.

SOUPS & VEGETABLES

CREATIVE VEGETABLE COOKERY

Vegetables add more than vitamins, minerals, and fiber to the diet. They can also add delightful color, texture, and taste to your meals. Combinations of vegetables enhance both eye and taste appeal. Try some of the following ideas or use your imagination to create special dishes for your family:
• Carrots, onions, and rutabagas.
• Cabbage, carrots, and red onion rings.
• Green beans and new potatoes with chicken-style seasoning.
• Grated zucchini steamed with fresh garlic, sweet basil, and dill weed.
• Small new potatoes with skin, layered and steamed with onion slices.
• Steamed broccoli and cauliflower, topped with a "cheese" sauce or gravy.
• Summer squash, sliced and steamed, with chopped onion, green bell pepper, diced tomatoes, and oregano. Add corn, if desired.
• Stir-fried vegetables, such as broccoli, carrots, cauliflower, onion, snow peas, spinach, bean sprouts, etc., in any combination. Add sesame seeds, cubed tofu, or slivered almonds, minced garlic, and Liquid Aminos.

SEASONING VEGETABLES

Salt is the most commonly used seasoning for vegetables, but it's a good principle of health to limit intake to 1/2-1 teaspoon iodized salt per day. Here are some suggestions for seasoning vegetables without using salt or fat:
• Fresh lemon juice added just before serving, perks up many vegetables, especially greens.
• Chopped onion, bell pepper, parsley, or minced garlic are taste enhancers.
• Chopped nuts or seeds, especially when lightly toasted, add flavor.
• One teaspoon of honey added to a large pot of greens or beans can greatly enhance the flavor.
• A pinch of herbs well chosen can be a delightful surprise. Experiment, starting with a small amount. Fresh herbs are best — use three times as much fresh as you would dried. Add about 5 minutes before serving. When using dried herbs, rub the leaves between your fingers to release the flavor and fragrance. Following is a table of suggested seasonings to try:

VEGETABLE	SUGGESTED SEASONINGS
Beets	Sweet basil, bay leaf,* cardamom, dill weed, lemon, tarragon.
Broccoli	Garlic, lemon, marjoram, oregano, tarragon.
Brussels sprouts	Sweet basil, caraway, dill weed, lemon, savory, thyme.
Cabbage	Caraway, celery seed, dill weed, savory, tarragon.
Carrots	Sweet basil, dill weed, marjoram, parsley, thyme.
Cauliflower	Dill, pimiento, rosemary, savory, tarragon.
Cucumbers	Sweet basil, dill weed, garlic, savory, tarragon.
Eggplant	Sweet basil, garlic, oregano, rosemary, sage, thyme.
Green beans	Sweet basil, dill weed, marjoram, oregano, rosemary, savory, thyme.
Greens	Sweet basil, dill weed, garlic, lemon, rosemary, sesame, thyme.
Lima beans	Sweet basil, chives, marjoram, savory.
Onions	Sweet basil, oregano, thyme.
Peas	Sweet basil, dill weed, pimiento, mint, savory, oregano.
Potatoes	Sweet basil, chives, dill weed, garlic, marjoram, parsley, savory.
Squash	Sweet basil, dill weed, oregano, savory.
Spinach	Garlic, lemon, oregano, rosemary, sesame, tarragon, thyme.
Tomatoes	Sweet basil, bay leaf,* dill weed, garlic, lemon, oregano, parsley, sage, savory.
Zucchini	Sweet basil, dill weed, garlic, onion.

MISCELLANEOUS

Coleslaw	Caraway, dill weed, lemon, marjoram, mint, savory.
Salad Dressings	Sweet basil, chives, dill weed, garlic, lemon, marjoram, mint, onion, oregano, parsley, rosemary, savory, sesame, tarragon, thyme.

Remove bay leaf before serving, or use ground.

COOKING TO CONSERVE NUTRIENTS

- Vegetables are one of the essential food groups and, when properly prepared, furnish a major portion of one's daily intake of protein, vitamins, minerals, and fiber.
- Boiling vegetables greatly decreases their nutrient value, as well as eye and taste appeal. Some cooks add baking soda to the water to preserve the color. However, this destroys thiamine (B_1).[30]
- Steaming is one of the best ways to cook delicious and nutritious vegetables. Waterless cookware, or a stainless steel colander that can be placed in the cooking pot to hold the vegetables above the water, are desirable utensils for vegetable cookery. Stir-frying in a nonstick skillet or wok is also an excellent way to cook vegetables.
- A microwave oven is a very handy way to steam vegetables without overcooking. Steam in a little water just until tender.
- Cook vegetables until they are tender-crisp, not mushy. Try to avoid lifting the lid during cooking, as this results in the loss of aromatic oils, which give vegetables their delightful flavors.
- It is best to cook vegetables just before serving. If the meal is delayed, chill vegetables and reheat later.

STEAMING TIME FOR VEGETABLES (In Minutes)

Vegetable	Minutes	Vegetable	Minutes
Asparagus tips	5-12	Kale	15-25
Artichokes, small	30-40	Kohlrabi	10-20
Artichokes, Jerusalem	25-35	Mustard greens	8-12
Beans, fresh Lima, shelled	25-35	Okra, whole	25-30
Beans, green	7-12	Okra, sliced	5-10
Beets, medium	20-30	Parsnips, sliced	10-15
Broccoli	7-10	Peas, green, shelled	5-10
Brussels sprouts	15-20	Peppers, green	10-20
Cabbage	15-20	Potatoes, whole	25-30
Carrots, sliced	15-20	Potatoes, sweet	25-30
Carrots, whole	30-40	Pumpkin	35-40
Cauliflower	10-20	Rutabagas, sliced	20-30
Celery	10-20	Spinach	5-7
Celery root, sliced	35-40	Squash, summer	8-10
Chard	5-10	Squash, hard	25-30
Collards	20-30	Turnip greens	20-30
Corn on the cob	5-7	Turnips, sliced	15-20
Eggplant, sliced	10-15		

FRESH GREEN PEA SOUP

2 1/2   cups boiling water
10   ounce package frozen peas, *or* 2 cups fresh peas
1/4   small onion, chopped,
      or 1 teaspoon onion powder
1   teaspoon salt (opt.)
1/4   cup clean, raw cashews or blanched almonds (opt.)
1/2   cup water

Add peas, onion, and salt to boiling water and quickly bring to a second boil. Cook 1-2 minutes. Process cashews in 1/2 cup water in a blender until very smooth. Gradually add cooked peas (with water) and continue blending until smooth and creamy. Serve immediately. **Serves 4.**

Per 1 cup serving: 51 calories; 3.3 g protein (25%); 9.3 g carbohydrate (72%); 0.2 g fat (3%); 60 mg sodium; 20 mg calcium; 0 mg cholesterol.

SPLIT PEA-LENTIL SOUP

2   quarts water
1   cup dried lentils
1   cup dried split peas
1/2   cup barley grain
3   carrots, grated or chopped
1   large onion, chopped
2   teaspoons salt
1   bay leaf

Combine all ingredients in a large kettle and bring to a boil. Reduce heat, cover, and simmer about 1 1/2 hours, or until barley is tender. Remove bay leaf before serving. **Serves 10.**

Per 1 cup serving: 182 calories; 11.4 g protein (24%); 34.2 g carbohydrate (73%); 0.6 g fat (3%); 410 mg sodium; 40 mg calcium; 0 mg cholesterol.

CHICKEN-STYLE NOODLE SOUP

1/2	pound noodles
1	cup chopped celery
1	onion, chopped
1/4	cup water
2	tablespoons All-Purpose Seasoning (p. 167)
1 1/2	quarts water
2	large potatoes, peeled and cubed,
	or 2 large carrots, sliced
2	cups garbanzos, with broth
2	cups scrambled tofu (opt.)
1	tablespoon chopped parsley
	food yeast flakes, to taste (opt.)

Cook noodles as directed on package. Drain. Meanwhile, simmer next 4 ingredients until celery and onion are tender. Add 5 cups of the water and the potatoes and simmer. Process garbanzos, broth, and remaining water in a blender until smooth. Add to vegetables and simmer slowly to allow flavors to blend. Adjust water and salt, as desired. **Serves 10.**

Per 1 cup serving: 164 calories; 5.8 g protein (14%); 32.5 g carbohydrate (79%); 1.3 g fat (7%); 408 mg sodium; 41 mg calcium; 0 mg cholesterol.

ALL-PURPOSE SEASONING

2	tablespoons onion powder
2	tablespoons parsley flakes
1	tablespoon celery salt
1	teaspoon turmeric
1/2	teaspoon garlic powder
1/4	teaspoon marjoram
1/4	teaspoon savory

Combine all ingredients and mix well. Store in an airtight container. **Yields 13 teaspoons.**

Per 1 teaspoon: 5 calories; 0.2 g protein (13%); 1.1 g carbohydrate (77%); .06 g fat (10%); 370 mg sodium; 11 mg calcium; 0 mg cholesterol.

CREAMY VEGETABLE SOUP

    3   cups steamed potatoes or mixed vegetables
    1   cup soy or nut milk
    1   tablespoon All-Purpose Seasoning (p. 167)
    1   clove garlic
    1/4 teaspoon onion powder
    1 1/2 cups broccoli tops, steamed

Process all ingredients in a blender, except broccoli tops, until very smooth. Pour into a saucepan and heat, stirring constantly, until thickened. Add broccoli tops just before serving. **Serves 4.**

Per 1 cup serving: 192 calories; 6.6 g protein (13%); 40.2 g carbohydrate (80%); 1.6 g fat (7%); 309 mg sodium; 53 mg calcium; 0 mg cholesterol.

CORN CHOWDER

    2   cups peeled, cubed potatoes
    2   cups water
    1   cup diced celery
    1/2 cup chopped onion
    1   teaspoon salt
    1   bay leaf (opt.)
    1/2 teaspoon celery salt
    1/2 teaspoon parsley flakes
    2   cups creamed corn
    2   cups whole kernel corn
    3   cups rich soy milk

Place all ingredients, except last 3, in a large kettle and simmer over low heat until potatoes are almost done. Stir in creamed and whole kernel corn and continue simmering for 10 minutes, stirring frequently. Add soy milk (for thicker consistency, decrease amount of milk). Turn heat off and let stand for 15-20 minutes. Remove bay leaf and serve. **Serves 12.**

Per 1 cup serving: 101 calories; 3.8 g protein (14%); 20.4 g carbohydrate (73%); 1.7 g fat (13%); 443 mg sodium; 15 mg calcium; 0 mg cholesterol.

VEGETABLE CHOWDER

6	potatoes
2	cups water
2	large carrots, diced
2	cups frozen corn
2	cups water
1	onion
1	teaspoon All-Purpose Seasoning (p. 167)
1	teaspoon onion powder
1/2	teaspoon sweet basil
1/4	teaspoon garlic powder
1/4	teaspoon turmeric (opt.)
1	bay leaf
2	cups soy or nut milk
1/2	cup finely chopped celery
1/2	cup finely chopped green bell pepper
4	ounce jar pimientos
1	teaspoon salt

Cook first 3 ingredients until carrots and potatoes are well done. Process next 8 ingredients in a blender until mostly smooth. Add to potatoes and carrots, along with bay leaf, and simmer for 1 hour. Add remaining ingredients and simmer for 5 minutes. Remove bay leaf and serve. **Serves 10.**

Per 1 cup serving: 140 calories; 4.9 g protein (13%); 29.7 g carbohydrate (80%); 1.2 g fat (7%); 281 mg sodium; 28 mg calcium; 0 mg cholesterol.

LENTIL VEGETABLE SOUP

2	quarts water
2	cups dried lentils
1/2	cup chopped celery
1/2	cup chopped onion
1/4	cup chopped carrots
3	tablespoons chopped parsley
2 1/2	teaspoons salt
1 1/2	teaspoons crushed oregano
1	clove garlic, minced
1	bay leaf
2	cups chopped tomatoes

Place all ingredients, except tomatoes, in a large kettle and bring to a boil. Reduce heat, cover, and simmer 11/2 hours. Add tomatoes and continue simmering, covered, for 5 minutes longer. Remove bay leaf before serving. Can also be cooked in a crockpot overnight. **Serves 9.**

Per 1 cup serving: 151 calories; 11.9 g protein (30%); 26.3 g carbohydrate (67%); 0.5 g fat (3%); 535 mg sodium; 43 mg calcium; 0 mg cholesterol.

SUPER STEW

2	cups water
1	pound tomatoes, chopped
1	cup sliced carrots
1	onion, chopped
2/3	cup sliced green bell pepper
1/4	cup chopped celery
1	clove garlic, minced
1	teaspoon salt
1/2	teaspoon oregano
1/2	teaspoon sweet basil
15	ounce can garbanzos, with broth
11/2	cups cooked spinach noodles
1	cup sliced zucchini
1/3	cup chopped parsley

Simmer all ingredients, except last 4, for 30 minutes. Add remaining ingredients and simmer an additional 15 minutes. **Serves 9.**

Per 1 cup serving: 168 calories; 6.8 g protein (16%); 31.6 g carbohydrate (73%); 2 g fat (11%); 429 mg sodium; 53 mg calcium; 0 mg cholesterol.

"CHILI"

2 1/2   cups dried red beans
2   quarts water
1   quart crushed tomatoes
1/3   cup chopped celery
1/3   cup chopped green bell pepper
1/3   cup chopped onion
2   tablespoons water
1   tablespoon McKay's Beef Style Seasoning (MSG Free)
1   tablespoon honey,
     or 2 tablespoons chopped dates (opt.)
2   teaspoons cumin
1   teaspoon salt

Soak beans in water overnight. Drain, then cover with fresh water until there is 2" of water over top of the beans. Simmer for 2-3 hours, or until beans are tender. Add remaining ingredients and simmer for 1 hour, adding water as needed, and stirring occasionally. For variation, use 2 quarts "V8" in place of water. **Serves 10.**

Per 1 cup serving: 175 calories; 10.9 g protein (24%); 32.3 g carbohydrate (72%); 0.9 g fat (4%); 505 mg sodium; 72 mg calcium; 0 mg cholesterol.

HOMEMADE "CHILI" POWDER

2   tablespoons paprika
1   tablespoon sweet basil
1   tablespoon dried bell pepper
1   tablespoon parsley flakes
2   bay leaves
1   teaspoon ground cumin
1   teaspoon onion powder
1   teaspoon ground oregano
1/2   teaspoon ground dill seed, *or* 1 teaspoon dill seed
1/2   teaspoon savory
1/4   teaspoon garlic powder

Process all ingredients in a blender until a fine powder. Store in an airtight container. **Yields 1/4 cup or 12 servings.**

Per 1 teaspoon: 7 calories; 0.3 g protein (15%); 1.3 g carbohydrate (62%); 0.2 g fat (23%); 2 mg sodium; 19 mg calcium; 0 mg cholesterol.

GAZPACHO

1 quart "V8" or tomato juice
1 cucumber, peeled and diced 1/4"
1 1/2 cups diced, fresh tomato
2 stalks celery, diced 1/4"
1/3 green bell pepper, diced 1/4"
2 tablespoons onion flakes
1 tablespoon parsley flakes

Combine all ingredients and chill several hours before serving. Do not heat. Serve chilled. Garnish with fresh parsley. For variation, add a small can of diced green chilies. **Yields 61/2 cups or 61/2 servings.**

Per 1 cup serving: 51 calories; 0.9 g protein (6%); 10.9 g carbohydrate (91%); 0.2 g fat (4%); 484 mg sodium; 35 mg calcium; 0 mg cholesterol.

MINESTRONE

1 1/2 quarts water
2 cups shredded cabbage
2 cups diced potatoes
16 ounce can stewed tomatoes
2 celery stalks, with leaves, diced
2 carrots, diced
1 onion, chopped
1/4 cup Liquid Aminos
3 tablespoons chopped fresh parsley
3/4 teaspoon Italian seasoning
1/2 teaspoon marjoram
1/2 teaspoon crushed rosemary
1 teaspoon salt, or to taste
15 ounce can kidney beans, with broth
1 cup uncooked macaroni
1 cup frozen peas

Combine all ingredients, except last three, in a large soup kettle. Bring to a boil. Reduce heat and simmer for 40 minutes. Add remaining ingredients and peas and simmer for 15 minutes. **Serves 10.**

Per 1 cup serving: 141 calories; 6.5 g protein (18%); 28.7 g carbohydrate (78%); 0.5 g fat (3%); 550 mg sodium; 57 mg calcium; 0 mg cholesterol.

BORSCHT

  3 beets
  3 carrots
  3 potatoes
  1 onion
1/2 small cabbage, *or* 1 cup beet greens (opt.)
1 1/2 quarts water
  1 cup tomato puree
  3 tablespoons fresh, *or* 1 tablespoon dried dill weed
  2 teaspoons salt
  2 bay leaves
  1 clove garlic, minced

Peel and cut beets, carrots, potatoes, and onion into chunks or strips. Cut cabbage into 2" chunks. Place in a saucepan with water. Cover and simmer until vegetables are tender (about 30 minutes). Add remaining ingredients and continue to simmer for 10 minutes. Remove bay leaves before serving. Serve with a tablespoon of the Tofu Sour Cream variation of Tofu Mayonnaise (p. 158), dropped in the middle of each bowl, if desired. **Serves 12.**

Per 1 cup serving: 60 calories; 1.7 g protein (11%); 13.9 g carbohydrate (87%); 0.2 g fat (2%); 381 mg sodium; 32 mg calcium; 0 mg cholesterol.

RICE SOUP

  2 quarts water
  3 stalks celery, chopped fine
  2 carrots, chopped fine
  1 small onion, chopped fine
  4 ounce jar pimientos
  1 tablespoon All-Purpose Seasoning (p. 167)
  1 teaspoon garlic powder
1/2 teaspoon sweet basil
  1 bay leaf (opt.)
  4 cups cooked brown rice

Place all ingredients, except rice, in a saucepan and simmer 20 minutes or longer. Remove bay leaf. Place 1/3 cup rice in each soup bowl. Ladle soup over rice and serve immediately. **Serves 12.**

Per 1 cup serving: 89 calories; 2.2 g protein (10%); 18.7 g carbohydrate (83%); 0.7 g fat (7%); 116 mg sodium; 25 mg calcium; 0 mg cholesterol.

POTATO CHIPS

4 large potatoes
1/2 teaspoon salt or onion salt

Wash potatoes thoroughly, scrubbing each with a vegetable brush. Run widthwise through the finest slicer of a food processor. Lightly salt while still wet. Place a single layer (may overlap slightly) on sprayed cookie sheets and bake high in the oven at 450° F for 15-20 minutes. Watch carefully to prevent burning. These can be microwaved—place on a glass or microwave-safe baking dish and microwave on high for 6-12 minutes, or until golden brown in the center of each slice. Let cool. **Serves 4.**

Per 1/4 recipe: 145 calories; 3.1 g protein (8%); 33.6 g carbohydrate (91%); 0.2 g fat (1%); 275 mg sodium; 10 mg calcium; 0 mg cholesterol.

FRENCH OR COTTAGE FRIES

4 large potatoes
1/2 teaspoon salt or garlic salt
paprika (opt.)

Wash potatoes thoroughly, scrubbing each with a vegetable brush. For French Fries, run potatoes lengthwise through the "French Fry" slicer of a food processor. For Cottage Fries, cut potatoes lengthwise into 1/8ths or smaller. Lightly salt while still wet. Sprinkle with paprika. Place on sprayed cookie sheets and bake at 450° F for 40-60 minutes, or until golden brown, stirring occasionally. **Serves 4.**

Per 1/4 recipe: 145 calories; 3.1 g protein (8%); 33.6 g carbohydrate (91%); 0.2 g fat (1%); 275 mg sodium; 10 mg calcium; 0 mg cholesterol.

SCALLOPED POTATOES

4	cups thinly sliced raw potatoes, with skins
2	cups water
1/2	cup clean, raw cashews
1/4	cup chopped onions, *or* 1 teaspoon onion powder
1	teaspoon salt
1/8	teaspoon paprika

Place potatoes in a sprayed baking dish. Process cashews in about 1 cup of the water in a blender until very smooth. Add remaining water and other ingredients, except paprika, and continue blending until smooth. Pour over potatoes, lifting potato slices to let sauce coat each slice. Cover and bake at 375° F for 1 hour. Remove cover, sprinkle with paprika, then return to oven and continue baking until browned (about 15 minutes). **Serves 4.**

Per 1 cup serving: 247 calories; 5.8 g protein (9%); 39.9 g carbohydrate (62%); 8.1 g fat (29%); 503 mg sodium; 24 mg calcium; 0 mg cholesterol.

YAMS WITH ORANGE SAUCE

4	large yams
1	cup orange juice*
1	cup pineapple juice drained from unsweetened, crushed pineapple
3	tablespoons honey (opt.)
1	teaspoon grated orange peel
1/4	teaspoon salt
1/4	cup chopped pecans or toasted coconut (opt.)

Bake yams at 350° F for 1 hour or until tender. Cool and peel. Slice into a casserole dish. Combine remaining ingredients, except pecans, and pour over sliced yams. Bake in a covered dish until thoroughly heated. Top with chopped pecans or toasted coconut. **Serves 8.**

*1 part orange juice concentrate to 2 parts water.

Per 1/8 recipe: 187 calories; 2.3 g protein (5%); 39.8 g carbohydrate (83%); 2.5 g fat (12%); 77 mg sodium; 27 mg calcium; 0 mg cholesterol.

BREADED ZUCCHINI

1   pound zucchini squash
1   cup whole wheat pastry flour
2   tablespoons McKay's Chicken-style Seasoning
    (MSG-Free)
1   tablespoon fine cornmeal
1   teaspoon Curry Powder (p. 178)
1   teaspoon garlic powder
1   teaspoon onion powder

Wash zucchini and cut into wedges. Mix remaining ingredients together. Dip zucchini wedges into breading mixture and shake off any excess. Place on sprayed cookie sheets and bake at 350° F for 40 minutes or until tender to fork. **Serves 4.**

Per 1/4 recipe: 148 calories; 5.2 g protein (14%); 31.4 g carbohydrate (81%); 0.9 g fat (5%); 306 mg sodium; 27 mg calcium; 0 mg cholesterol.

CRUNCHY GREEN BEANS WITH HERBS

1   pound fresh green beans
1   teaspoon salt
1 1/2   cups water
1/2   cup chopped red bell pepper
1/4   cup finely minced onion
1/2   teaspoon marjoram
1/4   teaspoon crushed rosemary

Rinse beans and snip off ends. Toss with salt. Bring water to a boil. Place green beans in a steamer and place over boiling water. Cover and steam for 3-4 minutes or until beans are tender, but not overcooked—they should be crunchy. Mix beans and remaining ingredients together in a large serving bowl. Serve hot. **Serves 7.**

Per 1/2 cup serving: 29 calories; 1.4 g protein (17%); 6.7 g carbohydrate (77%); 0.2 g fat (6%); 309 mg sodium; 37 mg calcium; 0 mg cholesterol.

BRAISED-DEGLAZED ONIONS

3   large onions
1/2   teaspoon Bernard Jensen's Protein Seasoning (opt.)
1/2   cup water

Chop, slice, or shred onions and place in a large nonstick skillet. Dissolve seasoning in water and add about 2 tablespoons to onions. Cook uncovered over high heat, stirring occasionally, until liquid evaporates and browned bits stick to pan. Deglaze pan by adding 2 more tablespoons broth. Stir or scrape to free browned bits. Stir often until liquid evaporates and browned bits form again. Repeat deglazing and cooking dry until a rich brown color develops. Use to season soups, pilafs, casseroles, etc. or as a side dish. Freezes well. **Yields 1 cup or 4 servings.**

Per 1/4 cup serving: 46 calories; 1.4 g protein (11%); 10.4 g carbohydrate (85%); 0.2 g fat (4%); 5 mg sodium; 25 mg calcium; 0 mg cholesterol.

GLAZED CARROTS

3   cups French Fry-style cut carrots
1   small onion, sliced and separated into rings
1/4   cup pineapple or orange juice concentrate
2   teaspoons chopped parsley

Steam carrots until just tender. Meanwhile, prepare onion rings as described in the Braised-Deglazed Onions recipe above. When vegetables are cooked, combine and toss with juice concentrate. Garnish with parsley. **Serves 6.**

Per 1/2 cup serving: 50 calories; 0.9 g protein (7%); 12.1 g carbohydrate (91%); 0.1 g fat (2%); 20 mg sodium; 23 mg calcium; 0 mg cholesterol.

POTATO CAULIFLOWER CURRY

1	onion, coarsely chopped
3	cloves garlic, minced
1	tablespoon cumin
1	tablespoon Curry Powder (p. 178)
1	teaspoon coriander
1/4	teaspoon turmeric
2	tomatoes, chopped
2	teaspoons salt
1/2	cup hot water
6	potatoes, cut French Fry-style
1	head cauliflower, cut in bite-size pieces

Spray a large nonstick pan or skillet with pan spray and preheat to medium heat. Brown onion, then add garlic and continue browning. Stir in next 4 ingredients and cook briefly. Add tomatoes and salt and cook until tomato becomes watery. Add water and bring to a boil. Add potatoes and cook for 2 minutes, then add cauliflower and continue cooking until vegetables are tender. Add water as necessary while you cook. Serve over brown rice, if desired. **Serves 10.**

Per 1 cup serving: 102 calories; 3.3 g protein (12%); 22.8 g carbohydrate (84%); 0.4 g fat (4%); 438 mg sodium; 40 mg calcium; 0 mg cholesterol.

CURRY POWDER

2	tablespoons ground Fenugreek seeds*
1	tablespoon ground coriander
1 1/2	teaspoons ground cardamom
1 1/2	teaspoons ground cumin
1 1/2	teaspoons ground turmeric
1/2	teaspoon finely ground bay leaf
1/2	teaspoon garlic powder
1/2	teaspoon paprika

Mix all ingredients together well. Store in an airtight container. **Yields 5 tablespoons.**

*Found in natural foods stores.

Per 1 tablespoon: 25 calories; 1.4 g protein (19%); 4.5 g carbohydrate (61%); 0.7 g fat (20%); 4 mg sodium; 25 mg calcium; 0 mg cholesterol.

CURRIED VEGETABLES

6	cups vegetables of choice, such as 2 cups carrots, 2 cups cauliflower, and 2 cups broccoli
3	cups water
1/2	cup shredded coconut
1/4	cup soy milk powder
1/4	cup whole wheat pastry flour
2	tablespoons blanched almonds*
1	tablespoon cornstarch or arrowroot
1	onion, chopped
1	tablespoon Curry Powder (p. 178)
1	tablespoon minced garlic
1	teaspoon McKay's Chicken Style Seasoning (MSG Free)
1/2	teaspoon salt

Cut vegetables into large chunks and steam until just tender. Process next 6 ingredients in a blender until very smooth. Simmer remaining ingredients in a small amount of water in a skillet. Add blended sauce and bring to a boil, stirring constantly, until thickened. Add vegetables. Serve on a large platter over a whole grain or pasta. **Serves 5.**

*Boil raw almonds in water for 1 minute. Drain and cool, then pinch off skins.

Per appr. 1 cup serving: 232 calories; 10.3 g protein (17%); 36.3 g carbohydrate (59%); 6.7 g fat (24%); 306 mg sodium; 106 mg calcium; 0 mg cholesterol.

VEGETABLE KEBOBS

1	red bell pepper, cut in chunks
2	6" zucchini squash, cut in chunks
12	cherry tomatoes
12	mushrooms
12	pearl onions
6	tablespoons Hollandaise Sauce variation of Golden Sauce (p. 90)
6	tablespoons Melted "Cheese" Sauce (p. 90)
6	tablespoons "Mustard" (p. 159)
6	tablespoons Tartar Sauce (p. 92)

Using 6 skewers, alternate vegetables and lay on sprayed cookie sheets. Broil until lightly browned, turning once. Serve on a large platter with sauces and spreads in bowls around the platter. **Serves 6.**

Per 1/6 recipe: 91 calories; 4 g protein (16%); 15.7 g carbohydrate (61%); 2.6 g fat (23%); 242 mg sodium; 38 mg calcium; 0 mg cholesterol.

EGGPLANT TAHINI BAKE

4	large onions, sliced
1	cup sliced mushrooms (opt.)
2	tablespoons Liquid Aminos
2	cloves garlic, minced
1	teaspoon salt
1/2	teaspoon sweet basil
1/2	teaspoon garlic powder
1/2	teaspoon oregano
1/2	teaspoon paprika
1/2	teaspoon parsley flakes
11/4	cups water
1/2	cup tahini (sesame seed butter)
2	tablespoons Liquid Aminos
2	eggplants, peeled and thinly sliced

Simmer first 10 ingredients in a large skillet. Add a small amount of water, if necessary. Combine remaining ingredients, except eggplants, and process in a blender until creamy. Pour a thin layer of tahini sauce into an 8 x 12" baking dish. Add a layer of sliced eggplant, and a thin layer of onion mixture. Cover with tahini sauce and repeat layering. Sprinkle extra paprika over the last layer of sauce, if desired. Cover and bake at 350° F for 45 minutes, or until eggplant is tender (test with a fork). **Serves 16.**

Per 1/2 cup serving: 53 calories; 2.3 g protein (17%); 5 g carbohydrate (36%); 2.9 g fat (47%); 312 mg sodium; 15 mg calcium; 0 mg cholesterol.

BROCCOLI & CAULIFLOWER WITH
TAHINI SAUCE

1	large red onion, coarsely chopped
2	tablespoons water
1	clove garlic, minced
1/2	cup tahini (sesame seed butter)
1/2	cup water
1/4	cup Liquid Aminos
1/4	teaspoon rosemary
2	pounds broccoli
1	head cauliflower
1	large red bell pepper, sliced thin

Simmer first 3 ingredients in a medium saucepan, for about 10 minutes. Stir in next 4 ingredients and mix thoroughly. Bring the mixture almost to a boil. Turn off the heat, cover, and let stand. Meanwhile, break the broccoli into stalks and separate the cauliflower into flowerets. Steam cauliflower for 10 minutes. Add the broccoli and bell pepper and steam an additional 6 minutes. To serve, mound the broccoli in the center of a platter, surround it with a row of cauliflower and then a row of red bell pepper. Pour sauce over the top. **Serves 8.**

Per appr. 1 cup serving: 168 calories; 9.5 g protein (20%); 17.4 g carbohydrate (37%); 9.2 g fat (43%); 245 mg sodium; 66 mg calcium; 0 mg cholesterol.

ORIENTAL VEGETABLE TREAT

1	clove garlic, minced
1	teaspoon salt
1	onion, chopped
1	cup chopped cauliflower
1	cup chopped broccoli
1	cup diagonally sliced carrots
1	cup diagonally sliced celery
1	cup diagonally sliced green beans
1	tablespoon cornstarch or arrowroot
1/4	cup cold water
2	tablespoons Liquid Aminos, or to taste

Simmer garlic and salt in a small amount of water. Add vegetables, one at a time, in the order given. Simmer each for one minute before adding the next vegetable. Stir cornstarch into cold water, then add to vegetables. Continue cooking until a clear gravy has been formed, stir frequently. Stir in Liquid Aminos and serve immediately. **Serves 8.**

Per 1/2 cup serving: 34 calories; 1.8 g protein (19%); 7.2 g carbohydrate (76%); 0.2 g fat (4%); 478 mg sodium; 32 mg calcium; 0 mg cholesterol.

ORIENTAL VEGETABLES WITH GARLIC SAUCE

1/4	cup water
3	cloves garlic, minced
1	tablespoon Liquid Aminos
1	onion, chopped
1	head broccoli, chopped
1	red bell pepper, sliced
1	cup mushroom halves
1	cup sugar snap peas
2	stalks celery, sliced diagonally
1	cup frozen green peas
1	cup water
2	cloves garlic, minced
2	tablespoons Liquid Aminos
2	tablespoons cornstarch or arrowroot
2	tablespoons toasted sesame seeds

Simmer first 3 ingredients. Over high heat, add vegetables, one at a time, in the order given, stirring as each vegetable cooks. Cook each vegetable for about a minute before adding the next vegetable. Set aside. Bring 3/4 cup of the water to a boil. Stir in 2 minced cloves garlic and 2 tablespoons Liquid Aminos. Mix cornstarch with remaining 1/4 cup of water and add to sauce. Lower heat and simmer until thickened, stirring constantly. Pour over vegetables, sprinkle sesame seeds over top, and serve. **Serves 6.**

Per 1 cup serving: 92 calories; 5.2 g protein (21%); 15.2 g carbohydrate (62%); 1.9 g fat (17%); 401 mg sodium; 78 mg calcium; 0 mg cholesterol.

KOREAN VEGETABLE PATTIES

2	cups soaked, peeled mung beans*
1	cup water
1	tablespoon toasted sesame seeds
1	teaspoon garlic powder
1	teaspoon onion powder
1	teaspoon salt
1/2	teaspoon Bernard Jensen's Protein Seasoning (opt.)
1/2	green bell pepper
1/2	red bell pepper
10	snow peas
3	green onions
1	carrot
1/2	onion
1	cup bean sprouts

Process first 7 ingredients in a blender until very smooth. Shred or slice vegetables julienne-style into long, thin 11/2-2" strips. Combine all ingredients and mix well. Drop by spoonful onto sprayed griddle or skillet, heated to medium-low. Cook well to a golden brown color on the bottom before turning and browning other side. **Serves 10.**

*Soak 11/2 cups mung beans in 3 cups of water for several hours. Remove bean skins by rubbing beans between hands, in the bowl of water. As skins rise to the top, they can be poured off. Repeat process until all skins are removed. (Ready-peeled, dried mung beans can be found in Asian markets.)

Per three 2" patties: 66 calories; 3.9 g protein (23%); 11.7 g carbohydrate (68%); 0.7 g fat (9%); 219 mg sodium; 34 mg calcium; 0 mg cholesterol.

HELPFUL HINTS

MENU PLANNING

SAMPLE MENU

BREAKFAST:
- Main dish, such as hot cereal, waffles, scrambled tofu
- Two fruits, one fresh
- Whole grain bread
- Spread, such as nut butter, preserves, avocado
- Nut, grain, or soy milk (for cereal)

LUNCH:
- Main dish, such as patties, loaf, or casserole, made with legumes, nuts, or seeds
- Two cooked vegetables
- Raw Salad
- Whole grain bread
- Spread, dressing, or gravy

SUPPER:
- Whole grain bread, cereal, or crackers
- Soup or salad, *or*
- Fruit or fruit dish, such as apricot crisp

Note: For best digestion, meals should be regular and spaced 4-6 hours apart. Two meals a day are adequate for many people. If you eat an evening meal, make it simple and light. Choose easily digested foods, such as fruits and grains, and eat early in the evening so that the digestive system can finish its work before you retire. This will enable you to sleep soundly and awaken refreshed in the morning. Here are some simple supper ideas:

- Fresh fruit and popcorn
- Fruit Smoothies* and Coconut Crackers*
- Apple or Apricot Crisp*
- Corn Chowder* and melba toast
- Golden Fruit Soup* and bagels
- Gazpacho* and Crispy Corn Chips*
- Apple Walnut Salad* and raisin bread
- Spinach Salad* and Oven Toasties*

Recipes in this book.

PLANNING AHEAD

The key to easy meal preparation is planning ahead. Find a quiet spot and plan a menu for your week, using the guidelines on pages viii and ix and in this section. Make sure you have a variety and abundance of fresh, whole plant foods. Cook double or triple quantities of grains and legumes for later use. On days when you're rushed, choose quick foods, such as soup and sandwiches or a main dish salad. Even a healthful dessert can be the centerpiece of a meal. Here is a suggested menu of main meals:

• **SUNDAY:** Make Mazidra* for your main meal. Cook three times as much brown rice and lentils as you need. Meanwhile, make Sweet Nut Milk* for the week.

• **MONDAY:** Steam chopped onion and garlic, add cooked brown rice and chopped black olives in a little water, either in a skillet or in a microwave. Serve with broccoli, topped with sliced, toasted almonds. Add a raw vegetable and bread with spread.

• **TUESDAY:** Lentil Links* bake in 30 minutes. Add a vegetable, salad, and whole grain bread or rolls. Before you sit down to eat, put on a large pot of millet, and by the time you've eaten, cleared the table, and washed the dishes, the millet will be cooked. Freeze in 1 cup quantities.

• **WEDNESDAY:** Use more of your rice for Garbanzo Rice Casserole.* This bakes for 35-45 minutes. Or, put together a loaf with your lentils, using the guidelines on page 105. While you eat, bake a few sweet potatoes for Thursday. If you don't use the rice for a casserole, use it in Fruitful Rice Pudding* for Thursday's breakfast, or for Breakfast Banana Splits.*

• **THURSDAY:** Reheat the sweet potatoes you baked previously, by splitting them and placing them under the broiler or reheat (covered) in a microwave. Serve with mixed vegetables and leftover Lentil Links. If you have some time you can prepare Tofu Walnut Loaf* for Saturday.

• **FRIDAY:** Warm up leftover Garbanzo Rice Casserole and the millet you cooked on Tuesday. Make Cream Pudding Delight* and a double recipe of Millet Butter.* Divide the Millet Butter into 3 parts and flavor 2 parts as directed in the Variations (Garlic Butter and Orange Butter).

• **SATURDAY:** Spread Garlic Butter on both sides of whole wheat bread, and heat in the oven while your loaf reheats. Serve with salad and steamed vegetables.

*Recipes in this book.

ONE-WEEK MENU

BREAKFAST	LUNCH	SUPPER
Delicious Millet*	Zucchini Spinach Lasagne*	Fresh Green Pea Soup*
Toast with fruit spread	Corn on the cob	Crackers
Orange	Celery sticks	Cucumber and tomato
Oat, Soy, or Nut Milk*	Whole wheat roll with	slices
	avocado spread	
Oatmeal with Raisins	Mazidra*	Peach Crisp*
Corn Muffins*	Whole grain bread with	Whole wheat bagel with
Millet Butter*	Millet Butter*	"Cheese" Whiz*
Grapefruit	Carob Chip Cookies*	
Ready-to-eat cereal	Tofu Walnut Loaf*	Lentil Vegetable Soup*
Toast with fruit spread	Baked potato	Crackers
Cantaloupe	Grandma's Favorite Gravy*	Zucchini and cucumber
Sweet Nut Milk*	Greens	sticks
	Carrot Salad*	
Cracked Wheat Cereal*	Tamale Pie*	Borscht*
Toast with nut spread	Pinto beans	Rye bread with
Fresh strawberries	Tossed green salad	Garlic Butter*
Fruit Milk*	Granola Crunchies*	Carob Chip Cookies*
Granola*	Korean Vegetable Patties*	Hot fruit cocktail
Toast with fruit spread	Rice	over toast
Banana	Brown Gravy*	Melon slices
Oat, Soy, or Nut Milk*	Tomato slices	
	Black olives	
Scrambled Tofu*	Bread Dressing*	Creamy Vegetable Soup*
Oat Biscuits* with	Cranberry Relish*	Rye crackers
Millet Butter	Yams in Orange Sauce*	Carrot sticks
Fresh fruit compote	Peas	
Hot Carob Milk*	Onion Rolls* with	
	avocado spread	
Waffles Perfect*	Pasta Italiana*	Fruit Smoothies*
Nut spread	Asparagus	Oven Toasties*
Applesauce	Jicama sticks	Popcorn
Fresh pineapple	Oatmeal Cookies*	

Recipes in this book.

FOOD COMBINATIONS

"It is not well to eat fruit and vegetables at the same meal. If the digestion is feeble, the use of both will often cause distress and inability to put forth mental effort. It is better to have the fruit at one meal and the vegetables at another." Ellen G. White, *Ministry of Healing*, pages 299, 300.

DEFINITIONS:
- **Fruit:** The product of a blossom containing the seed.
- **Vegetable:** The root, stem, leaf, or blossom of a plant.
- **Vegetable-fruit:** Agriculturists and nutritionists do not always agree on whether these are fruits or vegetables, though the botanical and Biblical definitions agree perfectly. If you tolerate them with fruit, use them with fruit.

FRUIT	VEGETABLE-FRUIT	VEGETABLE
Bananas	Avocado	Broccoli
Berries	Bell pepper	Carrots
Citrus	Cucumber	Cauliflower
Melons	Squash	Celery
Pears	Tomatoes, etc.	Greens
Stone fruit		Lettuce
Vine fruit, etc.		Spinach, etc.

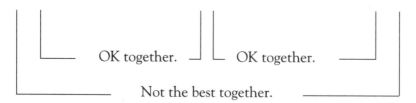

OK together. OK together.

Not the best together.

Grains, nuts, seeds, legumes, and olives combine well with fruits or vegetables.

VITAMINS AND MINERALS

Vitamins are necessary for the enzymes of the cells to perform their work of protein production and metabolism. Minerals are elements of the earth that are necessary for the electrical and chemical reactions in the body cells.

The best sources of vitamins and minerals are fresh, unprocessed fruits and vegetables, whole grains, legumes, nuts, and seeds. Seeds, especially, are good sources of trace elements. Many experts in the nutrition field believe that with a variety of natural foods, supplemental vitamins or minerals are unnecessary, except during illness. Self-prescription of some vitamin or mineral supplements can be risky, and in some cases can cause permanent damage to health. However, some vegans may need a B_{12} supplement. See following page.

CALCIUM

Many foods supply the nutritional elements found in dairy milk. Such common foods as greens (those low in oxalates, such as kale, are best), legumes (beans and peas), and whole grains, furnish adequate amounts of calcium. Medical studies have shown that the intake of calcium on a diet free of animal products is entirely adequate.[31]

Food	Quantity	Protein	CHO*	Sodium	Calcium
Almonds	1/4 cup	6.6 gm	6.9 gm	1.5 mg	83 mg
Blackberries	1 cup	1.0 gm	18.3 gm	0 mg	46 mg
Blackstrap molasses	1 T	0 gm	11.0 gm	19 mg	137 mg
Broccoli	1 cup	4.8 gm	7.0 gm	13 mg	136 mg
Butternut squash, baked	1 cup	3.7 gm	35.9 gm	2 mg	82 mg
Cabbage, cooked	1 cup	1.6 gm	6.2 gm	20 mg	64 mg
Carob powder	1 T	0.4 gm	6.5 gm	—	28 mg
Collards, cooked	1 cup	5.4 gm	9.8 gm	50 mg	300 mg
Dried figs	5	2.9 gm	61 gm	20 mg	135 mg
Kale, unsalted, cooked	1 cup	6.4 gm	8.0 gm	86 mg	270 mg
Mustard greens, cooked	1 cup	4.4 gm	8.0 gm	36 mg	276 mg
Oatmeal, cooked	1 cup	4.8 gm	23.0 gm	169 mg	23 mg
Orange	1 large	2.3 gm	23.4 gm	1.5 mg	76 mg
Pineapple juice	1 cup	0.8 gm	34.4 gm	2 mg	42 mg
Navy beans, cooked	1 cup	14.8 gm	40.3 gm	13 mg	95 mg
Soybeans, cooked	1 cup	19.8 gm	19.4 gm	4 mg	131 mg
Sunflower seeds	2 T	4.3 gm	3.6 gm	5.5 mg	21 mg
Tahini	1 T	2.6 gm	3.2 gm	17 mg	64 mg

*Carbohydrate

VITAMIN B_{12}

Vitamin B_{12} is made only by bacteria and certain algae, not by plants or animals. Animal products like milk, eggs, and flesh foods contain this vitamin. Bacteria grow in these foods, and if there is enough of the trace element cobalt, they leave B_{12} as a beneficial residue.

Civilized people thoroughly wash their food, their hands, and their cooking and eating utensils. Food is refrigerated. Water is filtered. Antiseptics, antibiotics and every possible method is used to avoid bacterial contamination. We must avoid harmful germs and their toxins. However, when we are fastidiously clean, we markedly decrease the amount of the essential B_{12} residue that we should be getting from the bacteria on our plant foods.

Our bodies can store a thousand times our daily need of B_{12}. However, these stores will gradually be depleted and nerve and other cell damage begin, unless we have: (1) enough of this B_{12} bacterial residue in our diet, (2) B_{12} readily available to combine with a polypeptide called "R-Binder," in the stomach, (3) a stomach that can make the necessary "intrinsic factor" to combine with B_{12}, and (4) a small intestine that can absorb it properly.

All people should be aware of potential vitamin or mineral deficiencies, whether they are vegetarian or meat-eaters. A diet too high in protein (specifically, methionine, which is common for meat-eaters), can place anyone in danger of Vitamin B_{12} deficiency.

When we avoid the use of animal products to improve our health, we should make provision for a source of B_{12} in our diet. Five micrograms of B_{12} a day is more than enough to supply all we need. You may wish to supplement your diet with a low-dose B-Complex tablet, a Vitamin B_{12} tablet (chew the tablet so that B_{12} can combine with "R-Binder" and be absorbed), or fortified food products. There is little danger of overdose by mouth. If too much is absorbed, it is readily excreted in the urine. A 50-100 microgram dose, one or more times a week should be sufficient. If this does not keep the blood level of B_{12} within the normal range (over 350 pg/ml), your physician may find that you have a problem in the stomach or intestines. You may need to take it by injection every 2-3 weeks.

Caution: Vitamin B_{12} may be converted to antivitamin B_{12} by minerals in a multivitamin-mineral supplement preparation. To avoid this problem, use a B-Complex tablet or B_{12} tablet. Also, the B vitamins work closely together. It is possible to become deficient in another B vitamin while taking a single B vitamin preparation. A B-Complex tablet helps you avoid this. Tablets should be crushed or chewed, to enhance absorption. For further information and references on this subject, write to: Medical Research Director, Weimar Institute, PO Box 486, Weimar, CA 95736.

SEASONING TIPS

Seasoning our food wisely is the best way to bring flavor to a recipe without using excess salt or fat. Mild herbs and spices used in traditional or creative ways can enhance flavor or provide taste-tempting variations. Some tips to keep in mind are:

- Add salt to soups at the end of cooking and to dried beans and peas after they have already softened.
- Cold foods may require more seasoning than hot foods.
- When doubling a recipe, don't double the seasonings. Increase by 1 1/2 times, taste, then adjust as necessary.
- Fresh herbs infuse foods with a greater depth of flavor than do dried. Store them in the refrigerator, wrapped in a paper towel, inside a plastic bag. Delicate herbs, such as basil, mint, dill, and cilantro may keep longer in a glass of water, stems down like cut flowers.
- When using fresh herbs, use only the leaves and tender stems. Adding them during the last 10 minutes of cooking enhances their flavor.
- Use 2-3 times the volume of fresh herbs as you would dried herbs.
- Dried herbs cost less and are more convenient. Use 1/3 to 1/2 the volume of dried herbs as you would fresh herbs.
- Experiment to find which herbs you like with which foods. Use a small amount to start, then adjust as necessary.
- For additional tips on seasoning vegetables, see pages 163 and 164.

Some common spices and baking ingredients are irritating to both the gastrointestinal and the genitourinary systems.[32] Some cause irritation to the nerves, increase blood pressure,[33] or break down mucus barriers in the stomach and bowel.[34] Some may be linked to cancer of the liver.[35]

Instead of these irritating spices, use mild herbs and seasonings that are kind to your system. Following are some suggested substitutions.

Irritating Seasonings:	Replace With:
Allspice, cinnamon, cloves, nutmeg	2 parts coriander + 1 part cardamom
Black, white pepper	Dried sweet basil, seasoning salt
Cayenne pepper, chili pepper	Paprika, cumin, bell pepper
Chili powder	Homemade "Chili" Powder (p. 171)
Hot curry powder	Curry Powder (p. 178)
Ginger	Cardamom
Horseradish	Sunny Sour Cream (p. 157), with lemon
Mustard	"Mustard" (p. 159)
Vinegar	Lemon or lime juice

EATING BETWEEN MEALS

For most people, eating is one of life's most enjoyable experiences. We enjoy it so much that we often find it difficult to eat only at meal time. Few of us, however, realize what takes place in the stomach when we eat between meals. A few brief insights into the digestion process will help us choose never to insult our stomachs again.

A study done at Loma Linda University some years ago revealed some startling facts. Students were given a typical breakfast of cereal, cream, bread, cooked fruit and an egg. Four and one half hours later their stomachs were x-rayed and found to be empty. A few days later the same students were given the same type of breakfast, and after two hours they were given such things as an ice cream cone or a peanut butter sandwich, or a piece of pumpkin pie and a glass of milk. After six to nine hours, a part of breakfast was still in the stomach. One person, after having breakfast, was given a little chocolate candy twice in the morning and twice during the afternoon. Thirteen and a half hours after breakfast, more than half of breakfast was still in the stomach–still undigested!

In all nature, we find harmonious rhythms, called circadian rhythms. We must live, eat, and work in harmony with these rhythms if we expect to be healthy and happy. In digestion of food, the stomach does not work in a haphazard way—taking care of food whenever or however it arrives. It works in a rhythmic, orderly way. When we eat a meal, the digestion process begins. When more calories arrive anytime during this process, digestion of the former meal stops. When digestion of the new substance reaches the level of digestion of the meal at the time of interruption, digestion continues.

The stomach is thrown into confusion when something new arrives every hour or two after breakfast, including more meals. What condition is that breakfast in after sitting in that moist environment for 12 to 14 hours? If we had the choice we would probably prefer not to have the stomach finish digesting it. We would probably like to open a door somewhere and throw it out! Unfortunately, we don't have that choice. Sometimes, of course, the stomach does rebel against such an insult and sends it back where it came from.

Having undigested food in the stomach at bedtime means that the stomach must work when it is needs to be resting. Every organ of the body needs rest and the only time the stomach can rest is when it is emptied of food. Some rest might be obtained between meals if they are sufficiently far apart. If the evening meal is early enough or light and easily digestible, when a person retires at night the stomach can rest, and sleep will not be disturbed by the digestion process.

Basic to living a healthy, happy, and abundant life, is the practice of eating regularly, contentedly, and with relish, but NOT between meals. Be good to your stomach, treat it kindly, give it adequate rest, and it will serve you well.

SHOPPING TIPS

Shop for fresh fruit and vegetables first. Try something new–ask someone purchasing it how they prepare it. Be sure you get a variety of fresh produce. As you shop, fill in your menu planner with fruits and vegetables. Ask yourself: "Do I have. . .
- something I can serve raw?
- something that cooks quickly (such as zucchini, grated)?
- something that cooks slowly, that I can prepare a day ahead? (You may cook tomorrow's slow-cooking vegetables while your family eats lunch today, then simply refrigerate and reheat tomorrow.)
- enough variety? (Supplement with frozen vegetables, if desired.)
- more than I can use at its peak of freshness?" (Beware of buying too much.)

LABEL READING

Every good shopper needs to develop the skill of label reading. Remember, it's the fine print that matters most, not the bold, catchy phrases on the front. Recent changes in label regulations provide consumers with helpful, detailed nutritional information. When shopping, keep these tips in mind:
- Ingredients are listed in order of predominance by weight. Enriched flour may be listed first and whole wheat flour listed second or third. This means there is more enriched flour than whole wheat flour by weight. The product label may read "made with whole wheat." It does not tell you how much whole wheat flour was used—it might be very little compared to the other ingredients.
- Manufacturers don't want to list sugar as the first ingredient, so they will often use more than one type of sugar. This "hides" the fact that sugar is the main ingredient. Some common sugars that are used are: corn syrup, maltose, dextrose, fructose, sucrose, etc. Look for the number of grams of sugar per serving.
- Avoid products with artificial coloring, flavoring, or preservatives.
- Determining the percentage of calories from fat is easy, especially with current labeling requirements. Look for the number of calories per serving and the number of calories of fat per serving. For example, Bleu cheese dressing has 77 calories per serving with 72 calories coming from fat.
  1) Multiply the calories coming from fat by 100:
     72 X 100 = 7200,
  2) Divide this number by the total calories per serving:
     7200/77 = 93.5,
  3) Round up to nearest whole number: 94.

This food has 94% of its calories coming from fat!

ECONOMY SHOPPING

Better nutrition for less begins with knowledge in shopping. Here are some suggestions:

• One of the most economical ways of providing for the family is to raise as much of your own food as possible. Whether in a garden, green house, or orchard, a few cents worth of seeds can produce a great deal of produce. If space is limited, have a mini-garden; try at least a few items in the flower bed, such as cucumbers or tomatoes. Greens such as kale or chard make a good background for bright flowers. In fully ripe, freshly picked food, you have optimum nutrient value, as well as economy.

• Prepare a week's menus in advance.

• Check refrigerator and freezer before shopping.

• Make a shopping list. Avoid impulse spending.

• Go alone. You will probably spend less.

• Shop when you are not hungry.

• Be familiar with prices so you know when a sale is a good buy. Read labels and compare prices. Compare brands—store brands often cost less then famous brands.

• First place on your shopping list should be given to fruits, vegetables, whole grains, and legumes. You may think dried apricots are too expensive, yet buy a bag of potato chips for over $2.00. Many snack foods are not only high in price, but also in calories, with few vitamins, minerals, or fiber.

• Buy fruits and vegetables at peak of freshness or near-peak. If the item is overripe and ends up being discarded, it is not a bargain.

• Buy groceries in quantity only if you have adequate storage space in a pantry, refrigerator, or freezer. An extra refrigerator or freezer can store bulk foods purchased from a wholesale distributor or farmers' market

• Use seasonal foods when in abundance. Can, freeze, or dehydrate foods.

• When choosing fruits, the largest item is not always the best. Medium size is often a better buy.

• Avoid restaurants except for special occasions. Eating out at noon may cost less than eating out in the evening.

• Don't waste leftovers. Use mashed potatoes in your next batch of bread dough or in soups. Season leftover cooked beans for refried beans or a sandwich spread.

• If possible, make your own bread. Better yet, grind your own wheat for bread-making.

• Using whole grains and dried legumes can result in big savings over ready-to-eat products.

• Make your own nut or soy milk.

STAPLES SHOPPING LIST

FRUITS
___Frozen strawberries
___Coconut, flaked and shredded
___Dates or chopped dates
___Raisins
___Canned unsweetened,
    crushed pineapple
___Apple juice concentrate
___Orange juice concentrate
___Pineapple juice concentrate

GRAINS
___Millet grain
___Brown rice
___Rolled oats
___Barley flour
___Whole wheat flour
___Whole wheat pastry flour
___Whole grain bread (can be frozen)
___Granola
___Grape-Nuts cereal
___Sesame or soy pasta

LEGUMES/NUTS/SEEDS
___Dry or canned garbanzos
___Dry lentils
___Raw almonds
___Raw cashews
___Pecans
___Walnuts
___Almond butter
___Peanut butter
___Tahini (sesame seed butter)
___Sesame seeds
___Sunflower seeds

MISCELLANEOUS
___Honey
___Cornstarch or arrowroot
___Emes Kosher Jel
___Minute Tapioca
___Powdered soy or tofu milk
___Active dry yeast

SEASONINGS/FLAVORINGS
___Sweet basil
___Bay leaves
___Dill weed
___Marjoram
___Oregano
___Parsley flakes
___Sage
___Savory
___Thyme
___Ground cumin
___Garlic powder
___Onion powder
___Paprika
___Turmeric
___Celery salt
___Salt
___Food yeast flakes (not Brewer's)
___Bernard Jensen's Protein Seasoning
___Liquid Aminos
___Lemon juice (if not making fresh)
___Ground cardamom
___Carob powder
___Ground coriander
___Almond extract
___Coconut extract
___Vanilla

VEGETABLES
___Garlic cloves
___Onions
___Potatoes
___Frozen peas
___Canned mushrooms
___Canned black olives,
    chopped and sliced
___Canned pimientos
___Canned tomato paste
___Canned tomato sauce
___Canned stewed tomatoes
___Canned whole tomatoes

HELPFUL ALTERNATIVES

Butter, Margarine, Oil — Millet Butter (p. 156); Garlic Butter (p. 157); nut spreads, avocado. For baked goods, use an equal amount of applesauce or pureed prunes (reduce any sweetening). For sauteing, use small amount of water or vegetable broth, or use a nonstick pan.

Baking Powder or Soda — Baking powders and sodas leave harmful, irritating residues in the stomach, as well as destroy thiamine (Vitamin B_1). Ener-G Baking Powder is made from calcium carbonate and citric acid, and does not have these harmful characteristics. Use twice as much as regular baking powder. For best results, add immediately before cooking. See Glossary.

Cheeses — See Recipe Index for "Cheeses" category. Commercial natural, nondairy cheeses.

Chocolate — Recipes and products made with carob. See Recipe Index for Desserts.

Cream — Cashew Cream (p. 38), Whipped Cream (p. 72), Coconut Whip (p. 71).

Cream Sauce/Gravy — See Recipe Index for Gravies/Sauces category.

Eggs, Scrambled — Scrambled Tofu (p. 33).

Eggs, for Binding — Process soaked mung beans in a blender until smooth and add to recipe. For a loaf or patties, process about 1/2 C of soaked mung beans with just enough water to enable the blender to work;
or use about 2-3 T of gluten flour in a loaf or in patties;
or use bread crumbs or oats;
or use Ener-G Egg Replacer, a natural, vegetarian product that can be used in place of eggs in most recipes. For each egg in your recipe, use 1 1/2 t Egg Replacer mixed thoroughly with 2 tablespoons water. See Glossary.

Eggs, for Leavening	Use 2 T of garbanzo or soy flour per cup of other flours. Increase water slightly to make up for fluid in eggs; *or* mix equal parts of soy flour and arrowroot powder. Use 2 T of mixture to replace 1 egg and add extra water; *or* process 2 T of almond or cashew butter with 1 T of lemon juice in a blender to replace one egg; *or* use Ener-G Egg Replacer. See Glossary.
Gelatin	Agar agar, Emes Kosher Jel, tapioca. See Glossary.
Meat Dishes	See Recipe Index for Main Dishes category, for burgers, loaves, casseroles, etc.
Milk	See Recipe Index for Beverages category. Commercially made nondairy milks (Pacific Foods, Vitasoy Light, Eden Soy, Rice Dream, and Soy Moo are good brands). Avoid those with added oil, sugar, or casein.
Sour Cream	Sunny Sour Cream (p. 157), Tofu Sour Cream variation of Tofu Mayonnaise (p. 158), plain soy yogurt.
Soy Sauce	Liquid Aminos, Aminotone, Mineral Bouillon. See Glossary for Liquid Aminos.
Spices	Herbs and herb powders, seasoning mixes. See Seasoning Tips (p. 193).
Sugar	Barley malt, date butter, date sugar, evaporated cane juice, ground dried fruit, fruit juice concentrates, honey, sorghum molasses, etc. Amounts will vary depending upon article used. Most conventional recipes can do with a reduction in total sugar. Begin with 1/2-2/3 the amount called for in the recipe and use one of the above sweeteners.
Vinegar	Lemon or lime juice. See page 193.
White Flour	Brown rice flour, barley flour. See Glossary for these flours.
Yogurt	Commercial soy yogurts, such as White Wave brand. Strawberry Cream (p. 71) is similar to strawberry kefir (yogurt drink).

EYE APPEAL

The saying, "We eat with our eyes," is true. The sight of an attractively prepared meal stimulates the flow of digestive enzymes. On the other hand, a carelessly prepared meal can actually hinder digestion. A thoughtful cook will choose pleasing color and texture combinations. If you're serving mashed potatoes, don't have creamed corn and cauliflower at the same meal. Not only should food look appealing on the plate, but the complete table setting should be attractive as well. A meal of something as simple as fruit can be served on china. On a table that is set tastefully, the simplest meal is elegant. Decorate your entree, vegetables, or salad with a garnish. Before each dish leaves the kitchen for the table, it should pass "beauty inspection." Is the bread on a bread plate or still in the plastic bread bag? Does each serving bowl complement the color of the food it holds?

GARNISHING IDEAS

• **Carrot Curls:** Wash and peel a medium-size carrot. With a potato peeler, slice long, thin strips down the side of carrot. Roll them into curls. Secure with toothpicks and keep in ice water several hours or until ready for use.

• **Carrot Flowers**: Use the end of a potato peeler like a drill and hollow out the center of the carrot. Fill it with something white, such as Tofu Mayonnaise. With a sharp knife, cut four or six "V" shaped nicks on the side of the carrot from top to bottom. Cut in slices and you have carrot flowers. Decorate with parsley sprigs or celery leaves.

• **Lemon Twists:** Cut a few slices of lemon 1/4" to 1/2" wide. Cut a slit in each slice, from the peeling to the center. With one hand, hold lemon on one side of slit and use the other hand to hold the other side. Draw one hand towards you and the other away from you, causing the lemon slice to twist. These look nice on a casserole dish or loaf surrounded by a few sprigs of parsley.

• **Mint Leaves:** Mint leaves are pretty garnishes for fruit dishes and desserts, such as parfaits, pies, puddings, etc.

• **Olive-Carrot Barrels:** Cut small matchstick-size pieces of carrot about 2" long. Poke 2-3 of these through the center of a pitted black olive. Serve on a platter with open-face sandwiches for a bright splash of color.

• **Parsley Sprigs:** One of the most versatile garnishes, these are a must for decorating entrees, vegetable dishes, etc.

• **Fruit Platter:** Arrange orange slices in an "X" on a round platter and fill in with four different fruits in season. Apples, bananas, peaches, strawberries, and blueberries are suggestions. Dried fruits could also be used—dates, figs, raisins and apricots, for example. Use your imagination and create your own fruit platter! *Note:* Banana and apple slices need to be dipped in pineapple or lemon juice, to prevent them from turning brown.

• **Elegant Grapefruit:** Rather than cutting a grapefruit in half the usual way, cut it in a sawtooth fashion. Place a raspberry, strawberry or blueberry in the center for color.

• **Fruit Kebobs:** Wash a whole fresh pineapple. Cut it down the center from top to bottom. Place half of the pineapple face-side down on a large platter. Peel the other half of the pineapple and cut the fruit into chunks to use on the kebobs. Insert 12" skewers through bite-sized banana chunks, cantaloupe chunks, kiwi chunks, watermelon balls, pineapple chunks, purple grapes, and whole strawberries. *Note:* Banana and apple chunks need to be dipped in pineapple or lemon juice before placing on the kebob, to prevent them from turning brown.

• **Orange Basket:**

1) Cut a strip across the side of an orange to the middle to make the handle for the basket.

2) If the orange does not sit straight on the counter, cut a thin slice off the "bottom."

3) Cut the top part of the basket in sawtooth fashion. Remove the orange skin between the scored sections for the handle. Remove the fruit of the orange from the upper part of the basket.

4) Leave the fruit in the basket portion. Place parsley and small flowers in the basket, inserting the stems into the orange flesh to hold them in place. This makes a lovely table decoration.

FOOD PRESERVATION

May to October is a busy time of year for storing food, beginning with strawberries and cherries in the spring and ending with applesauce and perhaps persimmons in the fall. What fun it is to satisfy the "squirrel instinct" and have the whole family work on the many projects, from picking or gleaning to freezing, dehydrating, and canning. How satisfying it is to look at the rows of canned food filling each shelf and the satisfaction of knowing the freezer is full and dried foods packed away in readiness for winter. In recent years, many have begun to realize the value of canning without sugar. Even the food industry caters to the increasing demand for items canned, dried, or frozen without sugar. Here are a few guidelines:

ECONOMY
• Select only high quality foods for freezing, canning, or dehydrating.
• Fruits and vegetables should be at peak maturity.
• Fruits should be firm and without defects to avoid waste.
• Buy fruits and vegetables on sale, in season, and freeze, can, or dehydrate for year-round savings.
• The most economical form of food preservation is dehydrating, since the only storage costs are inexpensive plastic bags or containers.

NUTRITION
• The quality of fresh food is best retained if food is processed within 24 hours of picking. Fruits and vegetables should be processed within 2 hours of harvest for maximum nutrient preservation.
• Frozen foods should be stored at 0° Fahrenheit or lower and used within one year.
• Dehydration and freezing causes very little loss of nutrient value, while canning causes a substantial loss.
• Dehydrated fruit makes a concentrate of natural sweeteners.

CONVENIENCE
• Home-canned, frozen, or dehydrated fruits and vegetables keep a variety of nutrient sources conveniently available.
• Frozen chopped bell pepper, onions, green onions, and parsley are convenient and timesaving.
• Dehydrated and canned foods are not dependent upon electricity and still retain their flavor well.
• Dehydrated food is the most easily and least expensively stored of the preserved foods, and takes up the least amount of room.
• Dehydrated food is an excellent emergency food supply.

TIPS ON CANNING

ADVANTAGES: Canned foods are economical and convenient. Some fruits and vegetables seem to have better flavor when canned, such as pears and plums. "Freezer burn" does not pose a problem, and canned foods are not dependent upon electricity. Here are some suggestions:

• **NEVER** use bruised or damaged fruit, or fruit that shows any sign of decay, such as a gray or black spot. If there is a spoiled spot on the fruit, the mold will have permeated the whole fruit, even if you cannot see it. Molds produce toxins that are carcinogenic.[36]

• **NEVER** use the open kettle method to can! You lose too many of your nutrients. The best method is the hot water bath. It is usually not necessary to process fruit as long as most books recommend. Try cutting the time by at least 5 minutes. You will find the flavor much better.

• **ALWAYS** can vegetables under pressure, especially green vegetables. Botulism is a deadly organism that forms easily in green vegetables.

• **NEVER** use canned vegetables that are discolored or have a peculiar odor. Do not even taste. Discard at once. Canned vegetables should be used within one year. Never keep them longer than two years.

Two Methods of Canning Without Refined Sugar:

1) Use very fresh, sweet fruit, pressing it until some of the juice "bleeds" out, then fill with boiling water. The natural sugars may be sufficient sweeteners.

2) Can with fruit juices (you may wish to dilute them). Use white grape, pineapple, or apple juice. White grape juice does not discolor the fruit but is quite expensive. Pineapple juice gives a good color but changes the flavor somewhat. Apple juice is the least expensive and has a minimal effect on color or flavor.

TIPS ON FREEZING

ADVANTAGES: Retains much of the natural flavor and nutrient value.

• Use only freshly harvested fruits or vegetables. Freeze as soon as prepared to minimize loss of nutrients.

• All vegetables must be blanched before freezing

• **NEVER** refreeze vegetables. They may be kept in the refrigerator for 24 hours after thawing.

• Dip apples, apricots, bananas, peaches, and pears in lemon juice, pineapple juice, or ascorbic acid, to prevent discoloring.

TIPS ON DEHYDRATION

ADVANTAGES: Dehydration is the least expensive method of preservation. Few nutrients are lost and dehydrated foods take up 1/3 of the space of canned or frozen food, and weigh very little. They are not dependent upon electricity for proper storage.

• Foods for dehydrating should be uniform in size and cut relatively small and thin. Fruits should have cores, pits, and/or seeds removed. The following foods need extra preparation:

Marinate these foods in pineapple juice, 5-15 minutes:

Apples	Bananas	Plums
Apricots	Pears	Prunes

Blanch these foods in boiling water for 2-4 minutes:

Beans	Cauliflower	Pumpkin
Beets	Corn	Squash
Broccoli	Peas	Yams
Cabbage	Potatoes	

• **Bananas:** Slice for chips or split lengthwise into thirds by inserting finger in one end and pushing downward. Soak in pineapple juice. These dry to the consistency of licorice. If any fruit is dried too long and becomes brittle, you can rehydrate it to chewy consistency by spraying a small amount of water into the container with the fruit.

• **Fruit leather:** Process any combination of fruit and spread onto trays that have been sprayed with a food release preparation. This is a good replacement for candy.

• **Lemon and orange peel:** Grate onto fruit leather trays and dry. Store in a covered jar.

• **Peaches:** Blanch in boiling water for about 30 seconds and remove skins. Slice and dry.

• **Backpackers** love leftovers that can be rehydrated by adding water.

• **Leftover bread** can be cubed and dried. Add seasoning for dressing, or process into crumbs for seasoned bread crumbs. For zwieback, thoroughly dry thinly sliced bread.

• **Onions, bell pepper, garlic, fresh herbs, etc.** All can be dried and, if desired, ground to make inexpensive single seasonings or seasoning mixes.

• **Soup mix:** Dry leftover vegetables and add seasonings.

• **Zucchini chips:** Sprinkle sliced zucchini with seasoned salt and dry.

• **Flowers:** Dry on fruit leather trays and make sachet packets, for lovely, inexpensive gifts.

FEEDING YOUR BABY HEALTHFUL FOODS

Opening a bottle or a can may be convenient, but it is not the best way to develop a healthy child. Most ready-prepared baby foods are inferior to your home-prepared foods.

Whole, unrefined foods contain the greatest number of nutrients, which make them the best food for babies as well as for us. We are all composed of what we eat. Fat cells develop in the first 2 years of life. Degenerative diseases which are evident later in adult life are largely due to the *type* and *quality* of foods eaten all our lives.

Feeding your baby food "as grown" is not difficult, nor terribly time-consuming. Here's how:

• You may begin introducing small amounts of solid food prepared for baby from your table at approximately six months of age. However, there is no need to rush babies into eating solid foods, if they are gaining weight at a reasonable rate. Teeth are a good indicator of the readiness for solid foods. New foods should be offered once a day in small amounts (1-2 teaspoons), for a few days. After that, the quantity can be controlled by baby's own appetite, but solid foods should not be offered more than 3 times a day.

• It is best for baby's digestion to have only one type of food at a meal when feeding first begins, then limited to two foods, such as grain and fruit, or grain and vegetables.

• New foods should be blended thin and smooth, using a blender or fork. **Never** give solid foods from a bottle—there is a danger of choking. Also, digestion begins with chewing, and baby will swallow, without chewing, from a bottle.

• Offer the same food until baby is accustomed to it. New foods should not be introduced more often than every 5-10 days. If the baby spits the food out, it does not mean that he doesn't like it, but rather that he has not learned how to transfer the food to the back of the mouth and to swallow solids efficiently.

• Spitting up or loose stools for a few days following introduction of a new food doesn't mean the infant has a food allergy. These are common and usually stop on their own. If they should persist, stop the new food for several weeks and reintroduce later to see if the reaction recurs. Some doctors prefer to introduce vegetables before fruits, since infants have a definite preference for sweet foods. Another line of thought is that fruits digest more easily than vegetables so are a better choice for baby's first food.

• Serve fruits and vegetables at separate meals.

WHEN	FOODS	HOW TO:
6 Months:	Brown rice	Remove your family's portion from pot, leaving about 1/2 cup for baby (to be used over a period of a week or so). Add 1/3 cup additional water and continue simmering while you eat (40-60 minutes).
Add at Weekly Intervals:	Millet	See brown rice.
	Grain milk	Reserve 3/4 cup cooked grain for grain milk. Process with 1/2 cup almond slices and 1 cup of water in a blender until very smooth, adding additional water slowly. Use enough water to make 1 quart. Grain milks are not suitable for bottle feeding, but are intended for thinning foods and mixing with formula.
	Nut milk	Process 1 cup nuts with 1 cup water in a blender until very smooth, adding additional water slowly, enough to make 1 quart. Almonds are an excellent choice, as they are a good source of calcium. Soak the almonds in hot water to remove the skins.
7- 8 Months:	Banana	Mash banana and add to cereal mixture when serving. Allow to stand 10-15 minutes.
	Pureed prunes, apricots, pears, peaches, applesauce	Basic Recipe: 1/2 cup cubed fruit, raw or cooked, to 2 T liquid, such as water, mashed, or blended with whole grain cereal. Use only 1 fruit for a meal with cereal.
	Barley, wheat	Cook well. Poorly cooked wheat can cause a food sensitivity.
	Oats	Dextrinize rolled oats on cookie sheet at 275° F for 20 minutes. Soak 1 cup of oats in 1 cup grain milk, nut milk, or juice, for 15 minutes or longer. Process in a blender until smooth. Adjust consistency with liquid or oats.

WHEN	FOODS	HOW TO:
9 Months:	Vegetables, green & yellow: carrots, squash, green beans, beets, broccoli, spinach, asparagus	Good sources of iron and B vitamins. Baby needs raw *and* cooked vegetables. Process 1/2 cup or more with vegetable broth or water. No salt, sugar or flavorings are needed. Surplus may be frozen in ice cube trays, then transferred to freezer bags. Thaw 1 or 2 cubes in a heat-safe bowl set in hot water, as needed. *NOTE: Always select fresh vegetables and fruits in season, without any signs of decay.*
10 Months:	Finger foods: green beans, oven-dried toast, pieces of fruit	Cook green beans, but do not strain. Cut strips of whole wheat bread, toast at 200-225° F until thoroughly dried.
11-12 Months:	Mashed sweet or white potato, pureed peas, limas, soybeans; spaghetti, toast	Amylase is being produced in salivary glands and starchy foods will be handled now. Baby is now able to chew and can have a wide variety of foods. He/she should begin drinking from a cup. Encourage self-feeding — it is an important step in teaching self-reliance. Put a large towel or machine-washable tablecloth under the high-chair and encourage your little one. Don't fuss over small messes.
	Most foods	

Aim for three meals a day by one year of age. Gently help baby to understand that "food is eaten only at mealtimes." Discipline yourself to offer nothing between meals — no juice, no fruit, no cookies — only water. This is for baby's best health.

CAUTIONS:

Mothers should remember that sweetened items are not necessary in the diet — white sugar contains no nutrients, only calories, and can depress immunity. Never add sugar to baby's food to induce him/her to eat it. No salt, sugar, honey or spices should be added. Honey should never be given to an infant under 6 months of age, because it has been associated with infant botulism.

Avoid giving your infant cow's milk (including pasteurized, whole, low-fat, and nonfat, and some formulas). It can result in food allergies,[37] as well as cause gastrointestinal blood loss, resulting in anemia.[38] The low iron content of cow's milk may also contribute to anemia. Infants fed dairy products can develop susceptibility to nervous system disorders.[39] Intake of dairy products seems to have an ominous connection with leukemia in children.[40] In addition, cow's milk is more concentrated in protein, sodium, potassium, and chloride, making the immature kidneys work harder at a time when they are unable to concentrate urine. Recently, over 90 studies have implicated cow's milk as the cause of juvenile (Type I) diabetes. The American Academy of Pediatrics has now advised that infants not be given cows milk until they are at least one year of age. Considering all the risks involved, cows milk is best left alone entirely.

Once a child is weaned, and milk or eggs are not used in the diet, a source of Vitamin B$_{12}$ should be added. Soy-based formulas and some cereals are fortified with B$_{12}$. Check with your pediatrician for assistance. Ideally, baby care should be under the guidance of a pediatrician sympathetic with a vegan diet.

Remember that food preferences are learned, not inherited. Babies' likes and dislikes often reflect our own preferences and attitudes. As babies become toddlers, great care should be taken to educate their tastes and appetites. However, be careful not to require children to eat something that is distasteful to them or to eat more than is needed. Don't get into a battle over food—it will likely result in more resistance. Mealtime should be a time of pleasant interaction. When introducing a new food, require only one or two bites. Be creative—if your child "hates" broccoli, try adding a small amount to a favorite casserole. Often this is enough to encourage a taste for such foods.

BASIC MEASUREMENTS

U.S. LIQUID MEASURES:

Pinch = about 1/16 teaspoon (t)
Dash = about 1/8 teaspoon
3 teaspoons = 1 tablespoon (T)
2 tablespoons = 1/8 cup (C),
    or 1 fluid ounce (oz)
4 tablespoons = 1/4 cup,
    or 2 fluid ounces
51/3 tablespoons = 1/3 cup
8 tablespoons = 1/2 cup,
    or 4 fluid ounces
8 fluid ounces = 1 cup,
    or 1/2 pint (pt)
1 pint = 2 cups, or 16 fluid ounces
2 pints = 4 cups, 32 fluid ounces,
    or 1 quart (qt)
4 quarts = 1 gallon (gl)

U.S. WEIGHT MEASURES

1 weight ounce (oz) = 1/16 pound
    (lb or #)
2 weight ounces = 1/8 pound
4 weight ounces = 1/4 pound
8 weight ounces = 1/2 pound
16 weight ounces = 1 pound

METRIC CONVERSIONS

U.S. TO METRIC LIQUID MEASURES (approximate):

Pinch = 1/3 milliliter (ml)
Dash = 2/3 milliliter
1 teaspoon (t) = 5 milliliters
1 tablespoon (T) = 15 milliliters
1 fluid ounce (oz) = 30 milliliters
1/4 cup (C) = 60 milliliters
1/3 cup = 80 milliliters
1/2 cup = 120 milliliters
2/3 cup = 160 milliliters
3/4 cup = 180 milliliters
1 cup = 240 milliliters
1 quart (qt) = About 1 liter (l)
1 gallon (gl) = 3.8 liters

U.S. TO METRIC WEIGHT MEASURES (approximate):

1 weight ounce (oz) = 28 grams (gm)
2 weight ounces = 57 grams
4 weight ounces = 113 grams
8 weight ounces = 227 grams
16 weight ounces,
    or 1 pound (lb or #) = 450 grams

APPENDIX

GLOSSARY

AGAR AGAR: A vegetable gelatin obtained from seaweed, available in large chunks, flakes, fine flakes, and powder. Amounts used vary depending on type. Use half as much small flakes as large flakes, and one fourth (1/4) as much powder as large flakes. Must be heated to activate. Look for it in natural foods stores, or in the Asian department of your grocery store.

ARROWROOT: A powder originally made from the root of a West Indian plant, but now also made from various plants with similar properties. It is used for thickening in the same manner and proportions as cornstarch. Arrowroot is not a refined product and has a better nutritive profile than cornstarch. Available in natural foods stores and Asian markets. Arrowroot, like cornstarch, should be mixed with cold liquid, then added to other ingredients and heated. Stir constantly to prevent sticking and lumps.

BARLEY FLOUR: Barley flour is a light-colored, mild-flavored flour, that performs well as a substitute for white flour in many recipes. Try this flour in place of white flour in your favorite pie crust, muffins, cakes, etc. It has some gluten, but not enough for use in yeast-raised recipes by itself. It can be used for 1/3 of the flour required.

BERNARD JENSEN'S PROTEIN SEASONING: A natural vegetable seasoning made from soybeans, alfalfa, corn, and whole wheat. It adds a savory taste to soups, patties, casseroles, etc. Look for it in natural foods stores. It is a good idea to transfer the seasoning to a tightly sealed, glass container, and store in the freezer, as it has a tendency to cake.

BROWN RICE FLOUR: Brown rice flour is another alternative to white flour in many recipes, other than recipes requiring gluten. Those with allergies to wheat may be able to tolerate brown rice flour better.

BUTTER FLAVORING: There are basically two types of butter flavoring available at present. One is an imitation product, which contains artificial flavor and color, usually in a liquid form. The other is a natural product, which contains real butter flavor, usually in a powdered form. Only a small amount of either is necessary to give the desired flavor. Two recipes in this book list butter flavoring as an optional ingredient. It can be left out of these recipes, if desired.

CARDAMOM: The dried fruit, either whole or ground, of an herbaceous perennial grown mainly in the Far East. It is sweet and highly aromatic and the ground seed can be mixed with ground coriander and used as a cinnamon substitute. (Cinnamon can be irritating.)

CAROB CHIPS: Carob chips and other processed carob candy should be used in moderation. Carob does have many benefits over chocolate, but manufacturers often process carob with oils, so that the product will perform more like chocolate. People with high lipid levels or degenerative diseases may wish to avoid these products. Carob *powder* is quite acceptable for those individuals.

CAROB POWDER: A powder made from the locust bean pod, also called St. John's Bread. Carob is naturally sweet and high in calcium, phosphorus, potassium, iron, and magnesium. Its flavor, especially when toasted, is reminiscent of chocolate. However it does not contain caffeine, theobromine, methylxanthines, or other undesirable components of chocolate. Available in natural foods stores.

CASHEWS: Cashews are actually a tropical fruit. They are available raw, roasted, or as butter. Contrary to popular belief, cashews are lower in fat than most nuts. Blended raw cashews give a creamy, rich texture and flavor to recipes, and have thickening properties when heated. They do need to be cleaned before using. Simply place them in a colander and rinse thoroughly with boiling water. Blanched almonds may be substituted for cashews in many recipes. However, the flavor and texture will be somewhat changed. In many recipes, the cashews can be reduced or omitted altogether.

CILANTRO: The leaves of the coriander plant are called cilantro (also called Chinese parsley). They are commonly used in Asian, Indian, and Mexican cuisines. The flavor of coriander is very different from the flavor of cilantro, even though they come from the same plant. Cilantro has a very distinctive flavor, so if you have not tried it before, experiment to find the right proportion for your taste. Look for fresh cilantro in the produce department of your grocery store, and dried cilantro in the seasoning department.

COCONUT: Coconut is actually a "drupe" (as are peaches and plums), not a nut. However, it is high in fat, most of which is saturated (although in short chains, which are not processed in the same way as long chain saturated fats, found in animal products). Its use should be moderate. Studies have shown that individuals who are not consuming any dietary cholesterol are able to handle vegetable sources of saturated fat without difficulty. However, it should be used sparingly by those individuals who have high lipids or degenerative diseases. While using coconut as a flavor enhancer and condiment in recipes is acceptable for most people, the use of refined coconut oil can be harmful, since the carbohydrate and fiber have been removed. (*Preventive Medicine, Volume 17*)

CORIANDER: The dried fruit, either whole or ground, of the coriander herb, grown mainly in the Far East. The ground seed can be mixed with ground cardamom and used as a cinnamon substitute. (Cinnamon can be irritating.)

DATE BUTTER: Date butter is used for sweetening in several recipes. Date butter also helps to give a moist texture to breads and cakes. To make date butter, simply soak dates in a small amount of hot water for a few minutes or more, until softened enough to process in a blender. Process until very smooth, adding more hot water if necessary, but not too much, so that it remains thick. Date butter is also a delicious spread for breads, waffles, muffins, etc.

DATE SUGAR: Date sugar is simply dried dates ground until semi-fine. It is an excellent substitute for white sugar, since dates are very high in sucrose and dextrose, yet are one of the most complete foods, containing abundant mineral salts, Vitamins A, B, C, and fiber. In some recipes, it may be a good idea to soften the date sugar in the liquid required for the recipe, before adding to the other ingredients.

EMES KOSHER JEL: (pronounced "emmes") An all-vegetable gelatin containing carrageenan, locust bean gum, and cottonseed gum. Available in natural foods stores and many grocery stores that feature a kosher foods department, in flavored, sweetened, and unflavored, unsweetened varieties. Recipes in this book call for the unflavored, unsweetened form. It must be dissolved in liquid and heated and will gel as it cools. One tablespoon of Emes Jel is required to thicken 2 cups of liquid.

ENER-G BAKING POWDER: This baking powder is made from calcium carbonate and citric acid. The company claims that it does not have the harmful characteristics of traditional baking powders. Ask for it at natural foods stores. If they carry Ener-G Foods products, they can order it for you. Or, you can order it from Weimar Institute. For more information, call Ener-G Foods, Inc. at 1 (800) 331-5222.

ENER-G EGG REPLACER: This egg substitute is made from potato starch, tapioca flour, leavening (calcium lactate, calcium carbonate, citric acid), and carbohydrate gum. The calcium lactate is not dairy-derived and does not contain lactose. For each egg in your recipe, use 11/2 teaspoons Egg Replacer mixed thoroughly with 2 tablespoons water. Ask for it at natural foods stores. If they carry Ener-G Foods products, they can order it for you. Or, you can order it from Weimar Institute. For more information, call Ener-G Foods, Inc. at 1 (800) 331-5222.

FOOD YEAST FLAKES: Also called nutritional or primary yeast. A yeast grown specifically for use as a food, high in B vitamins, and used as a flavoring. Often confused with Brewer's yeast, which is a by-product of beer-brewing and has a somewhat bitter taste. To add to the confusion, some companies are calling their food yeast, "Brewer's" yeast. Look for food yeast in natural foods stores. If you're not sure whether it's nutritional yeast or Brewer's yeast, ask the store manager.

INSTANT CLEAR JEL: A precooked starch, derived from waxy corn. It thickens immediately upon contact with liquid, needing no heating to activate, thus processing in a blender is best method for mixing, to prevent lumps. If you have difficulty finding it, you can order it from Weimar Institute.

LECITHIN GRANULES: Lecithin is a fatty substance used as an emulsifier. Commercial lecithin comes mainly from soybeans and is high in phosphorous. It is used in food release sprays to prevent sticking. As a recipe ingredient, it is often used to help keep bakery goods moist. Found in natural foods stores.

LIQUID AMINOS: An unfermented soy sauce substitute made from soybeans. It is high in amino acids and minerals, but is about 30% lower in sodium than regular soy sauce. Look for it in natural foods stores. Similar products are "Aminotone" and "Mineral Bouillon." If you use a regular soy sauce in any of the recipes, reduce salt accordingly.

MILLET GRAIN: Millet is the smallest of the grains and one of the most versatile. It is the only alkaline grain, and should be tolerated well by those who have allergies. Since millet is naturally very hardy and disease resistant, it is generally pesticide-free.

MUSHROOMS: Mushrooms are the fruit of edible fungi. Some are concerned about their safety. As with all produce, select fresh items, avoiding any that have bruises, black spots, or signs of mold. The common button variety of mushroom (champignon) is fresh when it looks plump with rounded caps folded around the gills. Fresh portobellos and shitakes are more mature mushrooms and will be flat, exposing the gills. Store fresh mushrooms in a paper bag in the refrigerator and use within a day or two of purchase. Clean them gently, holding them under running water to wash away dirt. There is some risk in eating raw mushrooms. They may become contaminated by handlers with poor personal hygiene (like other produce), or by having been grown in improperly prepared culture medium. Infection can be prevented by proper cooking. Hydrazines (substances found to be carcinogenic in animals) have been found in some species of mushrooms, such as the morels and the champignon. Cooking has been shown to reduce the level of hydrazines. If you wish to avoid mushrooms, try substituting diced eggplant in recipes calling for mushrooms.

PIMIENTO: A member of the sweet pepper family. Peppers are rich in Vitamins A, B, C, and E. Pimiento peppers are sweet and mild and can be found in small jars in the condiment department of your grocery store.

SMOKED YEAST: A product made from smoked nutritional yeast. Look for it in gourmet or natural foods stores. If you have trouble finding it, try substituting "liquid smoke" seasoning, found in some grocery stores, or substitute regular food yeast.

TAPIOCA: Tapioca is made from starch of the tuberous roots of cassava, or manioc, a woody tropical plant native to Central America. It is nutritious and easily digested. Tapioca comes in "pearls" of various sizes, as well as in a granular form, known as "quick" or "minute" tapioca, and must be cooked to activate its thickening properties.

TOFU: An inexpensive soybean product, high in protein, fat, phosphorus, potassium, vitamins, and a good source of calcium if a calcium-based coagulant was used in the processing (check label). Tofu is very versatile and can be used in both sweet and savory recipes. Look for it in the produce department of your grocery store. Select the varieties that do not contain soy protein isolate or concentrate. Use sparingly (2-3 times/week). If not using the whole package right away, keep it refrigerated, covered with water. Change the water at least every other day. Keeps 1-2 weeks.

TURMERIC: The rhizome of a perennial plant of the ginger family, grown in Southern Asia. It is valued as a food coloring and for its mustard-like flavor.

VEGEX: This is a natural, savory vegetable-yeast paste, used to give a hearty flavor to many foods. High in several B vitamins. Similar products are "Marmite" and "Vegemite." Look for them in natural foods stores or the gourmet department of your grocery store.

REFINED SUGAR GLOSSARY

"Hidden" sugar comprises 76% of our sugar intake. Only 24% is added in the home—the rest is added by the food and beverage industry. The consumer is confronted by a wide variety of sugars and other nutritive sweeteners, and there is no significant difference in the amount of calories each provides. A brief explanation of the more common sugars and sweeteners is given below.[41]

Brown Sugar: Consists of sugar crystals contained in a molasses syrup with natural flavor and color. Some refiners make brown sugar by simply adding syrup to refined white sugar in a mixer. It is 91-96% sucrose.

Corn Syrups: Produced by the action of enzymes and/or acids on cornstarch. High fructose corn syrup is a derivation of corn.

Dextrose: Also known as glucose or corn sugar. Made commercially from starch by the action of heat and acids or enzymes. Often sold blended with regular sugar.

Fructose: Known as fruit sugar, it occurs naturally in many fruits. Also known as levulose, it is a commercial sugar considerably sweeter than sucrose, although its sweetness depends on its physical form and how it is used in cooking.

Lactose: Also known as milk sugar; made from whey and skim milk for commercial purposes. Occurs in the milk of mammals. The pharmaceutical industry is the primary user of prepared lactose.

Maltitol, Mannitol, Sorbitol, Xylitol: Sugar alcohols or polyols, which occur naturally in fruits but are commercially produced from such sources as dextrose. Xylitol is a sugar alcohol made from a part of birch trees.

Sucrose: Obtained in crystalline form from cane and beets; a double sugar or disaccharide composed of two simple sugars — glucose and fructose. It is about 99.9% pure and is sold in either granulated or powdered form.

Total Invert Sugar: A mixture of glucose and fructose formed by splitting sucrose in a process called inversion, which is accomplished by the application of acids or enzymes. Helps prolong the freshness of baked foods and confections and is useful in preventing food shrinkage.

Turbinado Sugar: Sometimes viewed erroneously as raw sugar. It is refined to remove impurities and most of the molasses. Produced by separating raw sugar crystals and washing them with steam. Edible if produced under proper conditions. However, some samples have been found to contain contaminants.

ALTERNATIVES TO REFINED SUGAR

Amasake: Made from brown rice or barley grains inoculated with Aspergillus oryzae and allowed to ferment. Not recommended.

Barley Malt: Unquestionably a wholesome, nutritious, complex sweetener. It is made by partially sprouting barley grain, drying the sprouts, then grinding them into a fine flour.

Blackstrap Molasses: Made from sugarcane. It is more nutritious than white sugar, but the degree of refining is still rather high.

Brown Rice Syrup: Made from malted brown rice, which has been fermented. Not recommended.

Date Butter: See Glossary.

Date Sugar: See Glossary.

Evaporated Cane Juice: Tan to brown in appearance; coarse, granulated solid obtained from evaporation of sugarcane juice. Impurities, such as dirt and insect fragments, are removed. Sucanat is one brand, which lists an impressive nutrient profile.

Fruit Juice Concentrates: Minimally processed. Made by removing moisture from natural juices. These are simple sugars, so use in moderation.

Honey: An invert sugar formed by an enzyme from nectar gathered by bees. Its composition and flavor depend on the source of the nectar. Fructose, glucose, maltose, and sucrose are among its components. It is more nutritious than white sugar and is also sweeter, so less is required to give a sweet taste. The Scriptures give us good advice: *"Have you found honey? Eat only as much as you need. . . ."* Proverbs 25:16.

Maple Syrup: Made from the sap of the maple tree, which is boiled to evaporate moisture and concentrate the naturally occurring sucrose. It is more nutritious than white sugar, and is a good source of calcium, but use in moderation.

Sorghum Molasses: Made from sweet sorghum grain. Degree of refining is low to medium.

REFERENCES

1. *A Complete Summary of the Iowa Breakfast Studies*, Cereal Institute, Chicago, IL.
2. Trowell, H., "Definition of Dietary Fiber and Hypothesis that it is a Protective Factor in Certain Diseases," *American Journal of Clinical Nutrition*, 29:417, 1976.
   Anderson, J., *Plant Fiber in Foods*, HCF Diabetes Research Foundation, Lexington, 1981.
3. Burkitt, D., "Dietary Fiber and Disease," *Journal of the American Medical Association*, 229:1068, 1974.
   Gear, J., "Symptomless Diverticular Disease and Intake of Dietary Fibre," *Lancet*, 1:511, 1979.
4. Malhotra, S., "A Comparison of Unrefined Wheat and Rice Diet in the Management of Duodenal Ulcer," *Postgraduate Medical Journal*, 54:6, 1978.
   Rydning, A., "Prophylactic Effect of Dietary Fibre in Duodenal Ulcer Disease," *Lancet*, 2:736, 1982.
5. Piepmeyer, J., "Use of Unprocessed Bran in Treatment of Irritable Bowel Syndrome," *American Journal of Clinical Nutrition*, 29:1417, 1976.
   Manning, A., "Wheat Fibre and Irritable Bowel Syndrome," *Lancet*, 2:417, 1977.
   Editorial, "Management of the Irritable Bowel," *Lancet*, 2:557, 1978.
6. Ibid., Burkitt.
   Burkitt, D., "Varicose Veins, Deep Vein Thrombosis, and Hemorrhoids: Epidemiology and Suggested Aetiology," *British Medical Journal*, 2:556, 1972.
   Prasad, G., "Studies on Etiopathogenesis of Hemorrhoids," *American Journal of Proctology*, June 1976:33.
7. Burkitt, D., "Hiatus Hernia: Is it Preventable?" *American Journal of Clinical Nutrition*, 34:428, 1981.
   Capron, J., "Evidence for an Association Between Cholelithiasis and Hiatus Hernia," *Lancet*, 2:329, 1978.
8. Reddy, B., "Metabolic Epidemiology of Large Bowel Cancer," *Cancer*, 42:2832, 1978.
   Hill, M., "Colon Cancer: A Disease of Fiber Depletion or of Dietary Excess," *Digestion*, 11:289, 1974.
   Walker, A., "Colon Cancer and Diet with Special Reference to Intakes of Fat and Fiber," *American Journal of Clinical Nutrition*, 29:1417, 1976.
9. Trowell, H., "Ischemic Heart Disease and Dietary Fiber," *American Journal of Clinical Nutrition*, 25:926, 1972.
   Burkitt, D., "Some Diseases Characteristic of Modern Western Civilization," *British Medical Journal*, 1:274, 1973.
10. Haber, G., "Depletion and Disruption of Dietary Fibre, Effects on Satiety, Plasma-Glucose, and Serum-Insulin," *Lancet*, 2:679, 1977.
    Anderson, J., "High-Carbohydrate, High-Fiber Diets for Insulin-Treated Men with Diabetes Mellitus," *American Journal of Clinical Nutrition*, 32:2312, 1979.
    Miranda, P., "High-Fiber Diets in the Treatment of Diabetes Mellitus," *Annals of Internal Medicine*, 88:482, 1978.
11. Kijak, E., G. Foust, and R.R. Steinman, *Journal of Southern California State Dental Association*, 32:349, 1964.
12. *The Food Defect Action Levels*, U.S. Dept. of Health, Education, and Welfare, FDA Guidelines and Compliance Branch, Bureau of Foods, 200 C St., SW, Washington, DC 20204.
    Chocolate, Coca Cola, Cocoa, and Coffee, International Nutrition Research Foundation, Riverside, CA.

Journal of the Association of Official Analytical Chemists, 62 (5):1076-9.

American Journal of Clinical Nutrition, 6 (2) 1960.

Applied Microbiology, 20:644-654, October 1970.

13. McDougall, J., and M.A. McDougall, *The McDougall Plan,* New Century Publishers, 1983, pgs. 77, 79.

14. Davidson, P., "Insulin Resistance in Hyperglyceridemia," *Metabolism,* 14:1059-1064, 1965.

    Farquhar, J., "Glucose, Insulin, and Triglyceride Responses on High and Low Carbohydrate Diets in Man," *Journal of Clinical Investigation,* 45:1648-1653, 1966.

    Olefsky, J., "Reappraisal of the Role of Insulin in Hypertriglyceridemia," *American Journal of Medicine,* 57:551-556, 1974.

15. "Position of the American Dietetic Association: Vegetarian diets — Technical Support Paper," *Journal of the American Dietetic Association,* March, 1988, Volume 88, #3.

16. Barnes, S., "Effect of Genistein on In Vitro and In Vivo Models of Cancer," American Journal of Clinical Nutrition, 125:777S-783S, 1995.

    Kennedy, A. R., "The Evidence for Soybean Products as Cancer Preventive Agents," *American Journal of Clinical Nutrition,* 125:733S-743S, 1995.

    Shamsuddin, A. M., "Inositol Phosphates Have Novel Anticancer Function," American Journal of Clinical Nutrition, 125:725S-732S, 1995.

17. Robbins, J., *Diet for a New America,* Stillpoint Publishing, Walpole, NH, 1987, pg. 358.

18. Ibid., pg. 350.

19. Ibid., pg. 352.

20. Lee, H.P., L. Gourley, et al., "Dietary Effects on Breast Cancer Risk in Singapore," *Lancet,* 337:1197-2000, 1991.

21. Bahna, S., *Allergies to Milk,* Grune and Stratton, New York, 1980.

    Thrash, A., and C. Thrash, *The Animal Connection,* Yuchi Pines Institute, Seale, AL, 1983, pg. 107.

22. Ibid., pg. 100.

23. "A Multiple Share of Myeloma," *Medical World News,* May 16, 1969, pg. 23.

24. "More Clout for Human Cancer Virus," *Science News,* 103:121, February 24, 1973.

    "Virus-like Particles in Cow's Milk from a Herd with a High Incidence of Lymphosarcoma," *Journal of the National Cancer Institute,* 33:2055-2064, 1964.

25. McDougall, J., "The Case Against Milk," *Vegetarian Times,* March 1985.

    Fontaine, R., "Epidemic Salmonellosis from Cheddar Cheese: Surveillance and Prevention," *American Journal of Epidemiology,* 111:247, 1980.

    "Thermal Resistance of Salmonellae in Egg Yolk Products Containing Sugar or Salt," *Poultry Science,* 48:1156-1166, July, 1969.

26. Hulse, V., *Mad Cows and Milk Gate,* Marble Mountain Publishing, Phoenix, OR, 1996.

27. Wachman, A., et al., "Diet and Osteoporosis," *Lancet,* May 4, 1968, pg. 958.

    Walker, A., "Osteoporosis and Calcium Deficiency," *American Journal of Clinical Nutrition,* 16:327, 1965.

28. Heaney, R., "Calcium Nutrition and Bone Health in the Elderly," *American Journal of Clinical Nutrition,* 36:986, 1982.

    Paterson, C., "Calcium Requirements in Man: A Critical Review," *Postgraduate Medical Journal,* 54:244, 1978.

29. Bell, G., *Textbook of Physiology and Biochemistry,* 4th Ed., Williams and Wilkins, Baltimore, MD, 1959, pgs. 167-170. Adapted in McDougall, J., and M.A. McDougall, *The McDougall Plan,* New Century Publishers, 1983, pg. 101.

30. Harris, R.S., *Nutrition Evaluation of Food Processing,* 1960, pg. 477.

31. Ibid., Heaney.

    Ibid., Paterson.

32. Johnson, L.R., and B. Overhall, *Gastroenterology*, Volume 52, #3, March 1967.
   Schneider, M.A., *American Journal of Gastroenterology*, 26:722, 1956.
   Bridge's Dietetics for the Clinician, 1949, pg. 578.
33. Roth, L.W., and J. Blair, *Proceedings of the Society of Experimental Biology and Medicine*, 94:619, 1957.
34. Ibid., Johnson.
   Journal of the National Cancer Institute, 10:339-346, 1949-50.
   Gastroenterology, 18:269-285, 1951.
35. Hock-Ligti, C., *Acta Unio International Contra Cancrum*, 7:606, 1950-52.
36. Campbell, A.D., "Natural Food Poisons," *FDA Papers*, 1:23-27, September, 1967.
   Sittig, M., *Handbook of Toxic and Hazardous Chemicals and Carcinogens*, 2nd Ed., Noyes Publications, Park Ridge, NJ, 1985, pgs. 48, 49.
   Grasso, P., and C. O'Hair, "Carcinogens in Food," *Chemical Carcinogens*, American Clinical Society, Washington, DC, 1976.
   Conning, D.M., and A.B.G. Landsdown, *Toxic Hazards in Food*, Croomhelm, London, 1983, pg. 127.
   Altman, D.F., *Food Poisoning*, W.B. Saunders Company, Philadelphia, PA, 1988.
37. Bahna, S., *Allergies to Milk*, Grune and Stratton, New York, 1980.
   Bahna, S., "Cow's Milk Allergy: Pathogenesis, Manifestations, Diagnosis, and Management," *Advances in Pediatrics*, 25:1, 1978.
   Hill, D., "The Spectrum of Cow's Milk Allergy in Childhood," *Acta Paediatr Scand*, 68:847, 1979.
   "Polymorphic Allergy from Sensitization to Milk and Cheese," *Prensa Medical Argentina*, 37:1359, June 23, 1950.
   "Cow's Milk Allergy: A Critical Review," *Journal of Family Practice*, 9 (2) 223-232, 1979.
   "When a Child has Repeated Colds, Think of Milk Allergy," *Consultant*, January, 1968, pg. 41.
   "Complement Activation After Milk Feeding in Children with Cow's Milk Allergy," *Lancet*, 2:893, October 31, 1967.
38. McDougall, J., and M.A. McDougall, *The McDougall Plan*, New Century Publishers, 1983, pg. 50.
39. Agranoff, B., "Diet and the Geographical Distribution of Multiple Sclerosis," *Lancet*, 2:1061, 1974.
   Alter, M., "Multiple Sclerosis and Nutrition," *Archives of Neurology*, 23:460, 1970.
40. "A Multiple Share of Myeloma," *Medical World News*, May 16, 1969, pg. 23.
41. Chris Lecos, FDA Public Affairs.

RECIPE INDEX

ALPHABETICAL RECIPE INDEX

Pineapple Lemon Cream Pie	54		Super Stew	170
Pineapple Sherbet	68		Sweet & Sour Tofu	133
Pinto Enchiladas	122		Sweet Nut Milk	35
Pita Bread Chips	11			
Polynesian Fruit Bars	77		Tabbouli Salad	143
Poppy Seed Dressing	147		Taco Filling	120
Potato Cauliflower Curry	178		Tahini Dressing	149
Potato Chips	174		Tamale Pie	123
Potato Pancakes	31		Tapioca Pudding	63
Potato Pot Pie	110		Tartar Sauce	92
Potato Salad	143		Three Bean Salad	141
Pumpkin Pie	57		Toasted Avocado Sandwich	150
			Tofu Balls	133
Quick Hawaiian Dinner	135		Tofu "Cheesecake"	52
Quick Pizza Crust	9		Tofu Cottage "Cheese"	141
Quick Pizza Sauce	96		Tofu Cutlets	117
			Tofu Loaf	113
Raspberry Jam	42		Tofu Mayonnaise	158
Ratatoulle	127		Tofu Millet Burgers	116
Red Lentil Dal	131		Tofu Oat Burgers	116
Refried Beans	119		Tofu Walnut Loaf	113
Rice Crepes	32		Tomato Peanut Sauce	92
Rice Pudding	62		Tomato Sauce	91
Rice Ring	108		Tropical Fruit Fondue	78
Rice Soup	173		Tutti-Frutti "Ice Cream"	67
Rice Waffles	29			
Russian-style Pasties	131		Vegetable Cacciatore	129
			Vegetable Chowder	169
Salsa Ranchera	95		Vegetable Gravy	88
Savory Seed Mix	135		Vegetable Kebobs	179
Scalloped Potatoes	175			
Scandinavian Carob Cookies	76		Waffle Cake	60
Scrambled Tofu	33		Waffles Perfect	30
Seasoned Beans	118		Whipped Cream	72
Seasoned Bread Crumbs	13		White Sauce	91
Sesame Almond Sauce	89		Whole Wheat Crepes	32
Sesame Candy	78		Whole Wheat Bread	5
Soy Milk	36			
Spaghetti Sauce	96		Yams with Orange Sauce	175
Spanish Rice	124			
Spinach Salad	142		Zesty Mexican Sauce	94
Spinach-stuffed Manicotti	128		Zesty Tomato Relish	93
Split Pea-Lentil Soup	166		Zucchini Spinach Lasagne	128
Strawberry Cream	71			
Strawberry Jam	43			
Strawberry Slush	68			
Strawberry Topping	43			
Stuffed Green Peppers	109			
Summer Vegetable Enchiladas	121			
Sunburgers	115			
Sunny Sour Cream	157			

BUYING IN BULK

You can save significantly by buying your staples in bulk. You may want to form a co-op group with your friends so that you can take advantage of wholesale prices and share the cost.

For storing your staples, 1/2 or 1 gallon glass jars with airtight lids are convenient, impervious, and do not impart odors to the foods. Flours should be stored in a refrigerator, freezer, or root cellar. Whole grains, garlic, onions, potatoes, and hulled nuts, should be stored in a cool place, such as a root cellar. However, hulled walnuts and Brazil nuts should be refrigerated. Nut butters should be refrigerated after opening.

For ordering in bulk, or to order hard-to-find items, try the organizations below:

Weimart Natural Foods
  Product Orders
  PO Box 486
  Weimar, CA 95736
  (800) 525-9192
  Fax (916) 637-4722
  Catalog available.
  No minimum order.

Country Life Natural Foods
  P.O. Box 489
  Pullman, MI 49450
  (616) 236-5011
  Fax (616) 236-8357
  Catalog available.
  $25 minimum order
    for UPS delivery.

Mountain People's Warehouse
  12745 Earhart Avenue
  Auburn, CA 95602
  (800) 679-6733
  Fax (916) 889-9544
  Catalog available.
  $500 minimum order
    for delivery.

RECOMMENDED READING

DYNAMIC LIVING
How to Take Charge of Your Health
Aileen Ludington, MD and
Hans Diehl, DrHSc, MPH
Review and Herald Publishing, 1991
Hagerstown, MD

GET WELL AT HOME
Richard A. Hansen, MD
Shiloh Medical Publications, 1980
Poland, ME

HOME MADE HEALTH
A Family Guide to Nutrition,
Exercise, Stress Control, and
Preventive Medicine
Raymond & Dorothy Moore
The Moore Foundation, 1986
Camas, WA

HOME REMEDIES
Hydrotherapy, Massage, Charcoal,
and Other Simple Treatments
Agatha Moody Thrash, MD and
Calvin L. Thrash, Jr., MD
Thrash Publications, 1981
Seale, AL

McDOUGALL'S MEDICINE
A CHALLENGING
SECOND OPINION
John A. McDougall, MD
New Win Publishing, 1985
Clinton, NJ

NEW START!
Vernon Foster, MD
Woodbridge Press, 1990
Santa Barbara, CA

NUTRITION FOR VEGETARIANS
Agatha Moody Thrash, MD and
Calvin L. Thrash, Jr., MD
Thrash Publications, 1982,
Seale, AL

PREGNANCY, CHILDREN,
AND THE VEGAN DIET
Michael Klaper, MD
Gentle World, Inc., 1987
Paia, HI

THE MINISTRY OF HEALING
Ellen G. White
Pacific Press Publishing, 1905
Boise, ID

VEGAN NUTRITION:
PURE AND SIMPLE
Michael Klaper, MD
Gentle World, Inc., 1987
Paia, HI

All books listed above are available through Weimar Institute,
1 (800) 525-9192, Products Department.